Cultural Semiotics,
Spenser,
and the Captive Woman

Cultural Semiotics,
Spenser,
and the Captive Woman

Louise Schleiner

Lehigh
University
Press

Bethlehem: Lehigh University Press
London and Toronto: Associated University Presses

Associated University Presses
440 Forsgate Drive
Cranbury, NJ 08512

Associated University Presses
25 Sicilian Avenue
London WC1A 2QH, England

Associated University Presses
P.O. Box 338, Port Credit
Mississauga, Ontario
Canada L5G 4L8

The paper used in this publication meets the requirements of the American National Standard for Permanence of Paper for Printed Library Materials Z39.48-1984.

Library of Congress Cataloging-in-Publication Data

Schleiner, Louise.
  Cultural semiotics, Spenser, and the captive woman / Louise
Schleiner.
    p. cm.
  Includes bibliographical references and index.
  ISBN 0-934223-36-X (alk. paper)
  1. Spenser, Edmund, 1552?–1599—Characters—Women. 2. Spenser,
Edmund, 1552?–1599—Political and social views. 3. Literature and
society—England—History—16th century. 4. Women and literature—
England—History—16th century. 5. Semiotics and literature.
6. Sex role in literature. I. Title.
PR2367.W6S35   1995
821'.3—dc20   94-24491
                                                         CIP

PRINTED IN THE UNITED STATES OF AMERICA

To Diane F. Gillespie,
supporter of women's careers.
And to my other Washington State colleagues,
willing to think well of an unusual project.

Contents

Acknowledgements

I thank the administrators of the E. O. Holland Fund of Washington State University for the summer research grants and travel monies that supported this book. Initiation-completion grants from the Dean of Arts and Sciences helped me to write what became chapter 7 here and to get the index done. And my colleagues Thomas C. Faulkner and Rhonda Blair gave me computer help much beyond the call of duty, especially with generating and printing the line-numbered concordance I needed, of *The Shepheardes Calender.*

Thanks are due to the English Department and the Comparative Literature Program of the University of California, Davis, for the courtesies of visiting faculty privileges at the library, Instructional Media Center, and campus computer labs, and special gratitude to Richard A. Levin of that university, for the use of summer office space. Hoping that thanks can reach an unknown benefactor, I send them to the press reader whose careful organizational suggestions have, I think, greatly helped the book's coherence.

Cultural Semiotics,
Spenser,
and the Captive Woman

1

Introduction

Frederic Jameson in *The Political Unconscious* (1981) brought together concepts from neo-Marxist, psychoanalytic, and language theory to study certain patterns in nineteenth-century French and English political identity and writing; his approach seems highly promising for study of other periods as well, and I have here tried out something akin to it on early modern England. His ideas will find, I hope, elucidation and suggested modifications here, but let me offer an intitial sketch of them. He drew from A.-J. Greimas the concept of the semiotic square—a mapping of how two kinds of logical opposition, namely contradiction and contrariety,[1] interact with each other to define semantic categories—and he used it to elaborate his own version of something that he otherwise drew from Mikhail Bakhtin, P. N. Medvedev, and Julia Kristeva: a level or unit of meaning called the ideologeme (on Kristeva's sense of it see chapter 5, p. 104). In other words Jameson argued that the ideologeme as a unit of sociolinguistic meaning is internally structured according to the semiotic square. In his usage, the ideologeme becomes a set of interrelated oppositional possibilities whereby people of competing socioeconomic classes and class factions "talk" to each other,[2] as for example "aristocratic elegance vs. Napoleonic energy." Furthermore, his ideologeme is not only an economically based unit of socio-linguistic meaning potential but also a Deleuzean "desiring machine" or productive cultural fantasy (the idea coming from Gilles Deleuze and Félix Guattari's *Anti-Oedipus*). Any particular ideologeme thus bleeps and ticks inside a given society for some stretch of time, generating instances of its patterns, to enable people to put sexual energy into their expressions and productions.[3] The concept draws, as well, upon Jean-François Lyotard's *Libidinal Economy*, with its idea of cultural sites of desiring production.

Recently Jameson has urged scholars to attend further to Greimas, or go back to him for "spare parts."[4] In accord with that suggestion (though I came upon it after the present study was drafted), I have worked more closely than Jameson did with discourse theory.[5] I have also in my turn proposed some elaborations to the concept of an ideologeme although it remains for me both a macro-unit of ideological, socio-linguistic meaning potential and a syndrome with moving parts, for enabling and transmitting desirous utterance. One of these elaborations has the effect of highlighting its dimensions that bear particularly on gender study: I propose that the category or classeme of maleness-femaleness is characteristically part of the internal patterning of an ideologeme. And something of what women did in the face of a certain male-enunciated instance of this unit (in that age perhaps inevitably male-enunciated) is also considered here, in chapter 6.

I have further proposed that not only Greimas's basic semantic concept, the semiotic square, but also his basic syntactic concept—the narrative program—internally structures the ideologeme. (As Jameson observed, any given ideologeme can take both visual-emblematic and narrative forms [87].) The narrative program, as will be further explained in chapter 2, is an aggressional formula representing an agentive subject taking over or "governing" a second subject endowed with a mutually valued object—i.e., an object invested with a mutually conceived value.[6] In Deleuzean terms, I argue that the two "subject" positions in this narrative program formula represent "partial objects," generating desire in their interaction. The ideologeme, then, as a unit of libidinally invested political meaning, is an internally oppositional and internally mobile construct that enables speakers, writers, artists, or artisans using it to address their audiences in terms mutually sensed as valid—valid for contestation—by competing or conflicted groups.

I have assumed that one can study such conflicts between classes and factions, along with other interrelated efforts to attain or maintain domination, within the sphere of cultural semiotics, without speaking from an engaged Marxist viewpoint (see p. 181 below on Halpern).[7] In other words, I assume that class and class-factional identities and conflicts are one necessary factor to be studied along with others, if one tries to describe the functional processes of subject definition, writing, textuality, and reading within a society extensive enough to have economically differentiated social groups. Obviously I have taken up a perspective within language theory, but without trying to claim that it provides an ultimate horizon of explanation—I have only stood there a while, as it were, and reported some observations.

For a suitable text for a Greimassian discourse analysis, to be used as starting point in this study identifying a Renaissance English ideologeme, it seemed to me that Spenser's *Shepheardes Calender*—long considered the rallying cry that marked an emerging "golden era" of Protestant literary/artistic culture and political dominance in England—would provide indications for identifying such an instance. I also thought that the analysis might provide a new basis for addressing Spenserians' debates about the context out of which the *Calender* was written, the character of its unity, and how it functioned in the Elizabethan period. As this study has turned out, it provides an application of a semiotic model, though only provisionally posited, to a particular text *in toto*. Thus it is not only about Spenser's writings, though certainly it is about them—and indeed, concretely about many other Elizabethan writings and cultural productions as well (especially in chapters 5 and 6); it is also about the broader issue of how textual semiotics may relate and contribute to literary and cultural analysis generally, and they to it.

My study is addressed, then, to a number of readerships at once. The most obvious is scholars of early modern England, who I hope will ask whether the book offers worthwhile new perspectives, insights, or figurations (and they can make that determination by reading selectively, if they like). Another readership is people interested in textual and cultural studies theory, who may want to concentrate mainly on the reported discourse analysis itself, to see what might happen when Greimassian concepts are concretely applied to an influential literary text, and then the results are scanned for culturally semiotic implications. Yet another will I hope be feminists interested in semiotic dimensions of their work,[8] for I am arguing that gender— as the maleness-femaleness classeme, which always takes content as a local cultural construction (it like other classemes is a graduated or logically non-rigorous opposition)—is a system-level component of the kind of socio-linguistic unit that can be called an ideologeme; and I offer various suggestions about how gender worked in the one identified here. Of course I also, and primarily, hope for readers interested in thinking comprehensively about both theory (literary, textual, feminist, Marxist, cultural) and a particular stretch of a proposed history; for them the order of the chapters has been designed, as an introduction to the primarily studied semiotic model through the chosen text (the *Calender*), then a reporting of the application and certain of its results, then an extension of the analysis into further terrains of discourse pragmatics and of cultural interpretation.

In other words, the Greimassian model and the present application of it to *The Shepheardes Calender* are presented in chapters 2 and 3. Chapter 4 then explains a selected dimension of the results, namely the semantically pervasive imagery pattern or figurative isotopy of the *Calender*, whereby in this text expression pervasively figures as excrescence. Chapter 5 takes up the last phase of the analytical results—which come down to an instance of Greimas's "base narrative program" specific to the *Calender*—in order to identify and illustrate a particular Elizabethan ideologeme, that of the captive/repulsed/independent/tolerated woman (four terms of a semiotic square) as carrier of socio-political legitimation and hegemony. Chapter 6 traces several representative instances—or in the last case an evasion—of this unit of meaning: in Spenser's *Faerie Queene*, Sidney's *Arcadia*, Lyly's *Endymion*, a John Dowland song, a broadsheet ballad on shrew-taming, Shakespeare's *Taming of the Shrew*, the mysterious *Willobie his Avisa*, and two poems by the Countess of Pembroke. Chapter 7 moves on, methodologically, from discourse analysis to a related area, that of discourse pragmatics: it takes the perspective of Gerard Genette's *Seuils* (1988) on paratexts—prefaces, glosses, author interviews, etc.—and how they work politically through implying and then interactively shaping a book's readerships; it applies that paratextual perspective to the *Calender* to work out theories of both how it interacted with its contemporary readers and, scanning the process backwards, how it was composed in 1578–79.

On the *captive woman*, I propose that the *Calender* significantly contributed to the creation of that pervasive ideologeme of the last two Elizabethan decades. Spenser is therefore a culturally definitive strong writer (Harold Bloom's term) or "stylist" in Kristeva's usage, one who through calling into play the mirror-stage resources of his own "semiotic function," within a libidinally energized relation to ideological group identities of his historical moment, was able to coalesce and propagate viable macro-units of meaning or "desiring machines" for a given society and time span.[9] By thus recognizing the functioning of particular influential texts or cultural productions in contributing to the emergence of new ideologemes that will function for a limited time span, we can begin to work on questions of transition between periods and sub-periods—a matter that has proved difficult or impossible to theorize within most approaches to historical periodization.

As a motif, the "captive woman" of course existed long before and long after 1579 in various contexts (it is sometimes treated in feminist and folklore studies).[10] But what it became as a specifically Elizabethan, internally oppositional, libidinally invested, socio-linguistic unit of meaning within the English class and economic conflicts of the 1580s and '90s—that will be our historical topic. In concluding this initial overview, I should say that a piece of literary-historical spade work for the book was my article "Spenser's E. K. as Edmund Kent (Kenned/of Kent)" (1990, written 1986), arguing that Spenser himself kept control of and, in collaboration with Gabriel Harvey, largely wrote the *Calender's* "E. K." editorial apparatus—a view lately espoused by a number of other scholars as well, and now gaining widespread acceptance;[11] thus the whole *Calender* with apparatus should be regarded as one text or discourse. And finally, when speaking of "discourse analysis" *per se*, I am using the term "discourse" neither in the Foucauldian sense (which I do use in other passages) nor in the recent looser sense of "all the talk and writing about a certain subject matter" (e.g., "the discourse of Troy"—not a meaningful unit, in my view). Rather, when used here in the phrase "discourse analysis," it has the Greimassian sense of a discourse as *a* text with some measure of a posited kind of discursive unity, namely the kind identified by the aggressional formula of the "base narrative program." There are of course other modes of discourse analysis (and other modes of textual unity), but that is the one I am discussing here.[12]

METHODOLOGY: A BRIEF PLACEMENT

Before tackling the issues just presented, readers may want a brief account of the theoretical perspective of this study as compared with other approaches. My general assumptions are, first, that semiotic discourse analysis can offer help toward more convincing results in certain aspects of interpretation, especially for approaches analyzing the interaction of functionally literary texts with various other elements of their culture—such as Althusserian Marxism, feminism, and new historicism. Second, I agree with Kristeva's view of semiotics as a self-critical field of study, in part working toward empirical treatment of sign-systems, but with a continuous awareness of the epistemological difficulties that such efforts involve, including those of gender ideologies built into particular modes of analytical discourse. And third, I see value-saturated literary interpretation and commentary (still the bulk of Anglo-American literary study) not as outdated but as part of the processes of reception of literary texts in literate societies; it can, however, be framed and practiced with more recognition of the scholar's own ideological particularity and language-theoretical assumptions than has been the case heretofore. For example, when I speak shortly about a "theme" of the *Calender*—the inner conflicts of artists wanting to exercise power—I will try to do so not in general (as if one could talk such value-saturated talk in general), but from the defined fictional perspective of "Immerito" (the name Spenser in the *Calender* gives himself as ambitious new author), called into play as a fictional self by my own entering into that fiction, as a particular kind of reader and commentator in 1993.

An example of recent feminist ideas to which my project responds, although they do not specifically address the Renaissance, can be seen in Teresa de Lauretis's *Technologies of Gender* (despite its mistrust of quests for "wisdom" in the semiotic square, and of semiotics as a phallocentrist mode of discourse).[13] Modifying Foucault's idea of "technologies of sex" as "sets of techniques for maximizing life," de Lauretis calls for a new "subject of feminism" or a new kind of feminist perspective, from which to study how techniques or "technologies" of gendering work in a particular society, a perspective that is "at the same time inside and outside the ideology of gender" to be studied.[14] It must be so situated because particular women can never speak from the position of definedly silent "Woman" as that has been construed by French feminism (that is, as a non-speakable, alternative libidinal economy of discourse). To break out of that paradigm, de Lauretis thinks, feminists should work multi-dimensionally or from multiple contradictory perspectives at once. We should work, it seems, somewhat in the manner of Stephen Greenblatt's thick-descriptive cultural interpreter (see p. 19, below), who also wants to speak from both inside and outside of studied cultural formations. I see my effort here as relevant to the project of de Lauretis because identifying a given culture's ideologemes, with their particularly gendered enunciative and denotative positions (on which see also the discourse psychologist Wendy Hollway and the end of chapter 2 below)—such identifying and analysis of some of a culture's ideologemes would obviously be one contribution to study of its "technologies of gender," even if one must work partly by "speaking" some of the various male-enunciated discourses that we actual women often can speak (ventriloquize? infiltrate? appropriate?).

Mary Jacobus in *Reading Woman* offers another example, although my own procedures are different from hers; she plays off pairs of writers one against the other, dialectically and in deconstructionist fashion, in a series of chapters that create a kind of hitching, non-flowing or non-evolutionary history of emerging female writerly subjectivity, in nineteenth- and twentieth-century Europe and the U.S. I see my work as part of what Jacobus calls for because like de Lauretis she strives to break out of the bind of "privileging indeterminacy": she recommends as a new "feminist move" that one should "put in play a reading of the structures which produce and reproduce meaning, whether sexual or textual"[15]—such was also the project in my recent study *Tudor and Stuart Women Writers*.

As for new historicism, let me suggest something of this book's relation to it by commenting on Greenblatt's cultural poetics as theorized in *Renaissance Self-Fashioning* and *Shakespearean Negotiations*. He works, he says, toward a structural (though not structuralist) study of cultures by following Clifford Geertz, who proposed that anthropology should "address itself less to the mechanics of customs and institutions than to the interpretive constructions the members of a society apply to their experiences."[16] These constructions are to be, as it were, performatively mimed through a researcher's practice of interpretation, in a series of intuitively guided "thick descriptions," composed as if from the studied group's own point of view though also with infusions of the researcher's own self-recognized viewpoint. We might term this a perspectival polysemy. Likewise literary interpretation, Greenblatt believes, can "understand literature as a part of the system of signs that constitutes a given culture," although he says that in *Renaissance Self-Fashioning* he has not come far toward discerning such a system in Renaissance England: of its six writers in two triads of thesis-antithesis-"third term," he remarks that "such . . . schematic chartings are of limited value."[17] He has also made use of Foucauldian concepts for describing cultures, especially that of the circulation of social energy around power centers. Aspiring to a partly social-scientific mode of study, Greenblatt in effect practices value-saturated narrative commentary through eroticized scholarly storytelling (similarly, deconstructionist commentary has often been a reveling in aggressional, eroticized word play, revealing features of studied texts by miming generative self-oppositional strands in their writing process). Greenblatt's mode offers rousing critiques of modernist discourse formations, particularly psychoanalysis (in his studies of Renaissance identity formation) and certain aspects of literary canonicity (More was not a saint for all seasons but a divided and contingent self, often content with cruelties; Spenser was not the benign Christian moralist teaching right uses of power but an iconoclast in love with oppressive, colonialist power generated out of repressed sexuality—see chapter 6). Such libidinally energizing reversals of value-saturated assertions of one's professional predecessors show that literary interpretation, like the functionally belletristic writing on which it thrives, may also work revisionistically—in Kristeva's sense of intertextuality as revisionist transpositioning (i.e., inversions done on enunciative and denotative positions), or in Bloom's masculinist sense of Oedipal rebellion of writers against literary fathers. Greenblatt's procedure he says is as follows: "we seize upon a handful of arresting figures who seem to contain within themselves much of what we need, who both reward intense, individual attention and promise access to larger cultural patterns."[18] (Of course other new historicists do not necessarily proceed as Greenblatt does, but his theorizing can serve for orientation here.)

His points about "larger cultural patterns" and "the system of signs that constitute a culture," as well as his valuable critiques of untheorized application of modernist thought- and value-systems to earlier periods, lead me to suppose that my own project shares many of the characteristic aims of new historicist study. On perspectival polysemy—the effort to speak a value-saturated discourse self-awarely and *quasi* from the studied subject's or group's own viewpoint, also interlarded with one's own—I try out such commentary, as was mentioned above, in a number of stretches of this study. Indeed, the semiotic approach here does not claim to offer any complete alternative to subjective, value-infused interpretive study, but only to try complementing it with certain more empirical procedures. In short, I find much to agree with in new historicism as so far practiced, but I am looking for ways to be in part more systematic than it has been. Cultural semiotics can help literary and textual study to draw upon many concepts of ideologically engaged discourses such as Marxism and feminism;[19] that is, it can enable study of literary and other cultural production that does not neglect, but also does not merely isolate, its class-specific and gender-specific features. For study of textuality and culture, one needs more complex models of energized interaction among people and groups than the Benthamite pan-optical one favored in much new-historicist study—circulation of social energy around a magnetic center of monarch or court—although that model is of some value. While my study also focuses on the monarch and court, it seeks to portray them not as a center and concentric spheres but as a site of semiotic and material contestation by competing ideologies, and to study selected linguistic dimensions of how such contestation works.

An Althusserian Marxist book that similarly sees itself as complementing and partly overlapping with new historicism is Richard Halpern's *Poetics of Primitive Accumulation* (1991). Halpern critiques Foucauldian aspects of new historicism, especially what he considers an over-simplified view of the workings of power,[20] and he sees both Foucault and the new historicists, though for different reasons, as unable to theorize transitions from one cultural period-system to another (12–13). He describes Renaissance England (through some of its famous belletristic texts—including Skelton's "Elynour Rumming," *The Shepheardes Calender*, and *King Lear*) as reflecting the prehistory of capitalism in terms of Marx's concept of "primitive accumulation" of capital, through the nascent capitalist classes' separation of workers from control of the means of production. Some of what Halpern thus shows will be cited in Chapter 7 below.

And what of untheorized, positivist study of literary texts, contexts, and proposed intellectual history? Practices on the surface continuous with such modernist historicism will doubtless go on, although their institutional identity as a quasi-sacred discourse formation for moral training of moneyed and bourgeois students is changing. Investigators of cultures past and present will I believe always need to learn more about certain matters in contexts where, for the moment, neither theoretical elaboration, auto-telic verbal playfulness, nor absorbing intellectual storytelling serves the purpose. We must, for example, translate into our own terms particular systems of ideas that are from the investigator's viewpoint obscure but were or are current in the studied culture (e.g., legal or medical systems); or we must attend to archival matters not yet heeded, such as the traces of women's lives to be discerned by searching wills and ecclesiastical court records. These will be pointless activities unless there are some communally accepted standards of argumentation and evidentiary proceeding. Such study will always be needed because newly retheorized commentary on past or present cultures typically raises new questions and concomitant claimed answers, which then need to be critiqued for relative credibility by people who like to keep their noses close to interpretable records or primary evidence. If for example it is newly asserted, on the basis of an arcane passage in one medical treatise, that masturbation was viewed in the main positively in early modern Europe, someone should study what support the medical, casuist, or other texts conceivably treating the issue might offer for that view.[21]

Amidst the various modes of historicism now practiced, one can hope that improved graduate program curricula will lead future literary-historical and textual scholars to work from more broadly informed perspectives within language, literary, and cultural theory. When one looks at scholarship of an earlier generation (as I did for a Kristevan intertextual study of Shakespeare and Latinized Greek tragedy), one notices particular ways in which such work has dated, quite aside from the point that its supposed information has been revised: certain presuppositions (now discredited) are made about matters of method and fact; a tone and set of habits with diction reveal ideological biases that the writer was probably not aware of conveying; certain ways of using textual evidence to draw biographical inferences were then fashionable but no longer are, and so on. Despite the obvious point that scholarship of our own time will from future perspectives likewise date in such ways, many literary-historical scholars as yet evince no working awareness of that issue, assuming that their own untheorized scholarship represents some pure advance over that of earlier eras.

For example, although the view that Shakespeare was learned and competent with Latin goes in and out of fashion every third or fourth generation (alternate periods casting him as an inspired cribber of second-hand bits), the recent trend of making him learned again is fiercely defended, as if the matter will now be settled. In the paucity of trans-historic definitions of "being learned," the periodic reversals reflect little else but shifting usages of the Shakespeare *oeuvre* as supplier and validator of cultural codes and personal desires. (There are reasons why historical scholars now want to think again that Shakespeare was learned in the classics.) Perspectives incorporating aspects of text-linguistics and cultural semiotics could enable literary scholarship to leave behind at least some kinds of blind-sidedness. A capacity for careful description, for example, of such outmoding features of argumentation as those just noted could be worthwhile, even though we ourselves can no more stand outside our own conditioned moment than could earlier scholars.

Perspectival polysemy of several sorts is needed for literary and textual study to break out of its present methodological connundra. Perhaps we can set analytic frames of various kinds—feminist, psychoanalytic, ideological, socio-linguistic—around such value-saturated organizing questions as whether the hero of *Beowulf* died in sin, whether Milton accidentally made Satan his hero, whether the identity quest is the central theme of American literature, or if Hemingway was too bedazzled by sheer experience. They need not be left behind, but left, *as organizing questions,* to popular histories, student handbooks, and general audience book reviews. Such questions enjoy a certain lifespan within interpretive communities and then die off (or become "historical," as H. R. Jauss says), not of having been answered definitively but of having finished their useful life as triggers of the perpetually necessary newness in readers' confrontations with texts functioning as literary. It is not an ultimate answer that is important but, within a defined readership, the value-saturated question itself and the range of answers it provokes. But a new kind of scholar could learn to ask organizing questions that take into account and, at least in some limited way, offer to explain the conditions and processes of meaning-making within human cultures.[22]

My own effort has been to move toward a partially empirical—but also in some respects polysemically interpretive—mode of study, drawing upon textual semiotics for one clearly defined component of my study's evidence, with what result readers may judge by the ensuing chapters. Here no semiotic poetics—neither of Jauss, Kristeva, Eco, the new stirrings of Greimas offering possible materials for such (see below), nor any other—has been my subject, though I hope that efforts like this one can make a small preliminary contribution toward such a new poetics. Rather, I have worked with the model of Greimassian semiotic discourse analysis, considered as applicable to any discursively unified text, whether literary or other, so as to discover certain limited text-linguistic information that can, in this case, contribute to an interpretive reading of my chosen text and also to broader socio-cultural study of the Elizabethan period. I have proceeded by formulating, out of the Greimas/Courtés *Dictionary* definitions, a provisional set of algorithmic procedures (presented in chapter 2 and more technically in appendix 1) and applying them to the text of *The Shepheardes Calender,* then reflecting on the results.

Let us consider in conclusion what a semiotic cultural poetics might look like. A promising direction for it can be seen in Kristeva's idea that each particular "signifying practice"—e.g., literary writing and reading—works upon the basis of a system, a "semiotic disposition," which in the case of literary writing/reading is its set of deviations from a natural language's hegemonically defined (i.e., "standard") practices and patterns—phonemic, rhythmic, grammatical, lexematic; these are namely deviations from that standard "back towards [the language's] articulatory base, . . . consequently towards the drive-governed bases of sound production," towards the logico-symbolic categories that make language systems possible, and towards the pre-Oedipal psychosomatic functions that relate codes to the bodies of speakers or writers and their partners or imagined partners.[23] All of these elements relate closely to my way of working with Elizabethan belletristic texts here. But it must be stressed again that I am not claiming to propose such a full-fledged semiotic poetics. The current state of research seems to be still rather far from readiness for that enterprise, although certain studies generally based on such a view have been, for the last two decades, producing a new linguistically and psychoanalytically enriched brand of stylistics.[24]

Other developments are also pointing toward it. Greimas's most recent work on an oppositional category basic to much if not all of human meaning-making, which he terms the "thymic category" of proprioception (that of emotive claiming of something perceived as separate from the self, producing euphoria-dysphoria, or in activational terms attraction-repulsion), shows him moving in a direction that may eventually make possible an overlap or rapprochement between his project and the work of Kristeva, from the 1970s, toward a semiotic poetics: he is exploring the ways in which this thymic category—generating out of the body the human being's most basic dichotomy of urges—exists at the deep level of utterance and text generation and underlies all modal categories (e.g., 'having-to-be' or 'wanting-to-do').[25] In other words, he and his research group have begun to work, through step by step extensions of his theory of such modalities, on the sphere known to writing theorists (from their perspective in cognitive psychology) as affectivity in writing.[26] Kristeva treats this same area through what she calls the semiotic function: the workings of a surviving pre-Oedipal self or subject-in-process in each writer/speaker, that directs originally physical energies into the making of utterances and texts. Umberto Eco too shows himself headed toward this rapprochement of theories that could occur over the issue of a semiotic poetics, when he describes literary texts as the most telling instances of the "symbolic mode,"[27] i.e., instances of writing that does not only rely on writers' and readers' already existing, culturally evolved and situated competence with the given natural language of a text but innovates in such a way as to revise that very competence itself.

A semiotic poetics would be a field specializing in the most revealing kind of text for all such study of affectivity in the processes of speaking, writing, and textuality—namely those considered literary, artistic, or prophetic; such a poetics may eventually become part of an interdisciplinary meeting ground for a range of diverse studies of systems whereby meaning is generated. Perhaps in a few decades research teams will argue heatedly in French, Italian, German (for linguistically-oriented sociologists such as Jürgen Habermas will presumably get into the act), and other languages, working toward some measure of terminological consensus in this sphere of the fundamental affectivity of sign generation and sign use within human cultures. Will anglophone scholars wait until it is over and get a good translation done? Perhaps we can make some contribution by trying out cultural applications of concepts that have so far been well enough elaborated for that kind of effort. One such researcher in Renaissance studies is Keir Elam, who after publishing two books on Shakespeare and semiotics (using the speech-act theory of J. L. Austin and John Searle) has been working on a project involving correlation of Greimassian discourse theory—especially its handling of the thymic category—with concepts of the passions in Renaissance rhetoricians such as Thomas Wilson, Thomas Wright, and Pierre Charron, as well as with Elizabethan drama.[28]

Kristeva's view of semiotics mentioned above, namely that it is a definedly self-questioning set of projects that continuously critiques its own procedures and marks some of their limitations, is her version of a perspective that each researcher in semiotics needs to have in some form, and that distinguishes current semiotics from structuralism of the 1950s and '60s. In other words, each researcher will have some concept of both the exterior boundaries of semiotics—the borders of what it, as the study of potentially all human and animal sign systems, may usefully treat—and its interior distinctions between greater and lesser (and variant kinds of) reliability for different studies. Sometimes, as with Eco (who took the idea from Hjelmslev), it is a matter of distinguishing studies that can be grounded centrally in algorithmic, empirical handling of informant data from those that cannot be so grounded.[29] Thus Eco distinguishes between a "general semiotics" and particular instances of "specific semiotics": many of the latter can be empirical to a significant degree, he says, insofar as each can posit a limited sphere of systemically interrelated data "reasonably independent of" the observer: traffic signals functioning as a code, tribal kinship systems, or fashion codes. But more general and abstract studies, Eco proposes—e.g., of concepts of the sign *per se* (whether Peircean, Saussurean, Derridean, or other), or of areas of study falling between successful instances of specific semiotics—these should be considered philosophical rather than empirical. Eco's particular sorting out of these matters is not the only possible one; but the necessity for each researcher to have some such "sort" in mind characterizes the present state of semiotics, as it has responded to the epistemological critique of deconstruction.

For a view of the social processes of reading, I have for general perspective drawn upon Kristeva's concepts mentioned above—of strong writers ("stylists"), their revisionist (intertextual or transpositionist) relations with earlier texts, and their ability to interact with and shape culture[30]—as well as upon Bloom's concept of "misreading," Jauss's reception aesthetics, and Stanley Fish's account of interpretive communities.[31] But in this study the arc or circle of writer/ text/readership/social text/writer will be explored in other ways than those.

Greimassian analysis, being based on a model of text production that posits only an abstract "enunciator" behind the text and in itself takes no interest other than a lexical one in the historical contexts of a text's production and reception, has been denounced for viewing the text as artificially isolated, divorced from the politics, sexuality, and other material and cultural features of its writer and readers. In fact, however, the text's reflections of and participation in particular cultural processes and patterns, far from being obscured by textual semiotic analysis, can in many ways be elucidated by its results,[32]

for anyone who derives them carefully and then studies them from
political and cultural perspectives. Nor is Greimassian semiotic analysis, I believe, necessarily incompatible with active and inventive
readerliness if that is not privileged as being beyond critical scrutiny,
although obviously such semiotic analysis retains focus on text production and on what Eco has recently called the "intentions of the
text."[33] It offers to describe, with no more claim to absolutist accuracy
than is usually made for empirical formulations (that is, none), what
semantic and meta-syntactic features have through the production
process been built into a given text; and these descriptions are not
readings of any sort—as can be seen by the total result of chapter 3
here, which is merely one formulaic sentence—but rather are formularized results of repeatable analytic procedures performed on the
text, distillations as it were of its pervasive semantic features, as
these can be perceived by readers competent in the given language
of the text, consulted not as interpreters but as text-linguistic inform-
ants. The information they supply, if aptly questioned, spans through
and across particular subjective investments in readings. This is not
to say that the information transcends subjective investments, but it
allows us to describe a text in a way that we could cooperatively
refine and approach agreement upon, if such precision were desired
(i.e. the description procedure is algorithmic).[34] This kind of semiotic
discourse analysis, then, produces descriptions from only a very limited text-linguistic perspective and does not itself claim to offer
readings.

While the processes of reading are not to any great extent treatable
through such discourse analysis, it does offer a bridge from the text as
a discourse to the sphere of readers' "endless work."[35] This consists,
namely, of the several paired "actants of communication," that is,
sender-receiver pairs variously taking the forms of enunciator-
enunciatee, narrator-narratee, and interlocutor-interlocutee, and thus
variously situated within and relative to the diegesis of the text, that
is, relative to its surface flow of posited events and states. Within the
text these sender-receiver pairs become focal places of attention and
response for implied readerships; the third section of chapter 2, and
chapter 7 will treat such textual framing of the *Calender* oriented
toward implied readerships, which are in turn set in motion through
its evocation (or interpellation) of them, and its ensuing functional
interaction with them. (Greimas himself has begun to use such
sender-receiver pairs, in *Du sens, II*,[36] to develop analyses of cognitive
processes of "intersubjective communication.") Thus I believe semiotic discourse analysis can complement reader-response perspectives,
and my final chapter here illustrates that point.[37]

The Greimassian model of semiotic discourse analysis, as noted, proposes that certain kinds of structures will have been built into any discursively unified text, to the degree that it is thus unified, because of the nature of the discourse-making process. This exemplifies what Fish has called an "always possible . . . strategy," an approach "designed to make all texts one, or . . . to be forever making the same text," as Augustine did in proposing to read all texts as signifying God's love for mankind;[38] in this case, the repeated meta-text comes from linguistic study of certain mechanisms of sentence production, hypothesized to govern, with further elaboration, text production as well. We do not, however, find by applying this model to various texts that they all 'say' the 'same thing'—clearly in the discourse analysis here of *The Shepheardes Calender* (chapter 3) the results are specific to that text: rather we find a particular text's individuated versions of mechanisms whereby, at least in part, it became ready to 'say' whatever and multifarious things it can say for various readers. In such terms it might become possible to describe various kinds of reading practices more precisely than has been done so far.

A Recent Object of Pursuit: The Unity of the *Calender*

To come now to *The Shepheardes Calender*—mentioned above as promising for study of an ideologeme because it is often perceived to have marked the beginning of a literary and cultural era—let me first recall briefly what moment it marked in Queen Elizabeth's reign, and then what were my original questions about the writer, text, and political moment. Incidentally, we can note that the *Calender,* because of its multiple layers of personal, political, and readership reference, has already been found an especially suitable instance for the trying out of literary-theoretical models. It has been studied by Wolfgang Iser, the reader-response theorist, who concludes that it did (as most Spenserians now think) address Queen Elizabeth's French marriage prospect, though not strictly as Leicester party propaganda against the match but rather as a challenge to readers to engage themselves with the issue.[39] (For my part, I believe it was Leicestrian propaganda, but there is much more to be studied about its political positioning and complexity.)

Through the 1560s and '70s Elizabeth had been casting about for a workable balance among the major religio-political forces that could either threaten or maintain her rule; early on she even secretly discussed returning England to the Roman Catholic church in exchange for a papal declaration of legitimacy for herself (as Henry VIII's illegitimate daughter unrecognized by the pope).[40] Once the 1569 Catholic uprising of the northern earls had been suppressed and the pope had excommunicated her in 1570, that alternative was eliminated. Yet Elizabeth continued through the 1570s pursuing a difficult balance between conservative-prelatical forces, those who would keep the English church as Catholic as possible, and reformist forces, who wanted a less decorated liturgy, less wealth and judicial authority for bishops, more biblical education and interpretive homiletic training for local clergymen, and an end to absentee clergy holding of incomes from local parish tithes. With the revocation of the reformist Edward Dering's preaching license in 1572 and the suppression of the Parliamentary "admonishers" John Feild and Thomas Wilcox, the queen's government leaned the conservative-prelatic way; but then with the revulsion against the Parisian St. Bartholomew's Day massacre of Protestants and the appointment of Edmund Grindal as Archbishop of Canterbury, they leaned again toward the reformists; with the punishment of Grindal at the end of the decade over the issue of "prophesyings" (scripture interpretation meetings of clergy and laity that Grindal refused to forbid, despite the queen's order), they leaned again in the conservative direction. That last conservative-prelatical lean culminated in the queen's attempt in 1579 to marry a French Catholic royal scion, the Duke of Alençon and Anjou, a move that would probably have brought at least unofficial toleration for English Catholics (though the state would have remained officially Protestant) and also the possibility that a Catholic heir might eventually return England to the Roman fold, as Queen Mary Tudor had tried to do in the 1550s. From Elizabeth's pragmatic viewpoint, the marriage would have created an alliance with France bringing Anjou military forces to the aid of her Dutch allies against Spain, and also allowing England to free its worrisome prisoner Mary Stuart, Catholic rival claimant to the English throne, without thereby risking a French attempt to replace Elizabeth with that daughter of the Guises. But when the Catholic marriage plan proved simply too inflammatory, she abandoned it and at last ceased her effort at inter-confessional balance: she permitted the Recusancy Act of 1580 to impose heavy fines and penalties on practicing Catholics, and from then on defined herself as a commited Protestant queen, albeit by no means willing to weaken the episcopal authority of her hierarchical state church, nor indeed to give serious hearing to any further reformist measures within it.

The fall and winter of 1579–80 is the moment of this historically consequential decision, which the *Calender* addresses. Evidence of the unusual tensions at court during that time show that people of all viewpoints on the issues saw it as a moment of decision for the identity of the English church and nation. For two decades the aristocracy and gentry had been urging Elizabeth to marry and produce an heir. Now suddenly when the reformist party, despite the queen's rage at seeing her operational space constrained, scored a victory for its case against the Catholic marriage, the panic of the near miss left most of them determined to adore a Protestant Virgin Queen. The moment called out for a new ideologeme.

From Spenser's angle as a political nobody and new poet, wishing both to advance his secretarial career and to speak for reformism at that crisis moment, in those fall months he pulled together and readied for the press the eclogues and apparatus of his *Shepheardes Calender*, which appeared in December 1579, just as the queen began drawing back from her marriage negotiations (she put them on hold but did not yet abandon them officially until 1581). My initial questions were why did he publish, as his *debut* book, these pedantically framed, antiqued and anglicized eclogues circling around a depiction of himself as Colin Clout, a silenced poet with arms outstretched for admiring sympathy and support? And second, how—by what means and strategies—did the book safely address the politically defined audiences to whom it refers? It was a moment when rashness could get one executed, or at least a hand chopped off.

We come then to the issues of how to read *The Shepheardes Calender*. In the formalist decades of our century, it was usually seen as a static, thematically organized book, tonally correlated with the seasons of an abstracted any year, a timeless depiction of perennial conflicts within "the artistic temperament"—Spenser himself evoked that reading as part of his framing of the text, for example through the "December" epilogue verses: "Loe I have made a Calender for euery year,/That steele in strength, and time in durance shall outweare." Through a debate-of-the-month format the *Calender* has been said to treat the conventional Renaissance pastoral themes of poets' and clergymen's qualifications, dilemmas, and failures, as well as the pains of unrequited love. Clearly it does treat those themes. But how could a book timelessly addressing already conventional themes have served as trumpet call to a new age of literature and culture? Were its metrical experiments enough to make it so important as innovation? Bruce R. Smith has described it as one in a tradition of works that function as "the manifesto of an acutely self-conscious young artist," such as Virgil's *Bucolica*, Dante's *Vita nuova*, Wordsworth's *Prelude*, and Joyce's *Portrait of the Artist as a Young Man*[41]—works that, according to modernist patternings of literary history, mark the beginning of a literary era as well as of a particular notable career.

The last three decades have seen a widespread search for a new concept of the *Calender's* unity,[42] spurred by Paul McLane's 1961 identification of Colin Clout as, on the level of political allegory, Protestant England grieving over the iminent betrayal of him by his lady-queen's planned Catholic marriage (a view that has gradually won pervasive credence, even among Spenserians who try to discuss the *Calender* in apolitical ways). On the issue of the book's unity, a certain pattern of contrast among many recent studies can be noted: the interpreter focuses on the eclogues treating a selected two of the *Calender's* three major themes (the poetic, the political/ecclesiastical, and the erotic) and neglects or downplays the third. In other words, either one stresses the link between poetry and prophecy/politics, alluding only briefly to the erotic love theme (perhaps even declaring it a mere perfunctory generic necessity)[43] and focusing on "April," "May," "July," "September," "October," and "November"; or one stresses the link between poetry and eroticism, wishing away the political/ecclesiastical eclogues (as Mallette explicitly does)[44] and focusing on "January," "March," "April," "June," "October," and "December."[45] In light of this pattern, we continue wondering wherein if anywhere the *Calender's* unity lies. Beyond its own classification of the three central themes and which eclogues treat each of them (the listing of them by the glossator "E.K." in categories of the "plaintive," the "moral," and the "recreative"), is there a unity that subsumes all three?[46] Bruce Smith, after a thorough study of the *Calender's* generic components, concludes that there is no such principle.[47]

While musing on this state of affairs as I began this study, I was curious to see what a Greimassian analysis would turn up as the two thematized subject actants (or "actantial roles") standing behind the welter of "actors"—i.e., characters, concepts, and metaphorical figures at the surface of the *Calender* text. As noted above, the Greimassian base narrative program is a formula representing an infrastructural sentence of sorts, said to underlie the unity of any discourse to the extent that it is sub-structurally unified: an identified instance of this program will contain, besides a few other components, only two subject actants.[48] I thought that if such an analysis produced clear results, they would have a bearing on the question of the *Calender's* unity.

COLIN CLOUT: PROPHETIC PASTOR OR SICKLY DYING LOVER?

Let us consider more closely why there is perceived to be a problem about unity. Of course, at the level of generic convention, Renaissance pastoral itself combines the three major themes, each of which is treated in a separate set of eclogues within the *Calender:* that is, as Renaissance pastoralism had by 1579 interwoven classical and biblical imagery of shepherds into Christian bucolic modes (in various genres), a "pastor" could depict either a poet, a clergyman, or a courtier—or often a courtier poet, even a clergyman poet. And certainly the concept of poetry as delightful moral teaching inspired some poets of Elizabeth's reign, making them think their vocation prophetic and thus related to that of clergy.[49] Emphasizing this sense that "the poet aspired to fulfil the pastor's role in society," A. C. Hamilton's influential essay of 1956 noted the pairing of a number of eclogues (e.g., "June"–"July"), so that "what is first treated in terms of the poet is then expanded in religious terms."[50]

The present study will analyze the *Calender* in a way that reveals its portrayal of the emotional and political dynamics of a poet's attainment of pastoral, prophetic competence:[51] through finding a way to draw simultaneously upon the energies of personal eroticism, religious intensity, and socio-political engagement, the pastor finds his voice. In the face of potentially deadly political forces and drawing, for a political metaphorics, upon images of debilitating personal erotic failure (whether their basis was biographical or fictional), Spenser through writing the *Calender* became, and self-reflexively showed himself becoming, a mature poet.

But whether his fictive persona Colin Clout is likewise portrayed to have matured by "December"'s end has been a matter of debate. Few have disagreed with Hamilton that a central theme in the *Calender* "is the [poet's] effort to 'find' himself" through defining his calling as a high prophetic one. But a now extensively developed strain of interpretation (from Patrick Cullen to Joseph Wittreich and others) has disputed Hamilton's further claim that Colin suceeds in completing this maturational process by "December"'s end and that the hanging up of his pipe is then only a leavetaking of the pastoral as he ascends to epic.[52] On the contrary, Cullen, Wittreich, and others think that Colin has remained a failed and sickly lover/poet,[53] indeed dying at "December"'s end.[54] The latest version of this view seems to be Roland Greene's argument that, despite limited local moments of lyric "efficacy," as in "November" and "December," the *Calender* is a periphrasis, portraying needed conditions of what would enable fulfilled lyric utterance but programatically not being such itself; for "probably coming into existence from Spenser's sensation of contemporary poetic crisis, the *Calender* shows an impasse in the world of poetry, and settles it with poetry."[55] Why such a crisis existed Greene's essay does not consider.

Out of the analysis presented here, I believe I can propose a reading comprehensive enough to incorporate most major elements of these previous ones and some new ideas as well: Hamilton's emphasis on prophetic/poetic competence, valuable as far as it went, yet did not give enough account of the erotic theme's importance, while on the other hand Cullen and others have made Colin as erotic failure an ultimately defeated figure in whom Spenser is not likely to have portrayed himself. In fact he was an ambitious new poet. We have more to learn about reading the whole text in the dim, wintry light of "December," and how to give due weight to all three central themes: poetry-making, ecclesiastical/political pastoring, and love. Wittreich in *Visionary Poetics* profitably extended both Hamilton's and Cullen's perspectives by further exploring the *Calender's* prophetic/ political dimensions: taking McLane's view that its primary political reference is to the d'Alençon marriage threat, figured as Rosalind's betrayal of her Protestant people and church (Colin), Wittreich sees it as a "warning prophecy," whose "potential triumph . . . comes when it proves itself irrelevant because the prophecy is being listened to."[56] That is, by its veiled critique of Elizabeth's marriage plan, the *Calender* actually contributed, in some measure, to the Leicester party's successful efforts to change her mind.

While agreeing with Wittreich about the *Calender's* status as a "warning prophecy," I believe that Colin Clout in "December" is being portrayed as sickly and dying only in the seasonal sense that he and the vegetal world will go to their mother root, "where they together, / All the hard weather, / Dead to the world [will] keep house, unknown" (to take George Herbert's account of such death). Like the leafless trees Colin is dying, but only into a winter of discontent after the Queen's impending betrayal, when the holy cause—in some way that he can at this point only mystically project—will have to reconstitute itself; the trees' sap level registers a dormant health only waiting for springtime to call forth their vital signs again, and Colin's concluding hanging up of his repaired pipe, in direct reversal of his "January" breaking of it, registers an expectation of compe- tence to use it once more, when the season will be right.[57] How do we know that Colin is analogous to the dormant wintry trees? "December" says so, and also the analogy is part of a force field (or isotopy) at the center of the *Calender* as a semantically unified text (see chapter 4). My concluding chapter, proposing an explanation through paratextual analysis of how the *Calender's* parts came together for Spenser in late 1579, will show him integrating the themes of love, poetry, and religious politics by discovering how to separate his religio-political engagement, in the form of an imaged love for a woman, from the pervasive male affection of his education (for Gabriel Harvey and for Virgil and Chaucer); in those months he worked out how to achieve this separation in such a way as not only to maintain his friendship with Harvey but to intensify his erotic force as poet and activist.[58]

In other words, we need a reading of the *Calender* that will work at the level of an integrative emotional dynamics, beyond mere classification of the eclogues, remarking of their generic ingredients,[59] and elucidation of relationships among selected eclogues. Judith M. Kennedy's article on the *Calender's* concluding emblem, explicating *merce non mercede* (favor, not payment) in its erotic, poetic, and religious senses, points the way toward such an integrative reading for the whole *Calender*.[60] And Louis A. Montrose's insightful essays on the *Calender* have also taken steps in what seems to me the right direction, viewing it and some other Elizabethan texts as "pastoral in form, pervasively amorous in content, and intrinsically political in purpose."[61] But for exploring the issues I have been describing, we need a more penetrating and articulated analytical scheme than one of form-content-purpose. The useful question, I propose, is what happens in the *Calender*. Is there a central pastoral subjectivity— at once erotically, poetically, and socio-culturally activated—which underlies the various pastor-"actors" and, through the course of the twelve-eclogue sequence, undergoes a development of some sort? And if so, a development from what to what? In other words, is there a narrative or developmental dimension to the whole *Calender?*—more accurately in Greimassian terms, a semio-narrative dimension (i.e. a discursive succession of conceptual states, to be found in any unified discourse whether or not it tells a story *per se*). To answer this question, we will try out a Greimassian analysis and then consider its results. The effort will open a new range of possibilities for tackling the long-vexed problems of what are the relationships among the various aspects of the *Calender:* the E. K. apparatus, the ecclesiastical/ political topicality of the various shepherd figures, and the portrait of Colin Clout's woeful, for a time poetically incapacitating love failure. I believe my reading accords with Roland Greene's account of why Spenser took over the name "Colin Clout" from John Skelton, namely that he like Skelton wanted to fashion for his ecclesiastical critique a voice that would through most of the text be "deliberately factitious and empty speaking" but then would be brought "nearer to the center of things."[62] I would say, though, that Spenser's Colin is portrayed as having been deprived of an efficacious voice formerly possessed—until he regains it in "November" and "December."

We must focus (though not exclusively) on Colin Clout, not only because "E. K." says from the start that "under his person the Author selfe is shadowed" and that this new poet will soon be "beloved of all,"[63] but because his painful love plaints open and close the eclogues and because the penultimate, climactic one shows him (until then the silenced and impotent lyricist since "January") practicing, for a bereaved shepherd, the prophetic pastoral calling defined in the messianic prophecy of Isaiah: "The Lord God hathe given me a tongue of the learned, that I shulde knowe to minister a worde in time to him that is weary" (Isaiah 50:4, Geneva Bible). To the grieving Lobbin (referentially the Earl of Leicester and, by extension, the whole reformist faction of court and church)[64] Colin sings the consolatory word in good time for the weary, who are facing as they think the deadly fall of their Protestant queen and with it the death of what had seemed an undying cause, the Protestant English church:

> Whence is it, that the flouret of the field doth fade,
> And lyeth buryed long in Winters bale:
> Yet soone as spring his mantle doth displaye,
> It floureth fresh, as it should neuer fayle?
> But thing on earth that is of most availe,
> 　　As vertues braunch and beauties budde,
> 　　Reliuen not for any good.
> 　　　　O heauie herse,
> The braunch once dead, the budde eke needes must quaile,
> 　　　　O carefull verse.
>
> . . . .
>
> Why then weepes Lobbin so without remorse?
> 　　O Lobb, thy losse no longer lament
> 　　Dido nis dead, but into heauen hent
> 　　　　O happye herse
> Cease now my Muse, now cease thy sorrowes sourse,
> 　　　　O ioyfull verse.
> Why wayle we then? why weary we the Gods with playnts,
> As if some euill were to her betight?
> She raignes a goddesse now emong the saintes,
> That whilome was the saynt of shepheards light:
> And is enstalled nowe in heauens hight.
> 　　I see thee blessed soule, I see,
> 　　Walke in Elisian fieldes so free.
> 　　　　O happy herse,
> Might I once come to thee (O that I might)
> 　　　　O ioyfull verse.
>
> ("November," 82–92 and 167–82)

As prophecy, the elegy asserts a resurrective power that will outlive the dreaded catastrophe. Whatever reading one offers must account for the climactic, penultimate position of this Christian elegy for a beloved female figure, in which Colin—and Spenser could hardly have made the point any more explicit and emphatic than it is here— Colin returns to live performance after not "singing" since breaking his pipe in "January" (though he has spoken in dialogue). My reading sees this powerful elegiac affirmation, which sings the queen away most movingly to heaven, contained in a lead-wrapped coffin, as an act of political intervention (or if one prefers to be less dramatic, assertion) that at once restores the poet's competence and helps to set in motion what Jameson calls an ideologeme or unit of cultural discourse for an era (see chapter 5).[65]

A satisfactory reading must also account for the functioning of the E. K. apparatus. Two things can be affirmed without controversy (though as noted above, the view that most of the apparatus was done by Spenser himself with help from Harvey is now gaining broad acceptance): that in the editions of Spenser's lifetime and for many decades thereafter the apparatus was always printed in the *Calender* and considered integral to it,[66] and that E. K., whoever he may have been biographically, is textually a persona modeled upon the Renaissance publishing convention of the glossarist, implied by the text and taking part in its workings upon its readers—he is an informant, whose interwoven claims and explanations are part of the *Calender.* Ruth Samson Luborsky has demonstrated that Spenser himself either supervised or gave careful directions for the first edition of the *Calender* in late 1579; the text we have is thus very much as he wanted it to be, in a format unique in its time, with a scholarly apparatus that makes it look like a glossed, illustrated Renaissance edition of Virgil's eclogues, yet anglicized and rusticated, through its woodcuts and seasonal thematics, into the English calendrical tradition.[67]

THE MORALITY OF POWER

Let us pursue some hypothetical moral generalizations for a while. Let us try to conceive them from within the perspective of "Immerito," the unmeriting one, as Spenser signed the prefatory verse epistle to his anonymous book—a court secretary and hopeful, ostensibly humble new writer sending forth his first book, which probably felt like his first really important writing. That epistle begins, for the *Calender's* reader, a series of figures announcing themselves as private and humble while calling out for public and courtly recognition. Immerito's and Colin's self-contradictory proud and humble posing have long been seen as a new poet's witty method of publicizing his first

book by playing on the tradition of pastoral *personae* as humble folk
who yet "glaunce at great matters," as Puttenham put it. Richard
Helgerson proposes that Spenser was thereby becoming an anti-
Laureate Laureate in an age when poetizing was ranked ideologically
well below political careerism (though Richard Rambuss has recently
challenged this view, emphasizing Spenser's career as a managerial
secretary).[68] Either way, the *Calender* introduces him as determined
both to make a living and to function as a prophetic poet.

On the subject of Spenser's later relation to the queen's government, Stephen Greenblatt has strikingly described Guyon's icono-
clastic demolition of the "bower of bliss" (*Faerie Queene* II:12) as
showing that Spenser as a commited imperialist "loves" and "wor-
ships power," as a satisfaction replacing and displacing sexuality; thus
Spenser makes Guyon's violent display of power "an equivalent of
the erotic excess" it is suppressing.[69] I would agree that this point
formulates one aspect of the relationship between eroticism and
power in *The Faerie Queene*, though it should be noted (as a reviewer
of Greenblatt also observed, citing *Faerie Queene* VI)[70] that the poet
who in *Faerie Queene* I could show Redcrosse Knight conquered by
Orgoglio (Pride) through being "poured out in looseness on the
ground" with Duessa—that poet was a conscious, not a self-deluded
explorer of the linkage between sexuality and political power. He was
an explorer particularly of the linkage of sexuality to the colonialist,
imperialist power that Greenblatt focuses on (*Faerie Queene* V is all
about that, and more will be said on the issue in chapter 6). The
Calender has much to tell us about how Spenser came to love power,
and what he thought were kinds of power properly to be loved by a
national prophetic poet: in the *Calender* he had worked through the
power dilemma to perspectives that *The Faerie Queene* then mostly
takes for granted, though they are spelled out again in Guyon's Cave
of Mammon episode. Diverse modes of elaboration of the power-
sexuality linkage had been the *Calender*'s focal issue, with the
Queen's ostensibly calamitous French marriage plan serving as a
vastly fertile generator of diverse articulations of that linkage.[71] In
the *Calender* we even find Spenser agreeing with Greenblatt's point
that an artist's self-fashioning requires an enabling, functioning ideology and institution (or set of institutions) with which he can profitably
interact—this is the central drift of "October," which laments a poet's
inability, at a given time, to find that creatively enabling relationship
with the court. Chapter 6 will show my analysis agreeing with
Greenblatt's in seeing a fundamental divide between Spenser's and
Shakespeare's characteristic ways of relating their art to current Eliza-

bethan ideologies; but my discussion will ground that contrast in economics, class identity, and gender relations.

A prominent pair of terms for considering the power-sexuality relationship in Spenser's age was the slippery opposition of pride vs. humility. Awareness of the inherent contradiction in a humble man's quest for favor, fame, and intellectual reputation runs deep into the *Calender's* structure and internal dynamics. Beyond the Immerito who has written just a little book that he asks one of the kingdom's most intellectually respected noblemen (its dedicatee Sidney) to read and promote, beyond Colin who says he pipes "to please myselfe, all be it ill" ("June") yet writes a paean to the Queen, beyond E. K. the humble glossarist, who covers his identity yet declares himself to be selectively divulging what he pleases of the poet's secrets, beyond Cuddie of "October," who only wants to make a living yet dreams of pouring forth great tragedy, beyond Hobbinol whose green and "pleasant site" in "June" emblematizes political withdrawal, integrity and self-sufficiency yet who steps forward to sing Colin's paean to Eliza—where does it stop?

Not with the ecclesiastical "pastors," who are caught in the same dilemma of how to be both humble and proud. How shall we live out the gospel we preach of "blessed are the poor in spirit" while scrapping for and maintaining a power base—with its necessary attendant way of life—from which to influence the mighty and thereby make the correct moderate Protestant teaching prevail in the English church, under threat of a catastrophic Catholic marriage for the queen? How can we stay humble and charitable in the low dales and yet thunder potently against those cheerful pipers uphill with their saints and maypoles? Am I not making too much of the clerics' problem? Had not the church long ago resolved it with the doctrine that clerics' right to authority was given by their sacred function not by their degree of sanctity, and that a place of respect within or along side the ruling class was most practicable for the exercise of such authority? But that solution was one of the things against which Protestants deeply protested, throwing open a whole new late Renaissance arena for contested understandings of the societal roles of clergy. For most Protestants, a pastor's authority was to derive from his own evident progress toward sanctification, his own living out of the gospel, and he was to live simply and humbly among his flock. The built in danger in such a construct of clerical standing—of pride in one's humility—tended generally to escape their notice, despite the fact that materialistic pride and high living in the upper ranks of "pastors" was one of the reformist polemicists' constant criticisms, alike of Catholics and of conservative-prelatical Anglicans.

Reformist bishops were perhaps usually unaware of the potential for hypocrisy in their stance, just as broadcast evangelists today may cruise happily in their Cadillacs, the Beatitudes long since filed away, buzzing on their erotic power over people's psyches and purses. But Spenser was, I believe, keenly aware of it, exactly because he agreed that clergy should live humbly, yet recognized how little that ideal could be realized if reformist authority was to be wielded firmly. And just as keenly he saw that poets too had to gain access to some of the political influence of the proud if they wanted the chance to teach humility through delightful fictions. If we generalized away from Immerito's particular moment, we might find it an instance of Spenser's coping with the dilemma of any talented person discovering power structures and wanting to climb on them, yet neither trust them nor be found there.

Of course poets and thinkers of various eras have treated this theme of the problematics of the artist's or intellectual's relation to power. We could think of Dante alternately abasing and exalting himself, or of Milton—in "Lycidas," the work probably equivalent to Spenser's *Calender* as his career-defining, initiatory piece—calling ambition "that last infirmity of noble mind." But Spenser's *Calender* thematizes the power dilemma, portraying it as the case of a poet/intellectual who has been for a time disabled in his creative faculty, painfully disempowered, by a love failure. Colin's love suffering is unlike that of the conventional Petrarchan plaining lover—embodied in Perigot of "August," with whom Colin is deliberately contrasted by his refusal to enter the love plaint contest of Perigot and Willye, lest his plaints be mistaken for such conventional blessed sorrows; his suffering does not empower him as a poet but disables him, silences him. Through the course of the *Calender* he is seeking not so much to gain epic competence as to regain—and to gain on a new basis—his poetic competence per se. Thus the level of personal/sexual competence and power is subsumed into those of poetic and political/ecclesiastical competence and power. Or to see the case from inside out, from Colin's own viewpoint, the latter two are superimposed onto the former, as the young poet recovers and redefines his potency after a disabling blow (emblematically his "January" breaking of his pipe). Colin Clout is set moving in a world of Perigots and Palinodes and Diggon Davies, with the assignment to find a way of making acceptable the morally ambivalent and alarming power and powers essential to his poetic vocation. His pain is his motive force because he has experienced, in Rosalind's rejection after her initial acceptance of him, what it is to be weak and vulnerable and has found no spiritual exaltation in it.

Shee deignes not my good will, but doth reproue,
And of my rurall musick holdeth scorne.
Shepheards deuise she hateth as the snake,
And laughes the songes, that Colin Clout doth make.

Wherefore my pype, albee rude Pan thou please,
Yet for thou pleasest not, where most I would:
And thou vnlucky Muse, that wontst to ease
My musing mynd, yet canst not, when thou should:

Both pype and Muse, shall sore the while abye.
So broke his oaten pype, and downe dyd lye.

("January," 63–72)

Spenser handles the generic pastoral conventions very originally—
in his strong focus on a silenced singer surrounded by proxy lament-
ers, in his calendric temporalizing of Colin's competence story with
its emblematic illustrations,[72] and in the strategically placed emphatic
reminders throughout the *Calender* of the link between Colin's love
pain and his poetic incapacity. These features should leave us in no
doubt that this plaining love motif (whatever may have been the
biographical experiences behind it) is no mere prop on the pastoral
scene: it is at the center of the *Calender*'s emotional dynamics.

It is also true that Colin as a fictive thwarted lover is acting like a
"pensife boy halfe in despight" ("January"), whom Immerito and we
readers are to regard from an assumed perspective of greater matu-
rity.[73] But if we should adopt an attitude of condescension toward a
case of first love's woes, we would fail to perceive how Colin's love
pain generates and underlies the whole *Calender*. The poetry works
to make us feel his disempowerment. Rosalind has hated his expressions of desire "like a snake"; she has blasted the "timely buds" that
his "braunch of youth did beare"; she has even made him unable to
respond to his dear friend Hobbinol's affection, "Albee my loue he
seeke with dayly suit" ("January," 56). At the level of what is immediately perceived in reading (the diegetic), the hurt has caused in
Colin a general sense of failure and sexual self-contempt that is expressed in repeated images of castration, pruning, and cropping in
several eclogues. The love failure has been, though indeed characterized by naiveté and drawing upon Petrarchan conventions for its expression, no mere case of unreturned first love to be regarded with
bemusement, but the kind of blow that can bring on withdrawal,
self-searching, religious intensity, political activism—and poetry.

The whole *Calender* is thus a kind of *Notes from Underground*. From
the fictive Colin's perspective of personal incapacity, vulnerability,

and weakness, the eclogues pose the range of questions about power for artists, clerics, and intellectuals that naturally occurred to such a man of that time, in such a position. Can I let myself remain thus vulnerable? How can God's strength be "made perfect in our weakness"? Is incapacity the same as weakness? Can there be any capacity—"conning"—based only at the level of the personal? Or is it not a function of an interdependence between the artist and those in power? How can the meek "inherit the earth"? It seems nothing can be accomplished without recognition and power in some form. Yet how can I preserve my self-respect and write poetry while submitting to a queen who is threatening to destroy God's true church in England?

We must not underestimate the religious, the political, or the sexual intensity of this problematics of power for Spenser. He shows a young poet pausing, silenced, drawing back for a time, questioning whether he can continue in his calling. What then becomes of Colin inside the *Calender*, of his attempt to recover poetic competence and a sense of vocation? He does recover them:[74] in "November" at last, for the first time since his "January" pipe breaking, he "sings" again, in the liturgical month of the dead, a dirge. My analysis will later suggest, among other things, that he has made power acceptable by throwing down an ingeniously disguised challenge to the queen and her advisors, and by defining power as a competence that has been called for and justly recognized. He has defined it that way by persistently seeking a conjunction of *savoir faire* (knowing-how-to-do) with *pouvoir* (being-able-to-do), and necessarily with the ability to choose sometimes not to "sing" (being-able-not-to-do): *felice chi puo:* happy he who 'can do,' and also, says E. K. of that "August" poesie crowning the singing contest that Colin pointedly refuses to enter, happy he who can "leave off with the best" when the time is unripe.

SEMIOTICS AND THE RECOGNITION OF AN IDEOLOGEME

The treatment of the problematics of power in the present study will focus, however, not on moral generalizations such as those we have just considered (posed as from within the textual diegesis, from within Immerito's or sometimes Colin Clout's own viewpoint) but rather on linguistically and culturally semiotic analysis. That is, it has been shaped, as was explained above, by Fredric Jameson's neo-Marxist perspective, which, itself founded partly upon the Greimassian semiotics described in my chapters 2 and 3, supplies the central concepts of chapter 5. We will discover how it is that Colin as second-layer authorial persona becomes a strategy for prophecy, a way for Spenser to declaim to the queen from within this complexly framed or multi-walled text (a kind of fictive safe-house)—in an ingeniously veiled and thus self-preserving way to denounce at once her planned Catholic alliance and the entire conservative ecclesiastical party in England. We will see how he does that through a poetic calendar's submerged portrait of a grieving, rejected lover's aggressive recovery of ego strength, in the terms of Jameson's "ideologeme." The particular instance of it here was made viable, perhaps even invented, by *The Shepheardes Calender* for use in communication between the entrepreneurial, reformist-inclined, moneyed new-aristocrat party and the squirearchist, anciently aristocratic, theologically and liturgically conservative, economically old-fashioned party. (These interest-groups will be defined near the beginning of chapter 5.) They competed for the Queen's 'heart' and favor, and the *Calender* entered into that competition, thereby setting in motion a pattern for the culture of the subsequent Elizabethan period.

It will, however, be a while before we get to such political issues. For my premise here is that if one wants to do cultural semiotics as a form of cultural studies, it will be best to do some reasonably careful textual semiotics as part of the research process. As I carried out the discourse analysis here described, I was not looking for a predefined pattern (such as has, for rhetorical reasons, already been suggested by way of an introductory discussion on power and competence); I did not know what pattern would emerge—I simply watched to see.

Through the analysis in chapters 2 and 3 we shall come to see the *Calender*'s unity in terms of a Greimassian "narrative program"; then we can take the semiotic application into Jameson's scheme of socio-cultural analysis and also propose a certain semiotically derived, perhaps feminist, extension of Jameson, namely, that sememic definitions of particular ideologemes—necessarily conglomerates of many semes and sememic sub-groups—will typically if not always include a certain classematic opposition, maleness-femaleness. This is an ecclectic study: it assumes that one may propose a linguistics-based semiotic analysis of a particular text and then sit back and reflect on its results, tracking their implications through other, possibly compatible theoretical models.

2

The Greimas Model and the *Calender*'s Perspectival Framing

Using primarily the definitions in *Semiotics and Language: An Analytical Dictionary*, Vol. I, of A.-J. Greimas and J. Courtés,[1] one can describe a model of semiotic discourse analysis that turns out to be readily applicable to *The Shepheardes Calender*. The *Dictionary* correlates Greimas's own concepts (as developed and revised by 1979) with compatible or partially compatible ones from many other researchers.[2] Consciously hypothetical in their formulations of some concepts, the definitions are nevertheless complete enough to supply a provisional apparatus or algorithm (see appendix 1) for a whole-text analysis of the *Calender* that can contribute to study of the question about a semio-narrative dimension, considered in chapter 1. For readers new to such material, a suggested way of reading the following introduction to the Greimassian concepts would be to keep a slow, steady pace, not pausing much to ponder, since points that may at first seem hard to note will become more concrete in the subsequent application; and it may be helpful at the ends of sections to glance back through for the bold-faced terms and review their definitions. Readers scanning for particular commentary on Spenser should continue at least through the section on perspectival framing, which discusses specifically that aspect of *The Shepheardes Calender*.

The present chapter will review four fundamental, interrelated concepts used in the procedure I constructed and carried out: that of the generative trajectory, the actant, the semiotic square, and the narrative program, the last of these being the constitutive unit of discoursive structure. In this account, the *Calender* will already be cited several times for illustration; and, as noted, its perspectival framing through particular textual and paratextual viewpoints will be studied in some detail, through the concept of "actants of communication" or sender-receiver structures. Then in chapters 4 and 5 we can return to more exclusive focus on the *Calender*, through the new theoretical perspectives gained. A fifth important concept for Greimassian theory when applied as discourse analysis, namely that of the "semantic isotopy" and in particular of the "figurative isotopy," will be presented in chapter 4 when we examine the *Calender*'s imagery of "expression" as plant and animal production and reproduction.

Readers familiar with Greimas's narratology of the 1960s should note that his more recent work on discursive semiotics has made many gains in flexibility, especially through his accounts of predicative modalities (e.g., "knowing-how-to-do" or "wanting-to-do"); these are now seen as auxiliant elements of narrative or semionarrative structure, and are included in the "narrative program" formula as modal values, to be acquired or lost. Because of this work on modalities, he no longer proposes a third pair of actants along with the subject-object and sender-receiver pairs, namely the helper-opponent pair; instead he sees these last figures as actorialized instances of a subject's modal competence: "being-able-to-do/ not-being-able-to-do."

The materials to be presented here first, concerning the generative trajectory, are, as has been noted, based on Greimas's definitions in the *Dictionary*, vol. I, of 1979 (trans. 1982). An extended and in some ways revised view of the generative trajectory has since been presented in the *Dictionnaire*, vol. II (1986—not yet translated), by a member of Greimas's research group, Claude Zilberberg,[3] along with a second view, closer to Greimas' original one, by Daniel Patte, another group member.[4] (Indeed, volume II of the *Dictionnaire* is almost entirely the work of Greimas's co-workers and former students, the Group de Recherches Semio-Linguistiques.) Although at the end of this chapter we will also review these recent revisions, refinements, and extensions to the concept, we will here concentrate mainly on the "generative trajectory" as presented in 1979, which supplies an adequate basis for the level of detail required by the present study.

THE GENERATIVE TRAJECTORY

Before defining the "actant" through examining its place in the concept of the generative trajectory, we must first briefly review the generative theory of speech production, which in discoursive semiotics is extended to text production (generative linguistics, like other linguistic theory, has primarily studied units up to sentence size, but discourse analysis studies larger ones). In the Greimas/Courtés

Dictionary, I, the entry "**generative trajectory**" begins by noting that in generative-transformational linguistics, speech acts are seen as generated from a "deep level" (or deepest level, if more than two are identified) of virtual structures, to the "surface level" enabling realized speech. That is, they are generated along a trajectory from the most abstract to the concretely articulated, in such fashion that the progressions from one level or sub-layer to the next (the transformations) are effected according to "transformational" rules. But unlike Chomskyan transformational grammar, Greimassian discourse analysis is not concerned with formulating these rules in such a way that a discourse could be machine-generated; rather it offers *post facto* descriptive procedures, for taking an existing discourse and working back to its particular instances of certain hypothesized mechanisms of text production, not claiming to explain everything about the process. The model used here does not distinguish between literary and non-literary texts, although other aspects of Greimassian theory would admit of various ways of pursuing that distinction (see chapter 1 on Kristeva for her approach to it); the issue will not concern us here.

Greimas and Courtés adapt the generative model of sentence production as follows. To the original two posited levels—the fundamental and the surface—a third is added, resulting in a three-level generative trajectory; at each of these three levels the trajectory is shown divided vertically into two regions, the syntactic and the semantic (that is, so to speak, the region of the meta-sentence or semionarrative structure, and the region of meaning contents—the two representing the syntagmatic and the paradigmatic axes of language). This separation would of course be deceptive if one took its spatial representation too seriously; that is, the emerging text's acquisitions of semantic and syntactic features, at each level, are conceived to be happening simultaneously and interactively. The three levels are as follows:

I) the **deep level** of fundamental virtual syntax/ fundamental virtual semantics

II) the **surface levels** (sub-layers must be imagined within this region, though they are not shown on the following chart) of semio-narrative syntax and semio-narrative semantics (note: "narrative" is here used in a broad sense, as any evocation of a succession of events and/or mental states—all discourses, not just stories *per se*, have a narrative level in this sense. Thus we add the qualification "semio-")

III) the **level of textualization** or discoursivization, where we find simultaneously generated, 1) from the semio-narrative syntactic structures a) *personae* or characters, physical objects, or abstractions that are named—these can all be "**actors**" at the textual surface; b) a time frame; c) a spatial frame, and 2) from the semantic structures a) themes and their dispersion; and b) metaphors and other figures.

An overview of this trajectory is provided by the chart "The Generative Trajectory," from the *Dictionary* (134).

The Generative Trajectory

		syntactic component	semantic component
Semiotic and narrative structures	deep level	FUNDAMENTAL SYNTAX	FUNDAMENTAL SEMANTICS
	surface levels	SURFACE NARRATIVE SYNTAX	NARRATIVE SEMANTICS
Discoursive structures	DISCOURSIVE SYNTAX		DISCOURSIVE SEMANTICS
	Discoursivization		Thematization
	actorialization temporalization spatialization		Figurativization

(See p. 248, n. 12 below for a suggested, more elaborated version of the trajectory based on the *Dictionnaire* entry of 1986 by Claude Zilberberg.)

The model assumes that the structures at each level correlate with those at each other level, in a manner formulatable as production procedures of generative transformation or (for Greimas and Courtés) as procedures of "disengagement" from the implied writer/speaker, called the **enunciator**, though as noted above, the authors concede (*Dictionary*, 85) that thorough description of those procedures "is far from possible at the present stage of semiotic research" (see nn. 9 and 10 below). The charting of these three levels must be qualified by the point that the third one cannot be considered fully subsequent to the other two (as level 2 is subsequent to level 1); rather, it is a set of exigencies that may intervene in the projective, compositional process at each of the levels. For example, we must think of, say, a subject actant as already beginning to be thematized (i.e., to gain some semantic content, so to speak, for example as a pastoral maker) within level II even though thematization is diagrammed as occurring at level III and its dispersion through the text will occur there. This third level brackets together the processes of "textualization," of "putting into text that is linear" (temporally, spatially, or both—*Dictionary*, 133).

If we imagine, for example, a person busily engaged in writing experimental verse about, say, themes of sexual and artistic development and about the impact of a painful love conflict in a time of likewise painful political crisis, concentrating on what should come next, on defining the characters as disguised operatives within some intensely felt political commitments (but also as interactive fictional constructs), concentrating on spinning out metaphors that recurrently spring to mind in these processes (say, of the rejected lover as a tree with a broken branch), and all the while frequently backtracking, making insertions and deletions, fitting in portions that were written earlier, until some larger organizational structure emerges, then further adjudicating between earlier and later segments of that, sometimes frustratingly, linear text, to respond to occurences while the writing is in process, to correlate and rearrange parts, to make consistent, to make conformable to various intentions of revealing and partially concealing allusions for various audiences—if we imagine such a process, we can see that the semiotic model above offers the flexibility to account, in principle, for all the processes of text production. Chapter 7 will offer a more particular account of what I believe some of these were for the *Calender*. (For an oral discourse, the illustrated intervening of textualization at prior levels would work differently, consisting for example of retracings through formulaic reiterations with variation.)

THE TRAJECTORY'S SYNTACTIC SIDE, INCLUDING ACTANTS OF COMMUNICATION AND OF NARRATION

Having now roughly sketched in the frame of the generative trajectory, we next review it a little more closely, so as to define the "actant" and its other main component concepts. This time we take the three levels in reverse order, starting with matters already well known to us as readers, namely those at the immediate textual surface. We will first go through the syntactic side or region of the trajectory at all three levels, leaving review of the semantic side for later (remember that at each level it is, artificially, split into two regions, syntactic and semantic).

At the third level on the syntactic side, as was noted, two easily recognizable processes occur simultaneously: **spatialization** and **temporalization**—disengagement (from the implied enunciator) of a place or places "not here" and a time or times "not now": for example, there was "a hill . . . All in a sunneshine day . . . When Winters wastful spight was almost spent"—a certain late January thaw time in hill country. Along with these two processes, we also have simultaneously at the third level "**actors**" being generated (the process thus being called **actorialization**), as noted *personae* or characters, animals, objects, or named concepts.

Before these, at level 2 (semio-narrative syntax) and structuring their functions in the discourse, are the **actants**, any one of which can be represented by more than one surface-level "actor," as also conversely such an "actor" may have been syncretized from more than one actant.[5] The term "actants" derives from L. Tesnière, who defines them as "beings or things that participate in processes in any form whatsoever, be it only a walk-on part and in the most passive way," a definition that the *Dictionary* condenses to say that an actant is "that which accomplishes or undergoes an act" (5). The "actant" concept is based on the view that syntax is an interrelation of components "of the elementary utterance . . . such as subject, object, predicate" and that the predicate (to be referred to later as the elementary "**function**"—shown as "F" in formulae)—the predicate is "the nucleus of the utterance" (5). Instances of the four possible actants, **subject** and **object**, **sender** and **receiver**, are then, as it were, constellated around a predicate into a semio-narrative 'sentence' or meta-sentence representing the central structure of a given discourse, and called its "**base narrative program**." Since we are speaking now of level II's components in their syntactic, not yet in their semantic aspects, we should note that the four actants are what they are because they represent the four possibilities for the nominative positions of utterance syntax, which are defined in two patterns: either *subject*, predicate, *object* [i.e. complement—whether direct object or predicate nominative]; or *sender*-subject, predicate, object, indirect object [i.e. *receiver*]. (Obviously I am mentioning English word order for illustration, but these positions are conceived to be language universals, whatever may be the forms, sequences, or ellipsis patterns in which they occur in various languages.)

By the time a particular generative or writing process has moved into the last layer of level II,[6] these four actants have diversified into some of the following nominative positions, as defined by Greimas and Courtés (5–6). First, being usually versions of the sender/receiver pair,[7] the common **"actants of communication"** are the **enunciator/ enunciatee** and the **narrator/narratee**, occurring where the sender and receiver are explicitly installed in the discourse (for example as "I" and "you"), and the **interlocutor/interlocutee**, participants in "second degree interlocution" or dialogue.

Here let us pause to recall that (as noted in chapter I) while Greimassian discursive semiotics clearly focuses on text production rather than on reader functioning, it does offer an important bridge from the text as discourse to the sphere of reader activity, in this concept of the paired actants of communication; that is, enunciator-enunciatee, narrators-narratees, and interlocutors-interlocutees are by definition variously situated, as implied *loci* of attention/response, within and relative to the **diegesis** of the text (the flow of depicted states and/or events). They thus provide a fruitful model for studying the perspectival framing of a text, as we can shortly do with the *Calender*.

Besides communication actants, there are also at the same generative level (presumably the last layer of level II) the **"actants of narration,"** being mostly versions of the subject/object pair introduced above.[8] The subject/object actants are of two types, in accord with the two possible predicative forms of utterance: **subject of state**, often with the verb "to be," and **subject of doing**. That is, to give as example an excerpt from the results concerning the *Calender*, a sample 'subject/object of doing' pair might be as follows: a subject actant having been "thematized" at given moments of the text as a 'pastoral maker' comes to govern an object actant thematized as 'product of pastoral making.' These subject-object actants of doing are further subdivided into those of **pragmatic doing** and those of **cognitive doing** (i.e., subjects/objects "of doing [proper]" and those "of knowing"); for example, the cognitive subject actant can be actorialized by an informant such as our friend E. K.: the subject is the informant, the object is his information, which his "doing" may reveal or may declare concealed. In short then, within the syntactic side of level II of the generative trajectory, moving through different sublayers of level II the sender-receiver pair most often generates actants of communication, the subject-object pair mostly those of narration, although with certain exceptions.[9]

In the effort to present a relatively simple and straightforward account, I am making the "actant" sound like a more essentialist or substantialist concept than it is: we must bear in mind that an actant is no more than a syntactic position, at particular moments in the text being given loadings of various kinds. Thus the actant will at a given moment "be united with" a certain "thematic role" and a certain "actantial" (or syntagmatic) role—the two together wholly comprising its existence just at that moment or point within the narrative trajectory for potential readers. And it may also be conjoined with a value of some kind, a concept to be defined later.

Resuming our backwards review of the syntactic side of the generative trajectory, we come to the fundamental or initiating level, which is said to consist, in its syntactic dimension, of "a sort of organized space containing interdefined terms on which syntactic operations may be carried out, operations that give rise either to new organizational combinations (derived and complex terms) or to ordered syntactic strings" (*Dictionary*, 331). What the organization of that "organized space" consists of is something we must postpone until later for closer review, namely the set of oppositions known as the semiotic square; suffice it to say here that in the level-I realm viewed as syntax, each opposition on the square is seen not as a static relation between two opposed terms (as in logic) but rather as a potential action that some actant might *do* or suffer. For example, love and indifference are contradictory opposites (the presence of the one implying the absence of the other), but if love is imagined dying away, departing from someone's feelings to be replaced by indifference, we see that this static opposition can turn into a sentence, indeed a story line, and thus has the potential to generate syntax or meta-syntax.

The organizational pattern I am following dictates that we would next move into a reverse-order review of the semantic half of the generative trajectory, and soon we will do so. (Another glance at the above chart of the generative trajectory may be helpful at this point.) But let us first pause, before going on to semantics, for some application to *The Shepheardes Calender* of the concepts so far presented, in order to fix them more concretely in mind and also to begin illuminating a certain aspect of the *Calender* text.

COMMUNICATION ACTANTS AND THE *CALENDER*'S PERSPECTIVAL FRAMING

The actants of communication listed above can be seen "discoursivized" as certain "actors" in the text of the *Calender*, as it was consistently published and reissued in Spenser's lifetime and in the succeeding decades. Immediately after the title page, which indicates no author (thus the "enunciator" is not named), a first narrator speaks some verses "To His Booke" and to Sir Philip Sidney, signing himself Immerito, the unmeriting one. (A 'narrator' is a sender of discourse when "explicitly installed" there as an actor—*Dictionary*, 210.) Thus Immerito and "his book" constitute in this text the first narrator-narratee pair, with Sidney as its secondary narratee. At the start of the introductory epistle, a new narrator calling himself "E. K." takes the floor, claims for himself a status—as friend of the author—outside the eclogues' diegesis or fictive stream of projected states/events, and addresses himself to Spenser's close friend "Mayster Gabriell Harvey," thereby installing a second narrator/narratee pair of actors (E. K.—Harvey) that continues through the introductory materials as well as the prefatory "Argument" before each eclogue and the "gloss" after each. The actor E. K. syncretically combines this gloss-narrator actant of communication (as "sender") with the functioning of another, a "subject" actant, as we have already noted, namely that of the informant, a "subject of knowing," his "object" being his information. That is, declaring himself the *confidant* of the "new poet" who is "shadowed" in one Colin Clout, E. K. announces that he will clear up certain mysteries of the eclogues and will keep others secret (he says he has glossed them because he "was made priuie to [the poet's] counsell and secret meaning in them," but "as touching the generall dryft and purpose of his Aeglogues, I mind not to say much, himself labouring to conceale it"). E. K.'s character as a slippery and at times even disinformational informant is thus defined in his introduction. (Much confusion has arisen in Spenser scholarship for lack of recognition of this status of E. K.) His two actantial components or roles—as gloss-narrator (sender of purportedly editorial discourse) and as informant/non-informant (subject of knowing)—stand in a relation to each other of at least partial opposition rather than of accretion or complementarity: he has knowledge and at times withholds it, or withholds the "dryft" of it—we do not know at which times.

His epistle to Harvey proclaims that the "new poet" will through this book "come into the knowledge of men" and be "beloued of all, embraced of the most, and wondred at of the best"; this implies, besides the primary narratee of the actantial pair Gabriel Harvey, also a secondary narratee to his statements—the implied reader, named (thus installed) as "all" and "men." The narratee thus secondarily addressed by E. K. may be coalesced (since he or she is no more delimited than to be a general "all,") with the one directly addressed (thus being in that case the primary narratee) in the framing lines of "January" and in the opening of "December," as an implied, imperative-formation "you": "A shepherd's boy, call [you] him no better, . . . led forth his flock." (The other eclogues do not have such a framing voice addressing a "you" and speaking *about* the shepherds of the eclogue; rather they consist entirely of dialogue between named shepherds (as in a play script), thus actorializing the interlocutor/interlocutee pair of actants. In their case we can identify simply an "implied observer," another subject actant of knowing, implied by the fictive stream of events when no narratee is named, that is, from "February" through "November.") But in "January" and "December" an implied reader is explicitly represented as primary narratee for this introducer/concluder voice.

In sum, then, the implied readership is situated in the *Calender* text three ways: as a secondary narratee to E. K. the secretive informant addressing Harvey, as the syntactically implied "you" to the introducer-concluder voice piping up briefly in "January" and "December," and as absent implied observer (subject of knowing) in the other eclogues. It is small wonder that E. K. can play so many tricks on us: he is a doubly situated intermediary between the eclogues and this triply situated implied readership, from whose myopic perspective we as actual readers must come at the text, with all our best reading skills. Seldom has a text been so complexly framed and the readers thereby so schizophrenically situated relative to its diegesis. Then of course there is the innermost perspectival layering, when the shepherd-interlocutors of several middle eclogues themselves become narrators, and tell allegorical fables.

The first eclogue begins:

> A shepheards boye (no better doe [YOU] him call)
> When Winters wastful spight was almost spent,
> All in a sunneshine day, as did befall,
> Led forth his flock, that had bene long ypent . . .
> Tho to a hill his faynting flocke he ledde,
> And thus him playnd, the while his shepe there fedde.
>
> ("January," 1–6)

The speaker here, this general narrator of the "January" and "December" eclogues (and third narrator-actor to speak), will later conclude "January" with seven lines appended to the end of Colin Clout's "plaint," but then will withdraw entirely from the text until the opening of "December"—a pattern paralleling and thus deictically reinforcing the withdrawal of Colin Clout (the declared shepherd figure for the "author" Spenser) from live lyric performance, which lasts from late in "January" until "November." As we will see, this "January" narrator's statements turn out to supply clear confirmation of the actantial structure behind the textual surface, though my analysis will not initially refer to them in deriving its results.

These first lines show the narrator and the implied narratee ('you') as person-actors socially ranking Colin Clout, who is the first actorialization in the text of a "subject of doing" actant, defined or semantically invested for a start merely as "no better than a shepherd's boy." The eclogue narrator will, as mentioned, take the floor again to open "December"—which unlike "January" ends with Colin speaking, the fictive subject-'actor' having there finally usurped the role of the sender-'actor,' as if the portrayed and long veiled author himself at the end were in that constructed manner stepping boldly to the surface of the text—such is the effect created. By "December"'s opening, the narrator-introducer voice has named Colin not a mere hireling shepherd "boy" but a "gentle shepheard" who "wel could pype and singe, / For he of Tityrus [Chaucer] his songs did lere." Colin's thereby stated transformation between Eclogues 1 and 12 from a mere shepherd's boy—"call him no better"—to a "gentle shepherd" who can "sing" at the competence level of Chaucer defines what I shall later characterize and expand upon as the "narrative program" of a thematized actant, "pastoral maker" (i.e., a subject actant periodically evident throughout the text in coalescence with the thematic role "pastoral maker"). It is a subject actant that is actorialized most prominently as Colin Clout, but also as a number of other figures.

Thus we can identify several actants behind the text of *The Shepheardes Calender*, and it will be useful, for gaining a summary view of the "actant" concept through this illustration, to draw them together in a list.

ACTANT (2nd level, last layer)	*ACTOR* (textualized actant or coalescence of actants)
ACTANTS OF COMMUNICATION, SENDER/RECEIVER PAIRS:	
—enunciator/ enunciatee	—none [i.e. implied general sender of text/implied reader: blank position actants, by definition never *as such* "installed in the discourse"]

—1st narrator/ narratee and secondary narratee (of Immerito's verse epistle)

—Immerito/ his "Booke"—Sir Philip Sidney

—2nd narrator/ narratee and secondary narratee (of prose epistle and glosses)

—E. K./Harvey—implied reader as gloss narratee

—3rd narrator/ narratee (in "Jan." and "Dec.")

—introducer voice of "January" and "December"/ implied socially discriminating 'you' addressee

—interlocuter/ interlocutee

—1st shepherd/ 2nd shepherd of each ecologue

–"Feb." to "Sept." interlocutors as tertiary narrators/ narratees to each other

—when being tellers of allegorical fables

[ACTANTS OF COMMUNICATION] SUBJECT/OBJECT PAIRS:

—subject/ object of knowing (informant/ information)

—E. K./ the "poet's" private "counsell"

—subject/ object of knowing

—non-installed "observer" (the implied reader)/ fictive states and events in the ecologues (diegesis)

ACTANTS OF NARRATION
(to be described later)

—Sender (Emitter)/subject-Receiver

—"Pan that once did love" ("Jan.") and "God of Shepheardes all" ("Dec.")/ Colin as subject-Receiver

—subject/ object of doing

—pastoral maker (Colin Clout and other actors)/ product of pastoral making (their songs, sestina, etc.)

This list sums up my illustration of how the concept of actants can be applied to *The Shepheardes Calender*. All but the last two have just been discussed; explanation of the penultimate one will be left for later in this and the succeeding chapter where it can be better understood although it has here been generally defined in note 8, page 247. And of course the last one represents the primary subject-object portion of the narrative program analysis yet to come.

THE SEMANTIC SIDE OF THE GENERATIVE TRAJECTORY

The definition of the semiotic square—the fundamental "logico-semantic form" in Greimassian thinking—is rather extensive, but we must review at least some elements of it with care for the purpose of the present application, since the narrative structures we are going to see in the *Calender* and other texts cannot be grasped without it. Furthermore, since it structures the semantic/thematic dimensions as well as the meta-syntactic dimensions of discourse, an account of it shows clearly that Greimassian discourse analysis does not work only in a Proppian manner, identifying skeletally reduced fictive "events" and disguised "characters," as theory popularizers have sometimes claimed.

Represented at level I, the domain of fundamental semantics is "constituted by logico-semantic forms" or "categories" (*Dictionary*, 133 and 275), prior to any phonetic investment (which would enable representation of them in a given language), categories that "can be articulated on the **semiotic square**," i.e., as a set of interlocking relations based on two kinds of binary opposition that define the meaning of most fundamental semantic categories. The two kinds of opposition are **contrariety** and **contradiction**.

Signification, in this view, "rests only on a distinction of opposition which characterizes the paradigmatic axis of language" (*Dictionary*, 308): that is, a unit of meaning, a **seme** (the minimal unit of meaning, not further subdividable), is what it is only by virtue of not being every (and any) other possible unit of meaning in the given signifying system—say, the English language—where it occurs. A is defined by being "not non-A." Thus the definition of meanings is not substantial—as if words stood for things (a "pipe" meaning that particular tootling instrument over there)—but purely relational. Meanings are "points of intersection, results of relations" (*Dictionary*, 310). Of course this view does not deny that words will in many given utterances have particular "referents" in the phenomenal world; it asserts, however, that their meaning or semantic content is not determined by any particular referent but is a function of their position along the "axis of selection" or **paradigmatic axis**, from which at a given position in an utterance a speaker selects, out of a vastly extended string or "axis" of possible signifiers (in a language, words) that could fit into the given slot in the sentence, a certain one and no other. (Speech or writing involves the constant interplay of this paradigmatic axis [of selection] with the **syntagmatic axis** [of combination], along which units of meaning are strung out linearly, in classifiable patterns—the two axes are sometimes called the vertical and the horizontal.)

Semantic categories, then, are initially seen to be constituted by a binary relation of opposition, A is "not negative-A," negative-A standing for any other position than A's on the paradigmatic axis. But in logical terms there are two types of clear binary opposition: besides that of contradiction, there is also contrariety, and a given semantic category can be more than merely a two-term opposition. **Contradiction** means "the presence and absence of a definite trait" or in predicative terms the denial or negation of it, while **contrariety** refers to "the same trait, present twice in different [diametrically opposed] forms" (*Dictionary*, 308), that is, it is a trait, the existence of which implies that its obverse would also be possible.

The semiotic square, then, diagrammatically shows the set of logical relations generated by these two types of binary opposition—contradiction and contrariety—when they interact through taking the same term as starting point. Consider the following example:

In its predicative form, this is known as the deontic modal category:

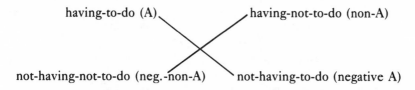

As was noted above under "syntax," contradiction, when seen in terms of process or action, is the act of negating the initial term; thus it is the relation of negation whereby the presence of one term implies the absence of the other. Contrariety, on the other hand, is the relation such that the presence of each term mutually presupposes the possible presence of the other (as its diametrical alternative); in the above example, if something can be prescribed, it is logically presupposed that it can as well be prohibited, and vice versa. The schematic way of drawing the square is

A possible square must be tested for another definitive relation if it is to be considered as representing a genuine semantic category, rather than as a mix of terms from different categories. That is, it must be possible to carry out the operation of assertion upon each of the two negative terms (-A and -nonA) with a resulting relation of one-way implication between it and the term above it on the square. Thus, moving from bottom to top on either side of our sample square, "permission to do," when asserted, implies prescription, and likewise optionality [to refrain], when asserted, implies prohibition. These two axes (sides of the square) are known, respectively, as the positive and negative deixes, while as we have seen the diagonal relations are the contradictory, the horizontal are the contrary. One must not think that for every semantic category all four positions of the square will necessarily exist (i.e., be lexicalized) in a given language—many times they will not, but they remain logical possibilities, for any category based on both contradiction and contrariety, as most fundamental categories are. Greimas and Courtés add that certain rare categories are not based on both kinds of opposition, but rather "their constitutive relation is [only] . . . contradiction" (309), and they thus have logically only two terms, as

Such a category is defined by the condition that "the negation of its primitive terms [A and non-A] produces tautological implications" (309). However, even these binary categories may usefully be mapped onto the semiotic square, since even though a sub-term may

be logically equivalent to the one above it, linguistically speaking it retains a trace of the operation carried out to produce it, as in

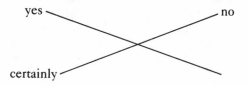

Any actant after initial semantic investment (i.e. at the level of "thematic role"—correlated with, on the syntactic side, the actantial grammar of communication and narration, as described above) "may be projected onto the semiotic square and thus articulated in at least four actantial positions (actant, antactant, negactant, negantactant)" (6).

As a last example of a semiotic square before we move on to the next level of semantics in the generative trajectory, we may revisit another modal one (cited in chapter 1, n. 1) that will later show us something about *The Shepheardes Calender,* namely love as desire, also called the boulemic or *vouloir* modality:

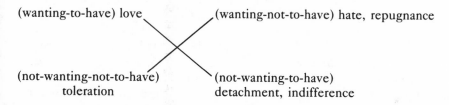

We have now surveyed the "first generation categorial terms" of the semiotic square. (The "second generation categorial terms" are relations between the relations on such a square—we do not need to consider them here.)

At level I, then, the semantic categories consist of the bare binary logico-semantic forms as constructs of multiple possible interrelations, while at level II, that of "semio-narrative semantics," they together become, for a linguistic semiotic system, the **semantic competence** of speakers/writers of a language—the semantic concepts that they know how to use. With respect to discourse generation, level II is where "available **values**—positioned on the semiotic square(s)" are selected and "actualized" by their "junction with subjects of the surface [semio-]narrative syntax" (*Dictionary,* 277). These values can be **modal** (i.e. a competence, such as 'knowing-how-to') or **descriptive** (including cultural, subjective, or objective ones, such as a pot of gold, or a social status); and two or more of them can at times be invested in a single actor. The syntactic "mold" where this investment of values occurs is the utterance of state, mentioned above in connection with the actant "subject of state" (as in 'my muse' is the source/locale of 'lovely layes' [poems]). Thus in the *Calender* a female subject actant of state (among other guises seen as the muse) is the subject that 'is' (is conjoined with) the achieved product of "making," which is invested with the value of competence. (See also below, p. 60 for further discussion of "values.")

At level 3 on the semantic side (discoursivization) we recognize two processes successively moving from the abstract to the concrete: **thematization** and **figurativization**. Thus at the same time as the dual subjective/modal value pastoral competence is being actorialized as Colin's object of quest (i.e., invested in the object half of a subject/object actantial relation, at the syntactic side of level 3), it is also being thematized as, among other thematic roles, poetry-making skill, and figurativized as, among other figures, Colin's pipe.

We have now moved through the generative trajectory of discourse twice, surveying first its syntactic then its semantic structures. Before we leave the concept of the "generative trajectory" behind and go on to the "narrative program," let me, as promised, give a brief update of certain research upon it, drawing upon the *Dictionnaire*, vol. II (1986). This material was not available when I first conducted my application, but consideration of it has contributed to my account here in a supplementary way. In the *Dictionnaire*, II, the entry *parcours génératif* presents, as its first half, a new essay by Claude Zilberberg on the generative trajectory, which assigns greater importance than was recognized before to the so called **thymic category**: **euphoria-dysphoria**, or attraction-repulsion. He there presents it as, we might say, a kind of third region within each level of the trajectory, mediating between the other two regions, those of syntax and semantics; and he proposes the thymic (in the form of the opposition category of tensiveness: i.e., tension-relaxation) to be the most fundamental level of fundamental syntax. He thereby adds to the generative trajectory a recognition of what we might term affectivity in the writing process.

The main disagreement between the two halves of this new entry "generative trajectory," *Dictionary*, vol. II—its second half being by Daniel Patte—concerns the question of which aspect of meaning-generation is ultimately more fundamental, syntax or semantics. Greimas has regarded syntax itself as ultimately semantic, and thus semantics as the more fundamental element (as Patte still does in his half of the entry). And Greimas has presumably considered the thymic category as a sub-component of the semantic side of the trajectory,[10] while Zilberberg seems to see it as either ultimately syntactic or at the interface of syntax and semantics.[11] Of course it has long been cited by Greimas as the activating category for the important step of valorization, the installing of values in the discoursivizing of narrative structure, but without reference to its particular place in the generative trajectory. In whatever way we might size up the disagreement between Zilberberg and Patte, both have expanded the older view of the trajectory—and here I think is the important point for now—by incorporating, in two different proposed schemata, impacts of the thymic category at each of the trajectory's levels.[12]

THE NARRATIVE PROGRAM

We complete our introduction to the Greimassian model with an account of the closely related concepts of the "narrative program" and the "narrative trajectory," which will enable us to analyze the *Calender* as a structured whole. The theoretical account so far given has, by way of example, identified Immerito, E. K., the eclogue-narrator, the shepherd-speakers, and god Pan as "actors" for various actants of communication (mostly sender/receiver pairs). Further, we have begun to identify the thematized actants of the subject/object pair (e.g., pastoral maker/ product of making). Such subject actants are said to inscribe in the discourse their narrative programs.

A **narrative program** is a meta-syntactic structure originating at the level of semio-narrative syntax and entering into the ordering of a discourse. It takes the form of an asserted transformation of a subject actant from one state to another with respect to a potentially value-invested object. (In overall effect, someone or something either gets a valued something, or loses it.) The concept was prefigured by the Proppian idea of a narrative progression from "lack" to "liquidation of lack," but is much more complex, and its interest lies in how it explains that process of discursive acquisition or loss.[13] In the *Calender*, the 'pastoral maker' subject (S_1) will through his transformative doing move from the state of not having the competence to make verse to the state of having that competence (lack of pastoral competence to possession of competence). This **base narrative program** or "NP" is globally at work in the *Calender*; the **instrumental narrative programs** (each of which reproduces the base narrative program's terms in alternative arrangements and shapes a sub-section of the text) and their manner of constituting the whole **narrative trajectory**, will be described in chapter 3.

Besides subject and object actants, narrative programs have a third necessary kind of element, that is **values**: as noted above, through an utterance or utterances of state (x is y), the discourse will have attached a value to the object to be governed by the subject of doing (i.e., it has concretized what is desired, and attached valorization to what was concretized). A value is a semantic category into which the thymic category (euphoria/dysphoria) has been invested, so that it is suitable for being "inserted into the frame which is foreseen for it within a surface narrative structure" (*Dictionary*, 365), namely, as an investment into the object-actant of an utterance of state. This combination of an object invested with a value-actorialization—say, the sestina of "August" for which Cuddie is vested with a "crown" as prize, here figuring pastoral competence—is represented formulaicly by the symbol "O_v." Values, as already noted, are either modal (such as 'being-able-to' or 'knowing-how-to') or descriptive (either entities such as can be stored up, or pleasures, states of feeling, and so on).

The new "narrative program" entry (*Dictionnaire*, II) includes a proposal by Francoise Bastide to account for the origin of this investment of value into an object (O): as the level II source of valorizing, she says, there is a sort of thymic instance of the sender actant, to be called the *emetteur* or emitter—in other words an emitter-receiver pair as the mechanism of transformation specifically for valorizing; that is, for investing the thymic category. This appears to be related, though perhaps it is broader in scope, to Greimas's earlier suggestion that there is one kind of Sender as an actant of narration, namely in literary, juridical, and certain other discourses, the transcendental Sender of a specific "program" of value to the S_1 subject of a discourse, as subject-Receiver. This instance was shown above in the list of kinds of actants in the *Calender* as god Pan with Colin as subject-Receiver, and will be illustrated further in chapter III (on issues related to the thymic category see also nn. 3, 6, 8, and 12).

To return now to the narrative program as a whole, it is said to be "composed of **an utterance of doing governing an utterance of state**" (*Dictionary*, 245). The "utterance of state" is the prior and presupposed assertion of equivalence or junction between a secondary subject (S_2) and the value-invested object (O_v), and the "doing" is the carrying out of the subject's transforming of that junction, either from disjunction to conjunction or vice versa. To continue the example from the *Calender*, Eliza (a 'respected woman'—in some text portions "the muse") is conjoined with the "April" lay in her honor, a poetic object thoroughly invested with "conning." The lay claims indeed to have engendered the queen-image it celebrates. This conjunction (of Eliza with the lay) is the utterance of state textualizing that condition of competence which the 'pastoral maker' (centrally Colin but also seen in other actorializations) is said to have lost at the diegetic temporal moment depicted in "January"'s conclusion, but that he eventually regains through his transformative 'doing.'

Greimas and Courtés's formulaic condensation of the narrative program concept is as follows. Besides the symbols already explained, one must know that -> stands for transformation (as just discussed),[14] that is, for the "doing" in that utterance of doing whereby the subject transforms the juncture between the S_2 subject and the valorized object, and that $^\wedge$ and U stand for, respectively, conjunction and disjunction. The formulation at this stage will not yet be complete but can be understood thus far as:

$$NP = S_1 \text{->} (S_2 U O_v)$$

That is, the narrative program[15] equals subject #1's "doing" or action that in effect transforms his (her/its) state from that of not having to that of having the value that was installed in the discourse through the assertion of its object's conjunction with subject #2. Alternatively, the NP may consist of S_1's losing of a value at first possessed— i.e., transforming himself to the state of non-possession of it, whereby the S_2 regains conjunction with it, thus:

$$NP = S_1 \text{->} (S_2^\wedge O_v)$$

As Greimas and Courtés explain, we are dealing with "a communication syntax between subjects (or a syntax of object transfers, since pragmatic, cognitive, or modal acquisitions of one of the subjects may be considered as so many losses for the anti-subject)" (*Dictionary*, 333). The S_1's action of governing or taking control of the S_2's juncture with a valorized object arises from the process of discourse generation: i.e., it "is" nothing but a transformation rule, explaining the movement of the meaning-generational process from the deep level of fundamental syntax to that of surface narrative syntax (see "Generative Trajectory" chart above, p. 45). Thus Greimassian semiotics explains language and textual utterance *per se* as an aggressional function.

One further refinement will complete the NP's representation. So far we have viewed it as a unit in isolation, but in fact it is a unit operating within the total functioning of the discourse. Therefore we bracket the formula (everything on the right side of the equation) and designate it with an "F" for "function," meaning that this pattern of a subject's transformation is a single function within the syntagmatic structure of the whole discourse. (That is, the base NP will commonly function through textualization of several variant instances of itself, which are called instrumental NPs, each of which is thus one among others, all of them together making up the text's **narrative trajectory.**) The completed formula for the narrative program, then, is

$$NP = F[S_1 \text{->} (S_2 \; {}^\wedge O_v)] \text{ or}$$
$$NP = F[S_1 \text{->} (S_2 \; U \; O_v)]$$

The total narrative trajectory of a given discourse is a "series of . . . narrative programs, . . . in which each NP is presupposed by another, presupposing, NP" (*Dictionary*, 207). In the narrative trajectory of the *Calender*, as we shall see, the NP of the pastor's acquisition of competence presupposes another NP, of his prior loss of love and thus competence.

A more detailed model of eight variant possibilities for instrumental NPs, as seen within a text's narrative trajectory, has been proposed in the *Dictionnaire*, II, by Peter Stockinger (cf. entry *programme narratif*, II:177–79). These eight include differing modes of creating or preserving a subject's [S_1's] control of a value, or making it latent (put back, as it were, to the level of the possible, the not yet discoursivized); the total model is said to comprise "a grammar of the narrative program" for charting exchanges and circulations of values.

The model of text production that we have now surveyed is a unified theory of interlocking concepts, which in the Greimas/ Courtés dictionary volumes receive fuller, more technical explanation than I have given here. But the dictionary is of course organized alphabetically by term, and nowhere summarizes the theory's set of fundamental concepts. Thus I have thought it necessary to do so in an introductory way here. Greimas has published accounts of many of them in books and articles in French and some in English, but the dictionary of 1979 (trans. 1982) revises and updates earlier work, presenting the central concepts of his theories, which he still generally holds, though as we have been noting, various modifications and elaborations of detail are proposed in the *Dictionnaire*, II (1986), by his Group de Recherches Sémio-Linguistiques.

IS THE "NARRATIVE PROGRAM" GENDER-SPECIFIC?

To end this chapter with a reflection from a different perspective, we might wonder whether recent feminist work on "women's ways of knowing" suggests a potential challenge to the claim of universality for Greimas's concept of the narrative program as fundamental to texts as unified discourses. The "narrative program" concept represents a view that any unified discourse, as such, is ultimately a sort of aggressional claim on rightness (thus a valorized motion into meaning, or a motion into meaning through valorization), wherein an agentive something/someone appears 'taking' a measure of that 'rightness' by means of taking over a valorized object from another someone/something—in short, a textualized piece of aggression—an assertion of some communication sent (in the sense of 'sending,' above), which has had to be paid for, as it were, within an economy of circulation of value, by a subject-(S_2)-and-object in conjunction, that have come under the governance of the S_1. Feminists may perhaps want to explore whether such a paradigm represents a characteristically male view of discourse, or whether it may typically apply just as well to women's discourse-texts.

The work of the psychologists Mary Belenky et al. presented in *Women's Ways of Knowing: the Development of Mind, Voice, and Self* (1986) proposes a pattern of typically female epistemological development that, if credited, might imply something about female discourse: if the thinking of women, as knowers and readers, works in certain ways, might not their thinking as writers, producers of discourse, also work in certain related, gender-specific ways? Belenky and Clinchy propose, as part of their 'map' model for epistemological development, a category of "separate knowing" (vs. "connected knowing"); two components of this "separate knowing" category are a habit of adversarial "reasoning against the other" and an agentive impulse to "mastery and control"; this kind of knowing they find to be characteristic not only of science and other putatively objective discourses but also of typically male thinking about ethical issues. The two components just cited sound reminiscent of the Greimassian narrative program: does not its S_1 subject by definition carry out an adversarial movement into mastery? In identifying the aggressive-acquisitive impulse (i.e., a proprioceptive instance) as the basis of discoursivity, is the "narrative program" concept claiming universality for a particularly male paradigm?

My own hunch is that it is not. I suspect that Greimas is indeed working at a level of production of semiosis prior to and cutting across the impact of gender categories. But this is only speculation. Dynamite-laced issues are here raised. Are women to be considered, at the level of functioning that makes up the very generation of language and discourse, non-aggressive? If Belenky et al. are (as they seem to be) tracing a pattern of culture-specific female socialization into certain "ways of knowing," those would presumably enter into discourse production at a level hierarchically subsequent to that of fundamental structures of discourse generation. The most I can say now is that the new research (cited several times above) of Greimas's team on the thymic category is supplying materials that would need to be taken into account in any exploration of this issue about gender. The question is not of immediate urgency for the present study since the gendering of the voices of the *Calender* seems to be unproblematically male, according to several dimensions of the culturally constructed maleness of its time.

3

The Shepheardes Calender Analyzed through the Greimas Model

We now review the analysis of the *Calender* text that the previous chapter has prepared for. The algorithm or set of description procedures that I followed comprises Appendix I below, in a version for readers who might want to consider its text-linguistic merit or applicability. The present chapter will summarize in less technical terms what the procedures consist of and what they showed about the *Calender* when applied to it.

STAGE 1: OBJECTIFICATION

Stage 1, the "**objectification**" of the text, we have in effect already accomplished in chapter 2. The task of that part of an analysis is to retrace and bracket out the first stage of the writer's textualizing process, namely the projection of a posited 'not-I, not-here, not-now': this objectification is done by terming the writer or "outer-level" category of person the "enunciator," by renaming any stated or directly referred to addressee of that enunciator the "enunciatee," by eliminating text portions addressed to that outer-level enunciatee, and finally by eliminating any referential time and place indications concerning the enunciator and enunciatee(s). Since the *Calender* is anonymous and has no direct addresses to readers or to its dedicatee, it programmatically subverts these common features of a discourse, by not naming the author and not directly addressing the intended readers (instead installing them as covert secondary narratees). Thus the task of objectifying it is to point out this state of affairs (that is, to describe the perspectival framing, as I did above), whereby the outermost sender-receiver pair is "Immerito" and "his book." As the 'enunciator' and 'enunciatee' are not referred to, we do not need here, as one often would for the procedures, to peel them away from the textual material to be taken as initial corpus. Spenser's political reasons for presenting himself to the reading public in this wrapped up state and inward-gazing posture are probably already well known to Spenserian readers of the present study but will be discussed for a new purpose in chapter 7.

STAGES 2 AND 3: SEGMENTATION AND EXTRACTION/INVENTORY

In proper order, one would proceed to stage two—segmentation of the text into sequences of the textual surface[1]—the results of which operation are then set aside until one completes the more laborious tasks of stages three and four, namely the discovery of, so to speak, the semantic core of the text. For the present summary, since the segmentation results come into play later, let us postpone reviewing them until they are needed (though in my carrying out of the procedures, I conducted the segmentation in prescribed order), and let us instead first review the nature of the procedures and the results of stage three.

Stage 3 is the **extraction of frequently occurring words** for a "corpus" of data. How does one extract the first frequent-words list? Using the whole-text method, as I did here, one begins with a complete concordance of the text, in alphabetical order showing each word, in its whole-line of occurrence (its context). The concordance I used was generated by a concordance program from a complete text of the *Calender*, with spelling standardized, and for all the words still existent in English, modernized. With the concordance in hand, my first two tasks were to coalesce the various forms of each inflected word (e.g., *conne, cunning, couth, kyth*, etc.) into a single entry-count, and to eliminate from consideration four categories of words: 1) grammatical words—i.e. "closed class" words of only grammatical semic content—such as articles, conjunctions, and prepositions (most of this had already been done by the computer program); 2) words that label something as approved of or disapproved of (euphoria/dysphoria tags), such as "good," "wicked," "delightful," "drearisome"; 3) qualifier and quantifier words, such as 'specially' or 'more,' and 4) general purpose words that, as used in the text under study, carry too little semantic information when extracted to be useful, such as 'say' or 'thing.'[2] After these jobs were done with the *Calender* concordance, the following relatively brief list of very frequently occurring[3] indicator words emerged, as the initial or first extraction word list, on the basis of which to conduct the next step. (That step would be the extraction of a further word list from the co-occurrence inventory of this one, i.e., from the set of all the words that occur within the whole line contexts of these first selected ones. Those will be called qualification variables.)

First Extraction, Number of Occurrences

shepherd 170	conne/conning [knowing how to] 36
love 130	aeglogue 34
poet 77	emblem 34
god 68	spring 34
sing 62	muse 32
flock 57	winter 32
verse 55	worth 32
learn 55	head 31
sheep 45	lust 31
poems/poetry 41	pipe 30
flower 37	eye 28
wit/weet 37	find 28
make [as craft] 36	hear 27
	honor 26

One's first thought is that this is a generically determined list, largely of words that would occur frequently in most Renaissance English pastoral works—and so it is. It is, however, only the starting point for a series of further **extractions and inventories** that will eventually—out of the whole-line contexts of these words—turn up a list of indicator words for something specific to this text, something that is itself not explicit at the textual surface, namely the "**semantic isotopy**," or what above I loosely called the semantic core, of the particular text.[4] The semantic isotopy will be a small set of sememes, some nominative (or rather, actantial), some predicative: for example in the results here to be presented, {pastoral 'maker' of artistic/prophetic expression}, and {having/governing}. "Isotopy" is a term Greimas borrowed from chemistry, where it means the relationship among slightly variant versions of the same atom or molecule—structurally alike but of slightly differing atomic weight. The semantic isotopy of a text is a set of structurally definable semantic constructs (sememes) that occur in the text in variant lexical versions (as an element occurs in variant isotopes): that is, they occur in a range of synonyms and para-synonymous words. The semantic isotopy of a text can be viewed as a **figurative isotopy** when one sorts its related sememic categories into metaphoric and metonymic groupings; this, in effect, is what we will do with the *Calender*'s isotopy in chapter 5, on the basis of word-group correlations shown in appendix 2.

How did I start with the initial word list and from there arrive at such isotopic sememes as the two sample ones just mentioned? Using the whole-text concordance, one goes through the (computer-selected) whole lines where each word from the initial 'frequent words' list occurs; one selects and lists all the co-occurring words (qualification variables) that are not excludable by any of the four exclusion categories above. Each of these selected words is listed along with its line number and with the base word from whose occurrence context it is being extracted. One next alphabetizes the resulting new list (thus making all the occurrences of each word fall adjacent to each other in the list and become readily countable); one then records a new occurrence count for each word,[5] and scans the list to determine what numerical level should now be designated 'frequent' for this new inventory stage. One can then draw up a new list of the frequent words that have thus emerged.

How does one determine what should be the **'frequent' level** at each inventory stage? I used the following principle: the level at each stage should be so defined that most of the already selected words will recur again as 'frequent,' along with a proportionately much smaller number of new ones. Because one is doing multiple extractions and inventories, casting the net slightly higher or lower at a given inventory stage will not significantly affect the outcome. I applied each time a further exclusionary criterion not so far stated[6]: for each of the newly identified, possibly 'frequent' words out of a given inventory, consider whether there are in the same inventory one or more synonyms or partial synonyms to it; if not, then eliminate that word. Thus if one has cast the net a bit low and picked up some words that do not reflect a widely recurrent sememe, they will be eliminated. If one has cast it a bit high and thereby missed some isotopic word, it may turn up later, or if not, some parasynonym of it will. (As mentioned earlier, the appendix may be consulted for a more precise account of the procedures just summarized.)

In the second-stage inventory for *The Shepheardes Calender*, then, along with most of the first list (see above), the following new words turned up as also frequent:

blossoms	oaten
break	reed
commend	rhyme
complaint/plain	show
fame	skill
mantle	tree
music	tune

One then continues extractions and inventories in this same manner until new 'frequent' qualification variables stop appearing. With *The Shepheardes Calender* this happened after five inventory stages. I then eliminated four words that had not recurred after the first list (probably these would be generically frequent pastoral words that had no particular bearing on the semantic isotopy of this text); the resulting list contained sixty-eight words that I assumed to be **isotopic indicators** for the whole text, here shown transcribed into noun form and alphabetized.

aeglogue	home	saving
blossom	honor	scorning
boy	lamb	shade
break	lass	sheep
calling [as calling out]	leading	shepherd
can/conning [having skill]	learning	shooting
commendation	leaving	showing
complaint/plaint	losing/being lorn	song
dance	love	skill
daughter	lust	sleeping
dread	maid/may	springing
emblem	making [crafting]	studies
fame	mantle	swain
feeding	muse	tree
feigning	music	tuning
flock	oat	verse
flower	pipe	warring
framing	playing	wasting
gift	poem/poetry	wolf
god	poet	woods
goddess	praise	working
grace	reed	wounding
hearing	rhyme	

The next step (an informal preliminary to stage 4) was to sort these sixty-eight words, provisionally, into groups of parasynonyms. For example, the largest grouping proved to be of words that refer to the product of pastoral 'making': aeglogue, complaint/plaint, emblem, music, poem/poesie/poetry, rhyme, song, verse. Such sorting cannot be done only by dictionary definition, of course, but must be based on a knowledge of prevalent and recurrent usage in the natural language of the text and its time (here, Elizabethan written English).[7] Sorting the sixty-eight isotopic indicator words, then, I came up with the following list of twenty-one preliminary or tentative sememic categories:

artistic/prophetic expression or 'making' (feigning, framing, making, tuning, working)

product of artistic/prophetic 'making' (words given above)

lesser (non-verbal) artistic expression (dance)

maker of artistic/prophetic expression (boy, poet, shepherd, swain)

being-able-to-'make' (conne/couth, learning, skill, studies)

figure of ability-to-'make' (pipe, reed)

reception of 'making' (hearing)

figure of reception/receiver of 'making' (feeding[8])

repose (home, sleep)

herd animal (flock, lamb, sheep)

canine (wolf)

plant (oat, grass, reed, tree, woods)

organic growth (blossom, flower)

respected chaste female (daughter, *dea*, goddess, grace [as person], lass, maid/may, and muse)

injuring/penetrating (breaking, saving [as contrary], shooting, wasting, wounding)

competition (leading, playing, warring)

recognition of competition (commendation, fame, gift, honor, praise, scorn [as contrary])

covering/hiding (mantle, shade)

opening/putting forth (calling [as 'calling out'], feigning [drawing, painting out], showing, and springing forth)

having/governing, in *vouloir* and *pouvoir* modalizations [wanting-to-have, being-able-to-have] (love, lust, loss, leaving)

virtuality of 'loss' (dread)

This sorting of the isotopic words into categories was only preliminary and provisional.

Stage 4: Structuration

The more proper next step was to analyze each of the sixty-eight words into component semes and sememes, or in other words to make a **semic/sememic inventory** for each word—a kind of profile of its semantic components, together representing its usual acceptation in the given text. One will then be able to sort those extracted words into groups of synonyms and **parasynonyms** (near or partial synonyms[9]), so that each group reveals as its common ground a **constructed sememe**. (To understand the concept, we must recall that the basic or minimal unit of meaning, not further subdividable, is the seme, and that two or more semes existing together in a more complex unit of meaning comprise a sememe.) In stage 4 that is, the extracted words will serve as material for identifying a small set of word groups, within each of which its words will have shared units of meaning that will be compiled together into a semantic profile,— a constructed sememe. These word groups are the ones that recur most frequently, and most frequently *together*, in the text and thus comprise and indicate its semantic and meta-syntactic individuality. Any given word of a natural language in its shared acceptations represents a seme, sememe, or set of sememes, but the profile that we can compile as representing the shared elements in a list of synonymous and parasynonymous words is an artificial contruct, an instance of meta-language, thus called a constructed sememe. This organizing of the selected frequent words into groups and identifying of their constructed sememes is called "**structuration**," the task of stage 4 of the procedures.

The seme and sememe definitions below, it must be understood, are not claimed to be naturally occurring language: they are constructs (sometimes stiff or bizarre-sounding) meant to allow for as precise an analysis as may be; devising them is an exercise in meta-language and in hierarchical sorting of the meaning components of a given lexeme. Rather than trying to present all sixty-eight semic/sememic profiles, let me offer two of the most complex as examples (most of the others were far simpler).

First, the word 'poet,' as used in the *Calender*, I analyzed as carrying the following semes and sememes. These components are variously indented or not indented to show their **hypotactic relation**s to each other (hypotaxis means "the relation linking two terms situated at two different stages of derivation . . . as between main and subordinate clauses, between modified and modifier"—*Dictionary*, 145). In other words, a category farther left governs those under and to the right of it. Substantive form is attributed to each term, and the sememic inventory is not exhaustively broken down to semes, but only far enough to show the structural outline of the total complex sememe represented by the word 'poet.'[10] Note that the two columns in the table below are distinct: we read down the left, or down the right; but each **classeme**[11] on the right is also linked with the lined up kernel seme or sememe on its left.

POET: *partially articulated semic/sememic inventory*

KERNEL SEMES/SEMEMES:	CLASSEMES:
producer [of]	humanness (not non-humanness)
	maleness (not femaleness)
	euphoria (not dysphoria)
fictiveness [veridiction modality]	
performativeness [fictive doing]	sound (not silence)
rhythmatizing/unrhythmatizing,	temporality (not spatiality)
controlling/decontrolling [of]	
language	
tones	
discoursiveness	
culturativeness	
units	
politico-culture	
participants	
enriching/impoverishing [of]	permanence (not transience)
language	
tones	
discoursiveness	
culturativenes	~~lowness (not height)~~
units	[shown canceled, as it is
	in only figurative
politico-culture	combination with the
participants	correlated category
	"culturativeness"]

In this notation, we show some of the elements lined-out when we want to express the concept that in a metaphoric complex sememe, the vehicle of the metapohor remains present but in a canceled state, having been neutralized by its governing set of semes. To take next a closely related word, 'shepherd' as used in the *Calender* (and perhaps in other Renaissance pastoral works) represents a figurative sememe—the shepherd as 'maker' of prophetic art.

SHEPHERD: *partially articulated semic/sememic inventory*

KERNEL SEMES/SEMEMES:	CLASSEMES:
producer [of]	humanness (not non-humanness)
	maleness (not femaleness)
	euphoria (not dysphoria)

performativeness [fictive doing,   sound (not silence)
  i.e. 'piping' to animal audience]
    rhythmatizing/unrhythmatizing,   temporality (not spatiality)
    controlling/decontrolling [of]
      herd-animals
    nourishing/starving [of]
      herd-animals

producer [of]   humanness (not non-humanness)
                                          maleness (not femaleness)
                                          euphoria (not dysphoria)

fictiveness [veridiction modality]
performativeness [fictive doing]   sound (not silence)

rhythmatizing/unrhythmatizing,   temporality (not spatiality)
controlling/decontrolling [of]
  language
    tones
  discoursiveness
    culturativeness
      units
  politico-culture
    participants

enriching/impoverishing [of]   permanence (not transience)
  language
    tones
  discoursiveness
    culturativeness   ~~lowness (not height)~~
      units   [shown canceled, as it is in
                                          only figurative combination
  politico-culture   with the correlated category,
    participants   "culturativeness"]

Once these inventories for the sixty-eight isotopic words have been
done, we can recognize a more precise set of relationships among
the above categories, into which the words were at first provisionally
sorted. For example, sememic structuration of the initial categories
of 'covering' vs. 'putting forth' reveals them to be two figuratively
articulated terms of the veridiction modality, namely 'secrecy' (being/
non-seeming) and 'truth' (being/seeming). The veridiction category
consists of the semantic category 'being' articulated to a second generation semiotic square (of relations between the relations), as shown
in the following diagram.

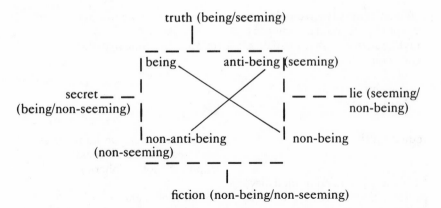

'Covering' in *Calender* usage is a figurative form of the concept 'secret,' while 'putting forth' represents 'manifestation' or truth. Since this same veridiction category has been found to occur in the semic inventories for 'poet' and 'shepherd,' (namely, in their term 'fiction': non-being/non-seeming), we can recognize their linkage at the level of the semantic isotopy with 'cover,' 'put forth,' and 'feign' (feigning = fiction: non-seeming/ non-being).[12] The *Calender*'s isotopy thus includes the set of the non-derogatory terms of the veridiction category (truth, secret, and fiction), excluding only the derogatory one of the lie.

Through identifying such semic and sememic overlaps of the isotopic concepts, we arrive, then, at the following small set of interactive constructed sememes, which include instances of shared semes and sememes recognized in all sixty-eight indicator words that resulted from the extraction inventories, and which therefore represent the "general semantic isotopy" of *The Shepheardes Calender*.

Actants (thematized):

> pastoral maker/producer of artistic/prophetic expression (includes vegetal and parodic animal figurativizations)
> product of artistic/prophetic expression (includes figurativizations as spiritual nourishment, and as vegetal and animal excrescence)
> respected chaste female
> consumer/sanctioner of artistic/prophetic expression

Value:

> competence for artistic/prophetic expression (includes figurativizations as emblematic objects and prizes, and as the concept of 'competing' at pastoral 'making')

Predicates (or "functions"):

> artistic/prophetic making (subsumes its contradictory, 'reposing' or not-making, and its veridictory modal figurativization as covering/uncovering,)
> rending/piercing
> having/governing (subsumes its modalizations, 'love,' 'loss,' 'leaving')

Having formulated the general semantic isotopy of the *Calender* as this list of sememes, we are now in a position to sort them into 'semic messages' and, after some further work, to propose a particular combination of them as a meta-sentence representing the *Calender*'s 'base narrative program.' That step will first require, however, a brief recapping of the narrative program concept as explained in chapter 2.

PROSOPOPOEIA AND STAGE 5: RECOGNIZING THE BASE NARRATIVE PROGRAM

Let us pause briefly for certain more concrete observations about the fundamental metaphoric configuration evident in the above sememic results. Chapter 4 will be, in one sense, an extension of this account of prophetic prosopopoeia. In *The Shepheardes Calender*, the pastoral 'maker'—the artist of musical, politically loaded and packaged language from the green-shaded pastoral world—is steadily set forth through a radical assumption of *prosopopoeia:* that is, the world of life, vegetal and animal alike, is fundamentally assumed to mirror his nature. Oaks and cypresses bear (as leaves) his curly locks and may speak his speech (cf. "February" and "November"). A fox, a wolf, or a briar may take over his actantial role when he is to be shown failing to live up to his calling. His budding branch (or his newly extruded velvety goat horns—cf. "July") of desire may be cropped/castrated by his much-respected nymph. His excrescences of fruit (say, hymns or *idyllia*) or thorns (plaints or curses), respectively, will feed or pierce his loved one or enemy. His central action of poetizing is figured as an oxymoronic activity of simultaneously covering and uncovering truth, just as a bush, in covering itself with foliage or blossoms, in the same process uncovers/discovers its particular nature. With this metaphoric configuration at the center of the semantic isotopy, we can easily see how the particular sixty-eight words indicate eight sememes, certain ones of which include animal and/or vegetal figurations, each of those in turn being embodied in various "actors" or particularizations—animate, inanimate, and abstract.

It will be recalled, from the presentation of the three levels of discourse generation in chapter 2, that actants formulated as are those in our eight-sememe list should be characterized as 'thematized' or outer-second level actants (situated just prior to the level of actorialization), which (still true to their first-level nature) function as subjects or objects, senders or receivers, the four 'first-level' or fundamental actantial possibilities, and may at the third level be particularized in both abstract and figurative as well as person "actors." Thus the 'pastoral maker' actant is actorialized as a tree or (parodically) a wolf, and also as Colin Clout, Cuddie, Palinode, and so on. The 'respected chaste female' is actorialized as a chopping, female husbandman ("February" woodcut), as Rosalind, Eliza, and Dido, as generally 'the muse' or source of inspiration, again as a soaring she-eagle braining a shepherd below with a shellfish, or again in some passages as the abstraction royal power. The modal value, pastoral 'making' competence (being-able-to-make), is actorialized figuratively as a pipe or bagpipe, as the abstractions 'conning' and 'skill,' and again as the competition or singing-match of shepherds.

But we have gone ahead of ourselves. Starting with the above list of actants, predicates, and a value—comprising the general semantic isotopy of the text—how does one (how did I) go about sorting them into the appropriate groupings or "semic messages," which one can in turn later sort into fully formulated base and instrumental narrative programs? For this task I used three sources of information from the results already in hand: 1) the correlation of semes and sememes (as shown in the semic inventories) shared by particular ones of the eight isotopic sememes; 2) patterns of word co-occurrence in the five inventories; and 3) the segmentation boundaries established in step II of the description procedures (see p. 248, n. 1, and appendix 1). After refreshing our memory of the definition of a narrative program, we shall refer to these sources for help in identifying and localizing (within the text) the *Calender*'s instrumental narrative programs. (As with any discourse under this analytical model, it will have one base narrative program and may have one or more instrumental or supporting narrative programs, which are instances of the base NP with one or another term reversed.)

As was noted in chapter 2, the narrative program is a formulaic sentence expressing "a change of state effected by any subject (S_1) affecting any subject (S_2)," whereby S_1 in effect goes from the state of not-having to that of having some value (v) invested in an object-actant (O) that has been conjoined with S_2. In other words and put

crudely, a unified discourse is fundamentally structured as someone/
something's (the S_1's) action of taking over a desired "value" by
taking over or governing an 'other' with whom/which that value has
been conjoined through an object (remember that actants may appear
in the text actorialized as either abstractions, figurative constructs, or
personae 'actors'). Where "F" = Function (or predicate), and u =
disjunction, the formula is F: S_1 -> (S_2u O_v). Note that the predicative
element or "function," the S_1's "doing," is represented twice in the
formula, as "F" (governing the utterance) and as "->" (in proper
syntactic position). Let us restate our eight sememes in alignment
with the terms of this formula.

Actants
  S_1: pastoral maker of artistic/prophetic expression
  S_2: respected chaste female
  O: product of artistic/prophetic expression
  [Sender: definer and consumer/sanctioner of the value
     'competence'][13]
Value
  v: competence for artistic/prophetic expression
Predicates:
  F: having/governing (in actualizing mode, i.e. 'taking control
     of')
  U: disjoining, or 'rending'/ 'penetrating'
  F with single actor (syncretically) as both the actantial subjects:
     [the performance NP of] artistic/prophetic making

This arrangement shows, first and most obviously, the alignment
between the 'pastoral maker of artistic/prophetic expression' (S_1) and
the product of pastoral making as object actant (O). For the product
of 'making' in *Calender* usage has sememically the same inventory as
'poet,' minus only the sememe of "producer." The same justification
holds for aligning the 'pastoral maker' as subject actant (S_1) with the
modal value of competence for 'making,' an alignment again justified
by the kernel semes shared by these two complex sememes. Pastoral
'making' competence, the only modalized sememe in the list, is the
only possible candidate to be the desired value that is seen to be
attached to its sememically matched object (product of pastoral making).[14] Furthermore, these linkages are reflected in certain clear patterns of high word co-occurrence frequency:[15] poet with feign (10
co-occurrences in the inventoried lines alone), with 'make' (4 co-
occurrences), with fame (6), honor (5), worth (5); and shepherd with
'aeglogue' (8), make (5), sing (4), play, skill, and pipe (3 each).

The position of S_2, the actant to be conjoined with/disjoined from the value-invested object (product of 'making') can be identified with that of the 'respected chaste female' on semantic grounds and in relation to the linkages that have already emerged. A distinct co-occurrence pattern proved to be that of 'dance' with words carrying the 'respected chaste female' sememe. At seven co-occurrences with such qualification variables, it is the next most common after the predictable 'shepherd' and 'love' at eleven each. Working from the other direction by counting the co-occurrent words in lines where we find the set 'dance,' 'heydeguys,' 'hornpipe,' 'miller's round,' and 'tripping,' we likewise find 'respected chaste female' words clearly prevalent: grace [as person] (3), maid (2), and daughter (1), while 'poet' does not appear, and 'shepherd' does so only twice.

In the usage of the *Calender*'s pastoral world, "music" or "song" (regarded in the Renaissance as an art essentially verbal as well as tonal) is interchangeable for poem/poetry/poesie—an "E. K." gloss explicitly makes this point, citing Terrence as authority ("December" gloss, "musick"). 'Dance' as a primarily non-verbal art of bodily motion (it might or might not have singing with it) cannot be so thoroughly assimilated to 'poem/poesie,' but does share important kernel semes with it and, by contrast, fails to share an important classematic element, maleness. As 'poetizing' is the especially appropriate activity for (male) shepherds, 'dancing' seems to be an analogously appropriate activity for their female goddess-grace-muse-daughter-nymphs. Consider this semic inventory for 'dancing,' which in *Calender* usage always includes accompanying music:

DANCING: partially articulated semic/sememic inventory

KERNEL SEMES/SEMEMES:	CLASSEMES:
fictiveness [veridiction]	humanness (not-non-humanness)
performativeness [fictive doing]	euphoria (not dysphoria)
rhythmatizing/unrhythmatizing,	sound (not silence)
controlling/decontrolling [of]	temporality/spatiality
tones	
motion	
corporality	
participants [in]	
sociableness	

enriching/impoverishing [of] transience (not permanence)
  motion
    corporality
  sociableness
      participants
      observers

The 'respected female' as dancer is linked with many of the semes for 'artistic/prophetic making' while yet being distinctly differentiated from S_1 with respect to the elements of verbality and absence of a gender seme; thus it is the natural S_2 with which the value-invested object (O_v) 'product of competent making' can be conjoined, so that S_1 may take control of it. Speaking more loosely, we might say that in the narrative program here emerging, the 'respected chaste female' is the transmitter of competence for the 'pastoral maker.'

The predicate sememes in our list of eight now sort themselves as functions centering the relations between the identified S_1 and S_2. As for the sememe of 'having/governing,' it is a lexicalization of a component central to the NP formula itself, if seen invested with a "realizing modality"[16]—that is, given the content of 'taking control' rather than simply of 'governing.' If one were in any doubt about that identification, a look at the occurrence frequency of such collocations as poet-love and shepherd-love would add further confirmation.

For the sememe that I termed 'injuring' in the initial list of categories, the parasynonyms (in inventoried lines alone) proved to include two sets for more specific actions of either 'rending' (break, carve, cut, cut off, gash, hew, lop, rend, tear) or 'piercing/entering' with instruments thereof (bite, pierce, prick, shoot, sting; arrow, bolt, dart, point, shaft); it was at first difficult to decide whether these represented the same sememe or perhaps two somehow related ones. Considering the NP formula, we see that they share the sememic content of disjoining (U). The third predicative sememe above, the activity of 'pastoral making,' when shown being engaged in, represents what Greimas calls a performance NP, described as a case of a single actor syncretically actorializing at once both S_1 and S_2; for example, Colin in "November," while he is performing, himself actorializes both the 'pastoral maker' and the 'respected female' (conjoined with invested competence). How this occurs we will see later.

For the base narrative program of the *Calender*, then, we arrive at the following version of F: $S_1 \rightarrow (S_2 \cup O_v)$: {pastoral maker (S_1)} {takes control of (F)} {respected chaste female (S_2)} [disjoined from(U)] {competence(v)}-invested {product of 'making' (O)}. That is, the pastoral 'maker' takes control of the respected chaste female thereby to disjoin from her (gaining for himself) the artistic/ prophetic-competence with which she has been invested. God Pan (as 'god' in the word list, who also 'hears' and 'feeds on' the object of 'making') represents a narrative Sender in a Sender/Receiver pair with the pastoral maker as subject/Receiver; the god is further, as [an actor of] the same Sender actant but in another semiotic-square position, the "passive Sender, receiving the knowledge about the subject-Receiver's doing and sanctioning it."[17] This process of closed or text-internal value circulation appears at the textual surface in Colin's "January" prayer, where he begs to be pitied by god Pan "who once did love" and again in his "December" prayer, where he offers his poetic work as food to "sovereign Pan."[18] Greimas, while suggesting this Sender functioning (see chapter 2), proposes no way to write it in relation to the NP formula because it is not part of the formula *per se,* but the following could, for our present effort at understanding, be suggested, combining with his point Francoise Bastide's suggested term "emitter" for this thymic Sender actant:

$$\text{Send}_1 \text{ (emitter)/Passive Sender (receptor)}$$

$$F:[S_1 \rightarrow (S_2 \cup O_v)]$$

Here it is worth recalling again (as mentioned a number of times) that we are understanding the two "Subjects," from the psychoanalytic viewpoint of Deleuze and Guattari, as "partial objects" whose quasi-machinic interaction produces desire.

THE INSTRUMENTAL NARRATIVE PROGRAMS

Finally, we must discern what instrumental narrative programs are the textualized instances of the above identified base NP, and where they are operative in the text. As was mentioned earlier, the segment boundaries determined at stage 2 will help us with this task, as will also the particular actorialized forms of the actants within each segment. Thus I now report what could have been presented above (the **segmentation** results), except that I have saved them for the point at which they become useful for the analysis, and we thus need to have them concretely in mind.

Segment boundaries in the *Calender* are of two sorts and marked with unproblematic clarity: first, between eclogues practically all the forms of categorical disjunction coincide (spatial [here/elsewhere], temporal [before/after], actorial [I-he-she/other], and referential [dialogue/narrative], and furthermore, they are reinforced by unvarying format anaphora (an "argument" to start, one or more "emblems" and a gloss to end each eclogue). Second, at the beginnings and endings of performed eclogue-internal segments (e.g., Colin's prayers, Thenot's or Piers's fables), again the **segment boundaries** are clearly marked by actorial and referential disjunction, as well as by temporal disjunction (e.g., "One day he . . . ") and other 'now-begins-a-fiction' signals. One cannot assume that each segment will correlate with one instrumental narrative program. But since both the segments and the instrumental NPs are units of the textual surface, one can assume that some of the segment boundaries will coincide with boundaries between the portions of text in which the particular instrumental narrative programs are inscribed, and that the segments may sometimes correlate with the NPs in a one-for-one relationship.

Working with the base narrative program established above, if we examine each eclogue for its particular actorialized forms of the actantial and value terms (pastoral 'maker,' respected female, product of making, and competence), we find patterns that show what and where the instrumental narrative programs are. That is, to start with "January," the pastoral maker is there Colin Clout, shown possessing a pipe (competence) and producing 'products of making' that he then loses, ceding the value of competence back into abstract conjunction with the lady Rosalind when he is scorned and rejected by her (an actorialization of 'respected female'); that is, his performed attempt at a hymn/prayer to god Pan (one of these 'products'—O) is a failure, bringing no blessing or "ease" and ending with the acting out of this re-conjunction of S_2 with O_v, as he breaks his pipe to emblematize the injury done him by his "muse." Formulaicly, the instrumental NP of "January" is then F: S_1 [Colin] -> (S_2 [Rosalind/Muse] $^\wedge$ O ['pipe'] v [competence]. That is, the pastoral maker loses the competence for prayer because in this segment he loses control of the valorized 'object of making' when it becomes, so to speak, re-conjoined with the 'respected female' who is rejecting him; i.e., he fails to retain competence, or F: $[S_1 -> (S_2 {}^\wedge O_v)]$. The presupposition of this opening instrumental NP is that the S_1 did formerly have the posited competence, a state of affairs that can be represented well by Peter Stockinger's more elaborated version of the possible instances of the narrative program in the *Dictionnaire* II. Under Stockinger's formulations, an NP can be shown reverting, so to speak, to the status of pre-textualization, where it is held in a kind of limbo of potentiality, which is of course not the same status as it would have if it had never yet been put into text (i.e., were first being generated).[19] But for our present purposes, I believe the above simpler formulaic representation will suffice, namely to depict the pastoral maker's loss of competence as the NP of "January."

The next instrumental narrative program has proved to be inscribed in the section of text comprising "February" through "April" and is more complex in its actorializations of the base NP's terms. From the perspective of diegetic time it represents a reversion or 'flashback': that is, it shows the pastoral 'maker' at an earlier, more youthful stage, formerly taking possession of the competence which in "January" he would lose.[20] The method I used for recognizing such a portion of text (i.e., of localizing a single instrumental NP as to what stretch of text it governs) is to keep listing the actorializations from segment after segment, until I could complete another version of the base NP formula with each of its components a positive term (not a contrary or contradictory thereof), and with either disjunction or conjunction of S_2 with O_v accomplished.

To illustrate this principle at work, we can begin with Cuddie, the first 'pastoral maker' actor in "February," who puts forth a "budding branch" of pastoral 'making' (O—product of making) which is at risk of being "cropped" off, although a "girdle of gelt" that he made (O—another product) has won him the love of Phyllis (S_2—respected female) for a few days. But Thenot, the other 'actor' of the pastoral 'maker' actant here and a contrary of Cuddie, scorns his product, his love, and his lady—i.e., does the opposite of giving him a prize or recognition—and thus there is no actorialization of competence (v). Indeed, as Thenot and Cuddie are then, in Thenot's concluding fable, replaced by two figurative actorializations of pastoral 'maker'— the "aged oak" and the young "bragging briar"—the efforts at 'making' (putting forth excrescence) by both of those actors fail, and again no 'actor' for competence (v) appears. As S_2 in this second, derived and figurative case of the "February" instrumental NP,[21] we have another 'respected female,' the chopping husband"man" of the oak and briar fable, whom we see to be female in the woodcut. She is distinctly not giving over a valorizing competence to either the oak or the briar: indeed she is chopping down the oak, and thus causing the briar also to die, for lack of its protection. Of the formula elements, 'v' (competence) thus still remains actorialized only in the contrary term (incompetence, as failure of excrescence or death) in "February," and since therefore the formula cannot yet be completely written, we assume that the instrumental NP in progress is continuing into "March," namely F: $[S_1 \rightarrow (S_2 \wedge O_v)]$.

Willye and Thomalin (and recountedly Willye's father) are the personae 'actors' of the pastoral maker actant in "March," and they are joined in that actantial role by a "hawthorn studde" that "bragly beginnes to budde / And vtter his tender head." Besides the hawthorn's utterance we have other vegetal products of pastoral making (O), notably the flowers rising up from their beds. As the respected chaste female terms, we have the contrary of the S_2 actant, the disrespected harlot goddess Flora—thus E.K. explicitly characterizes her in the gloss—and a human version of her, the "light" Lettice, whom the boys look for but do not find. This time the value (v) is actorialized, as winged Cupid with his piercing arrows. But instead of shooting the light Lettice with responsiveness to a shepherdish love plaint (which would have made the conjunction of anti-S_2 with O_v), he pierces Thomalin in the heel (the potential competence becomes a distinct weakness: anti-competence). Thus though "March" actorializes all the formula elements and with disjunction of S_2 and O_v, it does so with S_2 and v in the contrary terms, disrespected unchaste female and unsuccessful love longing. Again, as the complete formula cannot yet be written in the positive terms, we assume that the instrumental NP in progress continues.

"April" completes it, with the achieved product of pastoral 'making' clearly inscribed as the "lay," sung by Hobbinol, having been made by Colin (thus S_1 appears in doubled person-actors) as he sat beside a spring (O), his source of inspiration (v—competence) being the acquiescing virgin queen Eliza (S_2): F: [S_1 -> (S_2 U O_v)]. S_2 is here also actorialized as the adored Venus of Aeneas' vision (from Virgil's *Aeneid*), her subliminal whorishness (linking her to the Flora/Lettice of "March") being cancelled by her appearance "in likenesse of one of Dianaes damosells." The inverse temporal placement of this "February"–"April" instrumental NP is signalled (besides thematically by the youth/age motif) by the temporal and actorial disjunctions defined through Hobbinol's singing of a pre-dated piece composed by the absent Colin. Thus with "April" the base narrative program itself has been textualized, but in such a relation to the diegesis of the text that its "success" is cast into a hypothetical narrative past, and we sense that the story is not over.

Without going into so much detail as we just did with "February"–"April," we can see that, on the principle of 'when the formula can once more be written in its four positive actantial terms, the instrumental NP is completed,' the third NP runs from "May" to the opening of "November," and is the pastoral 'maker's' struggle through the period of continued missing competence initiated by the "January" NP (from which "February" through "April" represented a flashback).[22] An alternation pattern of inscribing the non-completed elements of the base NP formula organizes this instrumental NP into a set of three pairs of sub-segments: "May"–"June," "July"–"August," "September"–"October." That is, in each case the first month of the pair actorializes all the terms of the formula (F, S_1, S_2, O) except competence (v), while the second ("June," "August," "October,") actorializes and foregrounds pastoral competence, but implements the 'governing/possessing' of it in the contradictory term, not-possessing. Thus in "June," "August," and "October," respectively, we have Hobbinol's *locus amoenus* or "pleasaunt syte" of perfect poetizing (v), the mazer and cosset awarded to the song contestants (v), and the October Bacchanalian stream of inspiring wine (v), but in each case the primary pastoral figure, Colin or Cuddie, is emphatically shown not to have—to be cut off from—that particular actorialization of competence. In "May," "July," and "September," the mates of the three above, we have each time two person-actors and various abstract, vegetal and animal actors of the 'pastoral maker' (S_1), and various ladies and lasses actorializing S_2, while O appears as the nourishment supplied for the respective flocks (soft rich grass or weeds) in "July" and as the satisfactions held out in the moral fables of all three months—the 'goat and kid' story, the 'eagle and Grindal' story, and the 'Lowder sheepdog' story; but competence remains unactorialized in "May," "July," and "September," other than visually as the shepherds' staves in the woodcuts, reminders of the missing element. (The bleak scene of repression in the English church, as Spenser saw it, would be reflected in this pattern.) In other words, we see a thrice repeated sort of Tantalus alternation, between having no competence available and not having the apparently available competence.

With Colin's statement in "November" before he begins his elegy to Dido, we come to the end of this third NP: "my rymes bene rugged and vnkempt: Yet as I conne, my conning I will strayne" (competence being actorialized here in the concept "conning.") From "May" through "October," the pastor has hoped for competence then seen it appear but beyond his reach, hoped for it, seen it beyond his reach, hoped for it, seen it beyond his reach. (A notable negated actorialization of O in "June" is the piercing wooden arrow Colin produces, with a hope to shoot at the intransigent lady Rosalind (an effort to disjoin v from S_2)—he does not hit her. To summarize, the "May"–"October" instrumental NP was, in a form highlighting a few of the principal actorializations:

F :	S_1	$\rightarrow$ (S_2	$^\wedge$ O	$_v$)
taking	Colin/Cuddie/Thomalin	Rosalind/	trifles &	syte,
control	Hobbinol,	Flora,	bells,	mazer,
	fox, wolf	mother goat,	blossoms	wine
		'lady' shrine	of lust	

We have not yet taken note of the important actorial functions of the posie-emblems or mottos (themselves 'actors' in each case) attached to the shepherd interlocutors, each usually having such a motto assigned to him at the end of each eclogue where he appears. Colin's "January" emblem *Anchora speme* (Hope my anchor) is revised in "June" to *Gia speme spenta* (Hope already spent), serving as one among other signals that the narrative program of the "May" to autumn sequence, in relation to that of "January," is the continued non-possession of the hoped for good. Similarly, an effort to define and thus install competence as height (vs. lowness—classematically, as it were), running through a series of "July" *sententiae* and emblems (*Suorum Christus humillimus, Suorum Deus altissimus, In medio virtus, In summo foelicitas*), is ended by the term-shifting 'answer' of Cuddie's "August" emblem, *Felice chi puo.* The actant or actantial value can be actorialized as an abstraction, here a saying: 'high' *foelicitas* or felicity is superseded by felicitous cunning: "Happy he who can" rather than happy he who is high. The syntactic oddness of this motto is noted in the E. K. gloss, and the point of it thereby insisted upon. Thus besides serving as markers of segmentation, the emblems are also indicators for the nature of the narrative program(s) in progress.

Colin's "November" emblem, *La mort ny mord* (Death does not sting), points to the means by which he has at last recovered competence, by assimilating into himself a 'respected lady' cancelled, as it were, by death and apotheosized. When in "November" he at last sings after having been incompetent for lyric performance or 'making' since "January," we begin the portion of text inscribing the fourth NP, one of performance, formulated as a case of the same actor actorializing both the S_1 and S_2 positions.

$$\text{Colin} \quad \text{Colin-as-his-own-renewed-muse} \quad \text{elegy/pipe}$$
$$F{:}[\ S_1^| \rightarrow \qquad (S_2^{/} \qquad U \qquad \searrow O_v)\ ]$$

"November" begins with the old Thenot of "February," now humble and supportive, presenting himself as deferring to Colin just as a titmouse defers to a nightingale, then as a "lowly plant" being watered by a "higher tree" dropping dew. The woodcut triply actorializes Colin's recovered competence: he plays his pipe, his shepherd's staff is propped on his arm, and he wears a leaf-crown of honor on his head. The deceased Dido, the initial S_2 figure, is syncretically serving also as an O actorialization (she is "The fayrest floure our gyrlond all emong")—i.e., she syncretically actorializes both S_2 and O. In this vegetal form she becomes, as it were, a piece of visionary poetry, transferred to the green Elysian fields and "enstalled now in heavens hight," where Colin in visionary joy appropriates her to himself: "Might I once come to thee (O that I might) / O ioyfull verse" ("November," 181–82). This works as a kind of incantation in the lyric. In the act of performing the 'respected female's' funeral and apotheosis, the pastoral maker converts the initial S_2 actor (Dido) to a product of making (O—her lead-wrapped corpse), replacing her as S_2 with himself as performer, coalesced with the heavenly visionary lady, thereby acting upon his recovered competence.

"December" is then a reiteration of the base NP, again as a performance of Colin, with the S_2 figure now installed as a function of Colin himself: first as a group of "wiser Muses" lovingly chasing Colin (and superior to the "flocking nymphs" who may follow other shepherds), and finally as an unnamed female "One" contrasted with the "looser lass" he will no longer love ("The loser Lasse I cast to please nomore / One if I please, enough is me therefore"—"December," 119–20). Speculation about what, historically, is represented by this "one" restored, cleansed, and regained Muse lies beyond the scope of Greimassian analysis, and thus will be postponed until the following chapter.

The base NP has now been fully rewritten/reinstalled, with all terms in the positive: pastoral maker takes control of respected chaste female, gaining by disjoining from "her" a competence-infused object of 'making.' We have a set of instrumental narrative programs that can be summarized as the pastoral maker's loss of competence ("January"), his presupposed prior acquisition of it ("February"–"April"), his continued state of non-possession of competence ("May"–start of "November"), his repossession of competence in a performance NP ("November"), and his reiteration or continuation of his possession of competence ("December").

Formulaically, then, the *Calender*'s five (or one may consider them four, if the last is seen as a continuation of the fourth) instrumental NPs are as follows (each being, as described, a rewriting of the base NP):

"January"	$NP1 = [F:S_1 -> (S_2 {}^\wedge O_v)]$
"Feb."–"April"	$NP2 = [F:S_1 -> (S_2 \cup O_v)]$
"May"–early "Nov."	$NP3 = [F:S_1 -> (S_2 {}^\wedge O_v)]$
"Nov."	$NP4 = [F:S_1 -> (S_2 \cup O_v)]$
"Dec."	$NP5 = [F:S_1 -> (S_2 \cup O_v)]$

It may be helpful to end more concretely with five passages where each of these narrative programs finds explicit statement at the textual surface.

1. Wherefore my pype, albee rude Pan thou please,
Yet for thou pleasest not, where most I would:
And thou vnlucky Muse, that wontst to ease
My musing mynd, yet canst not, when thou should:
Both pype and Muse, shall sore the while abye.
So broke his oaten pype, and downe dyd lye.

("January," 67–72)

2. To her will I offer a milkwhite Lamb:
   Shee is my goddesse plaine,
   And I her shepherds swayne,
Albee forswonck and forswatt I am.

("April," 96–99)

3. a)
But if on me some little drops would flowe,
Of that the spring was in his [Chaucer's] learned hedde,
I soone would learne these woods, to wayle my woe,
And teache the trees, their trickling teares to shedde.
Then should my plaints, causd of discurtesee,
As messengers of all my painfull plight,
Flye to my loue, where euer that she bee,
And pierce her heart with poynt of worthy wight:
As shee deserues, that wrought so deadly spight. . . .
But since I am not, as I wish I were
Ye gentle shepheards, which your flocks do feede,
Whether on hylls, or dales, or other where,
Beare witnesse all of thys so wicked deede:
And tell the lasse, whose flowre is woxe a weede,
And faultlesse fayth, is turned to faithlesse fere,
That she the truest shepheards hart made bleede,
That lyues on earth, and loued her most dere.

("June," 93–101; 105–12)

b) Colin my deare, when shall it please thee sing,
 As thou were wont songs of some iouisaunce?
Thy Muse to long slombreth in sorrowing,
Lulled asleepe through loues misgouernaunce.

("November," 1–4)

4. She raignes a goddesse now emong the saintes,
That whilome was the saynt of shepheards light:
And is enstalled nowe in heauens hight.
   I see thee blessed soule, I see,
   Walke in Elisian fieldes so free.
    O happy herse,
Might I once come to thee (O that I might)
    O joyful verse.

("November," 175–82)

5. The gentle shepheard satte beside a springe,
All in the shadowe of a bushye brere,
That Colin hight, which wel could pype and singe,
For he of Tityrus his songs did lere.

("December," 1–6)

4

Isaiah: Excrescence as Expression and the Figurative Isotopy

"Let all the trees of the field clap their hands"

Before moving on to pursue the impact of the *Calender*'s narrative program as defining an Elizabethan ideologeme, let us first trace a more limited implication of the preceding analysis (chapters 2 and 3), one drawn from its semantic rather than its meta-syntactic dimension, that will complement the points to be made later about how the eclogues work together and what emerged socio-politically from their impact: that is, we will first examine the *Calender*'s particular elaboration of a field of traditional pastoral imagery, that of people as plants and animals.[1] In the terms of Greimassian discourse analysis presented in the previous two chapters, this material will represent what is called a figurative isotopy of a text, a certain plane of recurrence of meaning, created by the action of "figurativization" within the generating of a text: that aspect of the text-writing process that allows "actors" (figures at the textual surface, such as characters) to be formed with certain semantic components already built into them—namely those components necessary to the text's unity as a "semantic universe."

To begin spelling out this figurative isotopy, which the patterned correlations of most-frequent-word groups in appendix 2 below make clear,[2] let us consider what Sir Philip Sidney in the *Apology for Poetry* praised as the biblical prophets' "notable prosopopoeias," whereby the trees of the field shout and clap their hands. Metaphors of expression—sexual, artistic, prophetic expression—as plant (and sometimes animal) growth, excrescence, production, and reproduction run through all twelve eclogues of the *Calender* and its E. K. apparatus. For diversity and range of suggestion and application, Spenser varies the biological reference of such images, which may be of branching, foliation, blossoming, fruiting, horn sprouting, or herd growth and calving or lambing, yet all signify expression, which may either thrive or die. Our purpose in tracing the pattern will be not only to observe it, as something brought to light by the above discourse analysis, but also to note the particular sequence of emotional states that it enables the poet to string out, as one reads through from "January" to "December."

The pattern appears in "January" as part of the Petrarchan prosopopoeia of nature's sympathy with a love-sufferer, whereby Colin Clout addresses the winter trees as sentient sufferers like himself.

> And yet alas, but now my spring begonne,
> And yet alas, yt is already donne.
> You naked trees, whose shady leaues are lost,
> Wherein the byrds were wont to build their bowre:
> And now are clothd with mosse and hoary frost,
> Instede of bloosmes, wherwith your buds did flowre:
> . . . .
> All so my lustfull leafe is drye and sere,
> My timely buds with wayling all are wasted;
> The blossome, which my braunch of youth did beare,
> With breathed sighes is blowne away, and blasted
> And from mine eyes the drizling teares descend,
> As on your boughes the ysicles depend.
>
> ("January," ll. 29–34, 37–42)

The young pastor here laments his frost-killed blossoms of expressed love, then in conclusion to the eclogue despairingly breaks his bagpipe of reeds, another expressive piece of vegetal excrescence, prematurely destroyed. A metaphor here becomes, in a way typical of pastoral fictions, a narrative event: his failure of erotic expression (failure to win the favor of his desired lady Rosalind) breaks off his poetically expressive capability, represented as a reed pipe.

Before we proceed further with tracing this pattern of excrescence as expression and what it supports as events or developments in all twelve eclogues, let us consider a probable fund of images for Spenser's particular use of it as a metaphoric configuration, namely the messianic chapters of Isaiah, 54–56. Of course, the world of Renaissance pastoral commonly incorporates this kind of prosopopoeia, of a humanized, even eroticized, fictive landscape, where trees, flowers, and sheep have little other business than to image the psychic states of human characters. And other pastoral works of the time have metaphoric configurations akin to that we are observing. But in the *Calender*, the constant linkage of sex/excrescence/procreation/

production with prophetic art/expression points in several details to the metaphorics of these chapters of Isaiah. (Why that is so would be matter for speculation—perhaps the restoration moment in the national political life of ancient Israel to which the second Isaiah, as we call him, addressed his prophecy was of similar intensity to that of Protestant England in 1579—the continued existence of the Protestant English church perhaps indeed hung in the balance.)

The radical prosopopoeia of the *Calender*, with pervasive vegetal as well as animal figurations of the pastoral/prophetic 'maker' or poet, including especially, as we will see, the "September" fable of a sheep-dog named Louder, allies it closely to these chapters of Isaiah beginning

> Who hath believed our report? and to whom is the arm of the Lord revealed? For he shall grow up before him as a tender plant, and as a root out of a dry ground: he hath no form nor comeliness . . . we did esteem him stricken, smitten of God, and afflicted. But he was wounded for our transgressions . . . (Is. 53:1–4)

In these chapters, the bearing of fruit or offspring is repeatedly linked or equated with the creation of meaning or song, as when the eunuch is told not to consider himself "a dry tree," for in the Lord's house he will have "a name better than of sons and daughters"; and the formerly barren woman is told "Sing, O barren, thou that didst not bear; break forth into singing, and cry aloud, . . . for more are the children of the desolate than the children of the married wife" (Is. 54:1). The Lord's (as the prophet's) word from his mouth, it is said, will nourish the ground to make it bring forth seed, plants, and bread, and to make "the mountains and the hills break forth before you into singing, and all the trees of the field to clap their hands" (Is. 55:11–12). The conflation is so complete that not only do people sprout and blossom but trees grow hands and clap them.

The E.K. gloss says of the "February" Oak and Briar story that it is in the mode of Aesop's fables, and Spenserian commentary sometimes notes the strangeness of Spenser's practice of fabling with sentient plants, rather than with animals as Aesop mostly had (this "February" fable having no known source, I believe, as is commonly surmised, that it was specially devised to attack the Earl of Oxford—see chapter 7): a biblical rather than a classical metaphorics, particularly of Isaiah, would seem to be behind this narrative usage. In "February"'s fable, the treacherous young courtier as a briar bush no longer protected by the tall oak deservedly dies, while later (in "November") the recovered young pastor Colin is figured as a tall green tree dropping moisture over smaller plants below. In the back of Spenser's mind may have been a certain verse of Isaiah's: "Instead of the thorn shall come up the fir tree, and instead of the briar shall come up the myrtle tree: and it shall be to the Lord for a name, for an everlasting sign that shall not be cut off" (Is. 55:13).

More distinctly than was the case with this last example (which might be a coincidence), we have here in Isaiah, I believe, the literary source of "September's" brief—and again, original—fable about one "Lowder," the useless watchdog of the shepherd Roffy, who should have barked louder but did not. In the sleeping time of late night he vainly trotted out to search the far fields and woods for wolves while a disguised wolf feasted back in the pen. Thus he did not signal alarm when his barking was needed. The story must refer to some investigation of Catholic political activity, undertaken by one of Archbishop Young's (Roffy's) subordinates—a fellow employee of Spenser under Young—a misguided mission in which the investigator was duped into following a false lead while Catholic sympathizers worked elsewhere (see n. 16, p. 262). Isaiah had analogously, with bitter irony, invited the beasts to come and feed on the Lord's sheep, since His shepherds were proving so ineffectual:

> All ye beasts of the field, come to devour, yea, all ye beasts in the forest. His watchmen are blind: *they are all ignorant, they are all dumb dogs, they cannot bark;* sleeping, lying down, loving to slumber. Yea, they are greedy dogs which can never have enough, and they are shepherds that cannot understand: they all look to their own way, every one for his gain, from his quarter. (Is. 56:9–12)

The watchmen of the Lord are figured as at once greedy, failing shepherds' dogs and greedy, failing shepherds (the people being the Lord's sheep). The greedy shepherds appear in the *Calender* as Palinode of "May," Morrell of "July," and Diggon Davie of "September" (though the last is there penitent).[3] Certainly the dog owner of the fable, Roffy (Archepiscopis Hroffensis, Bishop John Young of Rochester, Spenser's own employer), is not one of them but a contrasting good shepherd. Yet even he has ineffective subordinates in his shepherding, such as this "louder" barking dog who yet does not bark where he should, and even has to be rescued by Roffy from the feigning wolf, who could lure the "dog" out because he "cond the shepherds call." Of course Spenser, in taking up this barkless dog metaphor (and turning it into a narrative), was not introducing something novel but rather adopting a biblical image already current in Protestant polemics.[4] But it remains, in the *Calender*'s central metaphoric configuration, a concrete link with the book of "Isaiah."

In working with the prophet Isaiah's metaphorics of radical proso-popoeia linking human, vegetal, and animal productive and reproductive capacities as vehicle for production of prophetic art and religio-political activism, Spenser created the *Calender*'s interlocking themes of the erotic, the poetic, and the moral-prophetic; for in the Hebrew prophetic tradition, a prophet could be figured not only as a shepherd or a springing tree but also as a rejected suffering lover or husband (as centrally in the book of "Hosea"). It appears that prophetic practices in ancient Israel included physical, gestural, and pantomimic systems of meaning, whereby a prophet might stand in public bleeding or dirt-covered to image the spiritual state of the nation, or give his own children names signifying a message they could spread as they merely moved about, or cry aloud in the street like an animal. For Spenser as Protestant poet wanting to speak prophetically in the England of 1579, the textual transmissions of this vivid biblical metaphorics seem to have proved especially appealing, and defined his handling of the pastoral genre.

The pastoral metaphoric construct of shepherding, sheep, and enemy wolves as both ecclesiastical and poetic needs a little sorting out. Church pastors, like the cult professional religious of Isaiah's day, are readily seen to have a flock of human sheep, but what exactly are a poet's or artist's sheep? As in Sidney's *Arcadia* poem "My sheep are thoughts" and in George Herbert's "Christmas" (where the poet claims "a flock of thoughts and words and deeds"), a poet's sheep are in the first instance his thoughts and words, which he must keep moving in ambling, rhythmic order with his metric and stanzaic piping.[5] (I may accurately say "he" and "his" in this context of definedly male poetizing.) This control of the word-sheep enables them to feed abundantly in well managed pastures of rich language and poetic tradition. From that point, by a metonymic extension of the pastoral poet as nourisher, we come to the concept that the poet's readers/listeners, along with the words they are given, are also "sheep" to be fed on his rich words. In one of Spenser's amusing formulations, the young listeners to be fed morally by the poet's words are "flocking fry" (sheep of the sea, as it were—"October").

The metaphor of the clerical pastor as shepherd has the same components, being constructed, however, from the opposite direction. The churchman's "sheep" are in the first instance human: his listener parishioners, who as in Psalm 23 are to feed on the pastures where he leads them, where his prophetic words of preaching will function as nourishment for them. By metonymic extension for him, then, his sheep may also be the words of his scriptural wisdom, learning, and preaching, which he is to order with skilled rhetoric and nourish and enrich with sound studies and with faithfulness to his calling. Thus, though the two constructs exist in hypotactically inverse forms, both poetic and clerical "pastors" are seen to have sheep (or flocks) that can function at once on two distinct metaphoric levels: as words/Word and as hearers of/feeders upon the said words. Analogously, as noted above in Isaiah, the Lord's guardians of sheep can exist on two metaphoric levels, as barking guard dogs and as the shepherd masters of those dogs.

In the biblical metaphorics of ancient agricultural Israel, the nourishing of human and verbal flocks ties in readily with imagery of excrescence/production as expression since the cultivated, nourished plants will naturally, like the animals, bear extrusions and offspring. Thus the *Calender*'s various pastors as lovers, poets, or clerics have been cast within a semantic universe defined by their own figural determinants, a possible world largely already available in pastoral tradition but also given internally consistent particular development and articulation within this text, at all its structural levels: of fable, lyric, dialogue, and editorial apparatus.

We return now to our tracing of the excrescence/expression field of imagery through the twelve eclogues. We saw that in "January" the pastor was portrayed being injured and even quasi-castrated by his love failure—his blossoms nipped by frost, his pipe of reeds, a vegetal excrescence (in the woodcut shown as a distinctly genital looking bag-pipe), broken off. In "February," by reminiscence we switch backwards in developmental time to an earlier stage of youth, where a young eager pastor, as yet untried in love, declares to a moralizing figure of old age that he intends to enjoy love since his "flowring youth is foe to frost" (l. 31); and he accuses the old man of a pruning, castration wish: "Now thy selfe has lost both lopp and topp, / Als my budding braunch thou wouldest cropp: / But were thy yeares greene, as now bene myne, / . . . Tho wouldest thou learne to caroll of Loue" (ll. 57–61).[6]

In "March" a youthful pastor, with a young interlocutor also interested in love and not blocked by moralizing old age, issues a call to the love-play befitting the spring season:

> Seest not thilke same Hawthorne studde,
> How bragly it beginnes to budde,
>   And vtter his tender head?
> Flora now calleth forth eche flower,
> And bids make ready Maias bowre,
>   That newe is vpryst from bedde.

Tho shall we sporten in delight,
And learne with Lettice to wexe light . . .

("March," ll. 13–20)

Flowers, the sexual organs of plants, with minimal metaphoric strain rise from flower beds to figure other organs rising from other beds, as Thomalin chases Cupid through the woods and bushes trying to catch him in a bird net. The hawthorne branch, as if articulate, "utters" its new bud. Sexual excitement energizes a springtime world of sprouting, rising, springing, and uttering.

Colin's "April" inset lay to Eliza creates the image of an ideal queen figure, herself a flower ("the flowre of Virgins . . . sprung" of her royal parents Pan and Syrinx), i.e., an excrescence of artistic/ prophetic "making," and the poem showers every part, garment, and ornament of that royal flower-lady with various ornamental and emblematic flowers. Later in the eclogue, Calliope and the other muses bring bay branches for Eliza's hands, making her into an Ovidian Daphne reincarnate, Apollo's beloved nymph-turned-tree that means sexual force directed into artistic creation (unattainable Daphne, chased by Apollo, became the bay or laurel tree, its garlands being awarded to winning poets at the god's festivals)[7]. Not Colin himself but Hobbinol (Spenser's tutor and best friend Gabriel Harvey) performs the lay, explaining that Colin once made it as he tuned his pipe to a spring's falling water, before he broke the pipe—the event depicted in "January";[8] thus narratively we are still in the reminiscence-of-youth time set moving by "February." With the doubled mythic instances here of Pan-Syrinx and Apollo-Daphne, which characterize Eliza's ancestry as a matter of desire directed into artistic creation (the same force energizing Colin's creation of this poetic image of Eliza), "April"'s presentation amounts to a bold claim: that the glorious queen being celebrated is really the poet's own creation—or we should rather say, excrescence, outgrowth, production.[9]

In "May" we again see an instance of ladies linked with imagery of vegetal growth, this time with the sexual implications nearer the surface: an adult pastor argues that he and his interlocutor should go out "to the greene Wood" with the May day revellers so as "to helpen the Ladyes their Maybush beare," to which the other replies with a tale of a kid whose "hornes gan newly sprout. / The blossomes of lust to bud did beginne, / And spring forth ranckly vnder his chinne" ("May," ll. 186–88). A beard as sign of sexual development appears as a patch of budding blossoms on the young goat's chin; visually, this is as strange and striking as trees clapping their hands. This budding lustfulness causes the kid to fall prey to a wily fox. Thereby

his youthful growth—and his very life—are "cropped." The suggestion of pruning as castration continues. (We should recall that wolves
in the *Calender* figure Roman Catholic operatives, while foxes, their
canine kin, represent Catholicizing or conservative Anglicans.)

"June" offers a maturing pastor a place in the central *locus amoenus*
of the *Calender*; Hobbinol's idyllic, unthreatened male "paradise" or
"pleasaunt syte" of perfect poetizing, characterized by "The grassye
ground with daintye Daysies dight / The Bramble bush, where Byrds
of euery kynde / To the waters fall their tunes attemper right" (ll.
6–8). Here no growth causes alarm, no efflorescence or excrescence
is cropped; instead, the muses sing to Pan among the holly bushes,
briars, and winding witch-hazel. Colin states his admiration for this
paradise of male companionship and unthreatened expression defined
by Hobbinol's scholarly and chaste "rymes and roundelayes," a place
where leafy boughs shelter birds who tune their "chereful cheriping"
to his poetry. But the love-sick pastor declares himself unable to live
there, hoping instead, if his poetic powers will suffice for the effort,
to make its woody reeds into love plaints that as sharp arrows will
"Flye to my loue . . . And pierce her heart with poynt of worthy
wight: / As shee deserues, that wrought so deadly spight" (ll. 99–101);
thus she would feel and know that her

> . . . flowre is woxe a weede,
> And faultlesse fayth, is turned to faithlesse fere,
> That she the truest shepheards hart made bleede,
> That lyues on earth, and loued her most dere.

In "June," then, the imagery of plant growth as expression takes
on a new range of connotations: a much beloved lady is said to have
become a "weed" instead of the "flowre" she was before. "February,"
"March," and "April" had traced a progressive flowering and foliation
of youthful sexuality into a state of cheerful though not yet fulfilled
love longing and into successful poetry. "May" had portrayed an
awareness that the love urge must unfortunately be denied sometimes, though still seeing it as appealing, and available for those
whose lofty calling does not in particular circumstances require absti-
nence. In "June," however, budding love as happy, manageable, and
unthreatened affection channeled into scholarly and poetic expression (Hobbinol's paradise) is set forth only to be shown as that condition in which the pastor whom love has injured is no longer at home;
as with "January"'s pipe-breaking, "June" shows that his love capacity has been broken off the vine of his health, and now has been
hardened and whittled into a piercing arrow pointed at the recalcitrant

lady's faithless heart—with full intent to hurt, though he laments that he may not have the ability to hit her.

In "July," the plants mentioned are those of the proud hills, condemned by the humble, lowland pastor and consisting of "bushes ranke" (l. 4), of "Melampode . . . and Terebinth good for Gotes" (ll. 85–86) but useless to sheep, and of "weedes" on which the sheep would be "glutted" (l. 112). Proper shepherds would be those "with fleshly follyes vndefyled," who by avoiding pride and heights, rises and risings, keep their flocks away from such rank and poisonous expressive growth as the fauna of Morrell's vaunted hills.

"August" portrays a productively love-sick pastor, Perigot, who through his improvised therapeutic singing of love plaints wins a carved maple goblet depicting a shepherd rescuing a lamb, over which scene is "spred a goodly wild vine, / Entrailed with a wanton Yuie twine" (ll. 29–30)—the goblet both emblematizes and rewards green and thriving poetic excrescence/expression, that grows out of artistically redirected sexual energy. But Cuddie, after awarding that goblet to the plaining Perigot, himself sings a contrasting harsher love plaint of Colin's, wherein the lovelorn pastor explicitly denies the worth of such happy and domesticated vegetal expression, imbued with artifice: a "bowre," he says, cannot contain his woes and cries, which must instead have the "wild woddes" to resound them (ll. 166–67.) And E. K. tells us that perhaps this Cuddie stands for "the author self."

"September" shows a pastor who has lost his sheep through unfortunate greed and a trip abroad, sitting "under the hill" with a sympathetic listener, taking shelter from "the Westerne wind [that] bloweth sore, / That nowe is in his chiefe souereigntee, / Beating the withered leafe from the tree" (ll. 49–51). The withered leaves of failed pastoral expression begin falling in the autumn winds.

From "May" through "September," then, we see a gradual process of dissociation or distancing of the central pastoral perspective (embodied in Colin and secondarily Cuddie and others) from the images of thriving, healthy vegetation that in "April" stood for achieved pastoral (sexual, aesthetic, prophetic/curative) expression. In "May" the distance is slight, the revels in the green wood being observed approvingly though the pastors do not participate. In "June" the vegetal world is even more beautiful, the suffering pastor's distance from it greater, and his inability to partake of it more grievous, as he turns it into an arrow for his lady's hurt. In "July" the vegetation acquires for him the import of something actively rank and harmful, thus to be rejected. "August" reembodies the "April" garland idea of positive vegetal excrescence/expression as a prize, in the lovely artifice of the vine and ivy cup, but only in order to show Colin's ever greater distance from it: at that point he can feel artifice not as the fruitful challenge of technique but only as constraint; he keeps to the wild woods, making them resound his incapacity for art. "September" blows the last leaves away from Hobbinol's happy retreat and represents the point of greatest distance between the pastor and his competence. In the temporal psychological sequencing, we have by the end of "September," when the last leaves are gone, arrived once more at the "January" condition (from which we flashed back to earlier youth): "my lustfull leafe is drye and sere, / . . . The blossome, which my braunch of youth did beare, / With breathed sighes is blowne away, and blasted" ("January," ll. 37–40).

"October" marks the turning point for the deflowered and defoliated pastoral consciousness. Cuddie, although still complaining of love's tyranny, of the corrupt times ripe only for satire, and of the absence of proper appreciation for high poetry (any "bud" of it that "shoots" must "wither," he says), and although taking no evident comfort in Piers's ideals about poetry's prophetic glory, yet ends by renouncing his dependence on love for inspiration and expressing a hope that he may yet, in great dramatic poetry, "throwe out thondring words of threate" and have his "temples . . . distain'd with wine, / And girt in girlonds of wild Yuie twine" (ll. 104, 110–11). The carved, vegetally decorated cup of "August" reappears as this prize garlond, though now only in Cuddie's wishes for a Colin of the future.

"November," as already mentioned, at last returns Colin, silenced since "January," to live lyric performance, and the laudatory vegetal image introducing him is noteworthy. To his suggestion that his interlocutor Thenot sing, Thenot—the old silencer of youth in February—this time replies that such as he should rather listen to learned pastors like Colin who have been "waterd at the muses well"; Thenot humbly casts himself as a lowly "little plant":

> The kindlye dewe drops from the higher tree,
> And wets the little plants that lowly dwell.
> ("November," ll. 31–32)

This image exactly retrieves the narrativized metaphor of the "February" Oak and Briar fable, now in a restorative form whereby the lesser plant does not destroy but admires its tree-protector. Colin has been rerooted as a tall and now Orphic tree, to put forth some of the dripping "boughes of Cypress" and "Eldre braunches seare" (ll. 144, 147) for Dido's funeral, rather than the "Oliue braunches" and "greene bayes" of love poetry that he formerly put forth for Eliza.

The singer of love has become instead a singer of death and the realm of the blessed dead, whose "fieldes ay freshe" and "grasse ay greene" cannot be frozen, cropped, or withered.

In "December" Colin reviews his life, in a lyrical prayer that unlike his failed prayer of "January" now succeeds in evoking a sense of divine presence and blessing[10] ("O soveraigne *Pan* thou God of shepheards all, / Which of our tender Lambkins takest keepe"— ll. 7–8). He continues to use the lyric competence restored to him in "November," again in an elegiac mood. His youth had "flowrd" into "Ioyfull spring" (l. 19), so gloriously he says that "Tho [then] deemed I, my spring would euer laste" (l. 30). But the god of Love, whom he had mistaken for "sovereign Pan" or God, burnt up this springtime growth and led him forth into hot summer, where "The bush my bedde, the bramble was my bowre / . . . The grislie Todes-toole growne there mought I see" (ll. 65, 69), a sick expressive growth not surprisingly generated by a god whom "Loue they called, . . . But better mought they haue behote him Hate." Colin reminds him-self how he learned herb lore in that summer of life, and "Kydst the hidden kinds of many a wede, / Yet kydst not ene to cure thy sore hart roote, / Whose ranckling wound as yet does rifelye bleede" (ll. 92–94).[11] Even other people's expressive growths (verbal art) did no good when applied to his wound. He sums up his case in often-quoted lines, which in full detail reascribe to him the "January" metaphorics of sexual and artistic expression as excrescence:

> Thus is my sommer worne away and wasted,
> Thus is my haruest hastened all to rathe:
> The eare that budded faire, is burnt and blasted,
> And all my hoped gaine is turnd to scathe.
>   Of all the seede, that in my youth was sowne,
>   Was nought but brakes and brambles to be mowne.

> My boughes with bloosmes that crowned were at first,
> And promised of timely fruite such store,
> Are left both bare and barrein now at erst
> The flattring fruite is fallen to grownd before,
>   And rotted, ere they were halfe mellow ripe.
>   My haruest wast, my hope away dyd wipe.

> The fragrant flowres, that in my garden grewe,
> Bene withered, as they had bene gathered long.
> Theyr rootes bene dryed vp for lacke of dewe,

> Yet dewed with teares they han be euer among.
> Ah who has wrought my Rosalind this spight
> To spil the flowres, that should her girlond dight?
>
> ("December," 97–114)

The pattern here is, as Patrick Cullen stressed, one of nature crossed or thwarted.[12] The promising pastor branched, budded and flowered in spring, as should naturally happen, but in summer brought forth not greenery but weeds and toadstools, in autumn not sweet fruit and ripe grain but rotten fruit and chaff. "May" through "October" have portrayed, as we saw, a time of absence from the successful poet's "April" garland of laurel and ivy, a prize which Spenser embodies again as the prize cup of "August," but there only in order to emphasize Colin's disjunction from it. And now after the autumn of the year "commeth timely death" approaching.

Yet, as we have also seen, in "November" the withered and failed love poet, spirit of the dying year, has already been rerooted, becoming a dark but thriving tree to drop dew beside the Elysian fields. Thus in the 'lifeless' Colin the sap will run all winter, and we expect that he may well flourish again beyond this 'death,' though we do not know what buds he will later sprout. In the metaphor of a person's life as one round of the seasons with winter being old age, the death Colin pictures now pending for himself implies his final end; and the interpretive tradition of the sickly Colin that I described in chapter 1 has wanted to take this person = year metaphor as literal and ultimate for the *Calender*. But since Colin has been subsumed into the imagery of pastor = plant occurring in every eclogue of the twelve, and most emphatically and explicitly so in the climactic "November," which E. K. declares the best of these eclogues and indeed of any he has ever seen, there is no reason to deny that the after-life theme of "November," where Colin speaks like some vegetation deity, spreads its force through the vegetal-seasonal metaphorics of the whole *Calender:* vegetation does not die permanently after winter marks its dreary end, and Colin too may rise again.

As noted, every eclogue has been part of this sequence elaborated through the shifting reference of imagery of growth as expression and production—not even just the love plaints and the celebrations of poetry, but the ecclesiastical eclogues as well. However, in following these images as parts of one sequence, I have so far said little about the divergent identities of the various shepherds. Can what happens to Piers in "May," to Thomalin in "July," to Cuddie in "August" and "October" make up part of a single sequence of images and psychological states devolving ultimately upon the pastoral consciousness embodied (or actorialized) narratively as Colin Clout?[13] A Greimassian discourse analysis of the *Calender* text and its narrative programs suggests that this is indeed the case, as was shown in chapter 3.

5

The *Calender* as Prophecy and the Captive Woman Ideologeme

Such a vision [of aristocratic elegance vs. Napoleonic energy] is not to be taken as the logical articulation of all the . . . ideological possibilities in the situation of the [French] Restoration, but rather as the structure of a particular political fantasy, as the mapping of that particular 'libidinal apparatus' in which Balzac's political thinking becomes invested—it being understood that we are here . . . asserting such fantasy or protonarrative structure as the vehicle for our experience of the real. When Greimas' system is used in this fashion, . . . it furnishes the graphic embodiment of ideological closure as such, and allows us to map out the inner limits of a given ideological formation and to construct the basic terms of this particular libidinal apparatus or 'desiring machine' . . . . The very closure of the 'semiotic rectangle' now affords a way into the text, . . . through its diagnostic revelation of terms or nodal points implicit in the ideological system which have, however, remained unrealized in the surface of the text . . . and which we can therefore read as what the text represses.[1]

Chapter 3 above has proposed the fundamental semio-narrative program that analysis appears to show in the *Calender* text when taken as a Greimassian discourse: the "pastoral maker" "takes control of" a "respected female" who is thereby being "disjoined from" "products of making" invested with "artistic/prophetic competence." Each phrase here (except "invested with," a sub-relation within the "narrative program" formula) represents a constructed sememe that emerged from lists of most-frequent-word groupings in the whole text of the *Calender*.[2] That formulaic sentence, that formularized scan profile of the text, is of course not a reading of the *Calender* in a literary-critical sense. It is not a reading at all but only a semantic and meta-syntactic distillation of the words of the text, as read by me, a reasonably experienced reader of the acceptations of Elizabethan English, reading them into twentieth-century English. Such a text-linguistic scan profile of a given text obviously has limitations of several kinds; but it may nevertheless be a useful piece of information for an interpretive reader to consult, along with other sorts of materials, such as descriptions of the English political situation in the late 1570s, and a neo-Marxist model of cultural semiotics that views literary texts as "symbolic acts," each taking its place in the antagonistic "collective discourse" passing among competing classes and factions at the time it was written.

As was noted in chapter 1, Jameson, in adopting Greimassian semiotics (even though he speaks of it as a system for "mapping out proto-narratives" and proposes narrative articulations of his ideologemes that perhaps in some way relate to Greimas's base narrative program formula), has not discussed that aspect of Greimassian thought and instead has drawn upon its semantic rather than its meta-syntactic concepts, especially upon the "semiotic square."[3] (The square is seen as constitutive of genuine semantic categories; it diagrams the relations of a term with two kinds of opposites to it, the contrary and the contradictory; and these are not essences but relations, i.e., they are what they are by virtue of not being possible double opposites of themselves, construed in a logically rigorous way—see chapters 1 and 2 above.) Jameson proposes that within a given nation or socio-political body at a given time, there are certain concepts around which people of competing or antagonistic classes organize their communication with each other—that is, shared versions of a certain basic unit of inter-class discourse, namely the ideologeme; and each of these ideologemes can take either static/semantic or narrative forms. In its static/semantic form, each one can be articulated into the four positions (term, anti-term, negated term, negated anti-term) of the semiotic square. Used as an analytical tool, such mapping, Jameson believes, can reveal which possible terms of the given ideologeme concept are being actualized and which are being "repressed" in a particular text. It can also reveal patterns of interrelation amongst the ideologically formed images that writers and other cultural producers will feel like inventing.

Whether Jameson has taken the ideologeme concept from Julia Kristeva or from its earlier mentions in her source Bakhtin/Medvedev, he does not say.[4] In any event it will be helpful here to look briefly at the respective uses of the term by Kristeva and Jameson, which are somewhat different even though they share some conceptual elements and both assume the formative power of ideological values in the generation of signs. Kristeva defined it as the unit of meaning through which the "social space" constructs the ideological values of its signs, and applied it in two related senses. On the broader level of application, it is a culture's most general, ideologically shaped mode of perception about knowing in general (equivalent to Fou-

cault's "episteme" of a given era and place), and she characterizes
Renaissance Europe as thinking by means of an "ideologeme of the
sign" (which she constrasts with the more mythically credulous classical and medieval "ideologeme of the symbol"). At a much more
concrete level, Kristeva's ideologeme of an era and society becomes
the unit through which the social space supplies ideological values
to any particular text. The idea of a "space" that "constructs" something is perhaps inelegant (and rather nebulous); perhaps we could
paraphrase to say that in her view, the socio-political force lines,
epistemically defining a social space, draw into patterns the ideological values of a text's signs, as these are generated within the culture's
sign systems. She thus conceives each text or utterance to have,
stretching along its length, its own particularized ideologeme—i.e.,
an operative loading of its values that shapes it to cohere with the
ideologically formed modes of knowing and valuing that are available
in its society and moment.[5]

Jameson, from a somewhat different perspective, uses the term
ideologeme to designate a kind of internally structured and recurrent,
as it were socio-linguistic, unit of meaning, instances of which can
be laid out on the semiotic square. Such units are free floating (as
contrasted with Kristeva's usage of a tailored, localized ideologeme
for each text): any one such ideologeme represents a cultural fantasy
that includes the terms of a semiotic square and can be found in-
stancing itself in many texts and productions. As for my own usage
here, while I am speaking of the ideologeme without Marxist engagement and expanding the definition of it to incorporate gender, I am
taking a view of it closer to Jameson's than to Kristeva's. The contrast
between their usages represents I think not so much disagreement
as a difference in the levels of generality of their observations.

Greimas would presumably consider Jameson's ideologeme (or any
ideologeme, as such matters can so far be recognized) sheerly speculative since the study of it cannot be based entirely on empirically
oriented linguistic procedures. Even so, we can pursue a provisional
exploration in literary and cultural semiotics, after the above Greimassian textual analysis of *The Shepheardes Calender*, by taking up the
ideologeme concept and investigating, if one does give it credence,
what ideologeme of Elizabethan England the *Calender* evokes and
indeed may itself have helped to create and set in motion.

To Jameson's definition (as discussed in chapter 1) I add a proposal
about the gender concepts involved in any such ideologeme or semiotic "desiring machine." For I think that most female analysts of
culture, and many male ones as well, will not be content with Jameson's dismissal of the supposed "false problem of the priority of the
economic over the sexual or of sexual oppression over that of social

class," namely, that sexism is only a "virulent survival of forms of alienation specific to the oldest mode of production, with its division of labor between men and women" (100). When one considers the importance of maleness/femaleness in Jameson's own described ideologemes (though his diagrams omit this classematic category) and in the ideologeme we shall here contemplate, one may suspect with Kristeva that sexism is operative at various semi-autonomous social levels, and in more ways than can be explained by a model of determinacy from modes of economic production.[6] Be that as it may, the gender opposition will here be included as a classematic category always operable within the proposed ideologeme's usages, as it evidently functioned for the writers, artists, and artisans (overwhelmingly male) who were able to claim a public voice, and who were libidinally invested in ideologies of the Elizabethan class factions here studied.

THE *CALENDER*'S POLITICS AND THEOLOGY

One could hardly find a better text than *The Shepheardes Calender* to illustrate Jameson's point that politics should be viewed as of the flesh and bone of literary texts. Indeed Jameson himself recalls Spenser, when saying that literary commentary should not regard politics as some mere "cobweb of topical allusion which the ahistorical and formalizing reader attempts desperately to brush away—that dry and intolerable chitinous murmur of footnotes reminding us of the implied references to long-dead contemporary events . . . in Spenser or Hawthorne" (*Political Unconscious*, 34). As was noted in chapter 1, the political situation in which Spenser completed and sent out his "little book" has been often enough evoked in recent Spenser studies: the anti-Catholic, anti-French paranoia of the decade after the Parisian St. Bartholomew's Day massacre of Protestants (1572); Spenser's engagement with leading figures in the militant Protestant Leicestrian faction (Bishop Young of Rochester, then the Earl of Leicester himself); their fears of the Queen's planned Roman Catholic d'Alençon marriage, which had reached a level of panic by late 1579 when Spenser saw the *Calender* through the press; and his printer Hugh Singleton's recent near loss of his hand (the sentence was commuted) for printing a tract by John Stubbs denouncing the proposed royal marriage.[7] Few now doubt that Colin Clout in the *Calender* is, at the level of political allegory, a figure of England as a grieving, faithful lover being betrayed by his lady the queen, though we need not go so far as to claim, with Paul MacLane, that Spenser had no personal lady-love in mind—that there was no personal referent for the figure of Rosalind, but only the political one, the queen.[8] Indeed, to deprive the *Calender* of a personal libidinal level of meaning would be to disempower it; instead we shall here see it, in Jameson's terms, as partaking of a "libidinal apparatus" or "desiring machine" exactly whereby personal eroticism is invested in political thought and action, and in turn is thereby intensified and made a fertile source of efficacious writing. The *Calender*'s mechanisms for doing this, with respect to male and female loves, are discussed in chapter 7.

One of the tasks I proposed in chapter 1 was to discover a reading that would treat all three central themes of the *Calender*—the poetic, the political/ecclesiastical, and the erotic—in an integrative way, rather than falling into the pattern of many recent readings, namely of stressing two of them at the expense of the third. We are now in a position to do that. For the base narrative program that has turned up in the *Calender* could not exist except as an integration of the three themes.

But before we can concretely apply this narrative program to a reading of the *Calender,* we must spell out a particular part of the ideological context in which it needs to be considered: that of the era's politically engaged theology. David Norbrook has especially well summarized the viewpoint of the Protestant party that Spenser supported: they were militarily aggressive and devotionally fervent, yet moderate in terms of sacramental issues and ecclesiastical governance. That is, they adhered to a Zwinglian moderate position on matters such as the nature of Christ's presence in the Eucharist and upheld episcopacy against Presbyterian decentralized church government; yet they attached little importance to claims of bishops' apostolic succession, or to vestments and other aesthetic elements of traditional liturgy, asserting rather that bishops should be learned, skilled at biblical exegesis for preaching, of good character, uninterested in riches, and devoted to diocesan governance. Further, they

> shared with the Presbyterians a strong sense of solidarity with Calvinists throughout Europe. Their theology was in fact more emotive and more heavily influenced by apocalyptic ideas than Calvin's own thought. They were conscious of a perpetual tension between soul and body in the individual and between pure doctrine and external forms in the outward church. For them the inner struggles of the individual and the apocalyptic struggle against Antichrist were closely connected. They viewed the English church not as a serene via media transcending the European struggles [its later self-image] but as part of the international reformed community.[9]

All these features accord with the fact that Protestantism had come to prominence in England through Henry VIII's humanist education, through his break with Rome over dynastic issues, and through the foothold that the movement gained among powerful courtiers and ladies during the brief reign of Edward VI; it had thus come primarily as a religion of the Henrician neo-aristocracy of new wealth, not as a peasant movement and only partially as a merchant import.

When faced with the prospect that Elizabeth would, as they saw it, betray at once the Dutch Protestant cause, England, and themselves by alliance with the Catholic d'Alençon (through whom she in her pragmatic way meant to arrange military aid for the Dutch and solve some other diplomatic problems so that her Protestant settlement would be freer from foreign threat),[10] the Leicestrians' sense of apocalypse and of prophetic denunciatory fervor were intense. We should not be surprised that Spenser turned to the prophet Isaiah's messianic "suffering servant" chapters, denouncing the wicked "shepherds of Israel" (see chapter 4), as source for the *Calender*'s particular configuration of pastoral imagery, in order to oppose the courtiers and prelatical conservatives who favored or tolerated the French marriage plan. There could hardly have been a more potent and suitable model for Spenser as poet/lover/prophet of England at that moment than, as we now call him, the second Isaiah, with his energized visions of righteousness, at once universalizing (or we might say imperialist) and intensely tribalist or patriotic.

In the fictions of the *Calender*, the personal and the moral-political realms of experience are, for both kinds of pastors (poets and clerics), suffused with eroticism, which when productively channeled supplies energy for artistic and clerical pastoring and itself must be energized by grants of attention and favor from the politically powerful. Furthermore, the relationship of artists and clergy to rulers is reciprocal: artists and clergy must try to claim moral high ground and to influence the politically powerful, while yet depending on them not only for a living but for the very cultural terms and socially symbolic possibilities of a "pastor's" functioning. That is, the ruler must be ideologically active in a way that a pastor's "libidinal apparatus" for creating art or preaching can draw upon and speak to. Thus Cuddie in "October" grieves that he cannot now make high poetry because the court offers him no ideological sustenance and because those in power are not ideologically suitable discursive partners for him. Within the *Calender*, "October"'s gesture of longing for an unrealizable high art is the last push in the pastor's unsuccessful effort, from "May" through "October," to regain competence without recapturing the lost lady. He has, as it were, made every effort to do without the ruler's denied favorable response to his love-suit, and now turns to an imagined takeover of the empowering lady, in "November."

The basic question is this: if Colin is grieving, rejected Protestant England, Rosalind his now treacherous lady/queen whose betrayal by marriage-commitment has robbed him of his competence to speak, then what is it that the *Calender* as a "socially symbolic act" does about his dilemma? What is its "plot," in both the literary and political senses? What do the various shepherd figures of the *Calender* contribute to this plot? And how does Spenser manage his symbolic act without danger of government retaliation?—the 'act' we discern here had to be covert, not explicit.

For the prophet Isaiah, great poet though he was in a modernist view of "the Bible as literature," the need to cry out his exalted visions presumably seemed sheerly a matter of prophetic, religio-political calling, rather than of verbal art or the will to 'make' artifacts: "Cry aloud, spare not, lift up thy voice like a trumpet, and shew my people their transgression" (Is. 58:1). For Spenser, a self-analytical man of the Renaissance operating within something like Kristeva's linguistically auto-reflexive ideologeme of the sign, a man who yet wanted to speak as the prophetic poet of embattled English Protestantism, the internal pressure of fervency may have been just as great as Isaiah's. But he also saw himself as an artist, in that position and cultural moment necessarily a satiric artist (so says Cuddie in "October"), who wanted to survive the crisis of the moment and live to write another day—and even wanted to make a living as a "professional" poet. Thinking in Richard Helgerson's terms of Spenser as pioneering careerist poet, we might in the present context speculate that the *Calender* did two related socio-political jobs at once, that of prophetically acting upon the queen and that of creating the possibility of a middle-class, careerist-functionary identification for non-theatrical poets; this suggestion would I think accord with the recent qualification of Helgerson's view of Spenser's professionalism proposed by Richard Rambuss.[11]

In *The Shepheardes Calender* Spenser brings off a masterpiece of feigning, that at once cries out its prophetic message, covers its tracks, and confesses the artist's painful dependency on the political power which must both feed and be fed by him. "To feign" in Elizabethan usage could mean either "to conceal" or the opposite, "to reveal": that is, it meant either to paint over (to cover or varnish acceptably) or to paint out (to image something[12]). When Hobbinol tells Diggon Davie not to speak "too plaine: / Better it were, a little to feyne, / And cleanly couer, that cannot be cured" ("September," ll. 136–38), he is not being a coward but is stating Spenser's strategy, at once artistic and political. Poetry as fiction (non-being/non-seeming) is also at times a covert activity or dissimulation (being/ non-seeming), close neighbor of lying (seeming/non-being), that is, with an address directly across a two-generation semiotic square from that of the lie;[13] it can tell painful truth (being/seeming), but only circuitously. The claim was doubtless a politic and political lie, but by veiling, feigning, and coloring made a fiction, when E. K. says of the "September" 'Lowder' fable that we studied in chapter 4 (about a failure of one of the agents of Spenser's recent employer Bishop Young): "This tale of Roffy seemeth to coloure some particular Action of his. But what, I certeinlye know not." Jonathan Goldberg has pointed out that the poets of this age, as well as the rulers, operated by the principle of the Emperor Tiberius: *Qui nescit dissimulare nescit regnare.*[14] By extension, whoever does not know how to dissimulate does not know how to poetize.

Why must the prophetic poet operate so slyly, as Jameson says "tilting" his fiction "powerfully into the underside or *impensé* or *non-dit*"? Not only does he (I say "he" advisedly, for this context) want to save his neck or his hand, but as new-historicist studies have often noted, he cannot otherwise construct a means of influencing the power centers of his society; the new point here is that he must set in motion a particular "libidinal apparatus" or "desiring machine," which will in Jameson's terms be an "imaginary solution" to a "real but insoluble conflict."

The New Ideologeme and the *Calender*'s 'Solution' for the Insoluble Conflict

Recalling the set of plot-segments, defined by "instrumental narrative programs," identified by the analysis in chapter 3, and also the set of explicit indicator passages at the end of that chapter, we can see that the *Calender*'s plot, that which it does or "acts" to achieve an imagined solution to an insoluble conflict, is indeed tilted down, but not irretrievably down, into the *non-dit*. We want to discern how the disempowered Colin of the "May" through "October" segment regains the lyric competence which he is suddenly so well able to exercise in "November," where he finally comes out of his silent incapacity and performs—he sings a new song. For all the dozens of evocations of the pastoral maker's love for his lass, very seldom is there any mention of hate; but in one of these, at a crucial point in the final instrumental narrative program (the reiteration of Colin's performance), he says that Cupid the god of Love ought rather to be named god of Hate:

> The shepheards God (perdie God was he none)
> My hurtlesse pleasaunce did me ill vpbraide,
> My freedome lorne, my life he lefte to mone.
>> Loue they him called, that gaue me checkmate,
>> But better mought they haue behote him Hate.
>>> ("December," ll. 51–55)

If the god or essential power of Love in "December," the concluding articulation of the *Calender*'s "base narrative program" or overall plot (the 'maker's' regaining of competence), is rather the contrary, Hate, then all those many declarations and protestations of love for Rosalind are, by a code revision, rewritten. And all those many love plaints, "causd of discurtesee," are to fly to the lady, "where euer that she bee, / And pierce her heart with poynt of worthy wight: / As shee deserues, that wrought so deadly spight." The will to have the first actorialization of the beloved lady (Rosalind) reverses to its contrary, the will to repel her. Rosalind is bade farewell, Dido in her stead controlled, in a lead-wrapped coffin.

The function in the *Calender* of the semantic category of 'having/ governing,' most frequently lexicalized as we saw in the words 'love,' 'lust,' and two of their opposites 'loss,' and 'leaving,' is clear in the above passage, read in conjunction with a further one from Colin's "December" meditation (ll. 109–20):

> The fragrant flowres, that in my garden grewe,
> Bene withered, as they had bene gathered long.
> Theyr rootes bene dryed vp for lacke of dewe,
> Yet dewed with teares they han be euer among.
>> Ah who has wrought my Rosalind this spight
>> To spil the flowres, that should her girlond dight?
> And I, that whilome wont to frame my pype,
> Vnto the shifting of the shepheards foote:
> Sike follies nowe haue gathered as too ripe
> And cast hem out, as rotten and vnsoote.
>> The loser Lasse I cast to please nomore,
>> One if I please, enough is me therefore.

Like the suffering servant who grew up before the Lord as a tender plant with a root in dry ground, the prophetic 'pastoral maker' has been bruised and afflicted; he has suffered from a deadly thwarted desire (a 'wanting-to-have') for a loose lass, whom he lost and finally must give up on, as Diggon Davie scorns the riches he mistakenly sought. In the form of the unwholesome clerical pastors, he desired either Flora (unredeemed sexuality—desired by Palinode) or *dea mo-*

neta (the money goddess—by Morrell and Diggon). As Colin he desired an approved, euphorically tagged form of the potent lady, a queenly power, and when he lost her ('was-not-able-to-have,' in the sememic results) his own competence was "lorn" or lost, so that he had to get rid of his desire for her by getting rid of her. This last point is what is repressed or *non-dit*, namely the repelled lady term of the ideologeme. He had to grieve for her and to find a replacement lady, a reclaimed, for a while interior muse, who could preside over a new kind of competence or power to make, that was not a matter of heights and depths (along the old hierarchy of the queen's courtiers) but of interiorized "conning." *Felice chi puo*—"happy he who can"—the final "August" emblem, this clearest "actorialization" of pastoral competence, is glossed by E. K. to mean "eyther him that can win the beste, or moderate him selfe being best, and leaue of with the best" ("August"). As was noted above, it answers the debate question of "July" by replacing its opposition of height-lowness (*in medio virtus / in summo foelicitas*) with the modal one of competence / non-competence. Thus when Colin is done, he can take leave of the queen. He can choose to "leave off" poetizing under her and pack away his restored pipe for a winter of inactivity prophetically expecting some new, resanctified ruler to come after her. "July" has problematized height / lowness by showing that even proper elevation is dangerous, and then abolished it with a concluding term shift.

In other words, the *Calender*'s imaginary solution to the real problem of Spenser's insouciant lady/queen with her imminent French marriage—so appealing to her, so horrifying to the Sidney-Leicester party, so psychically disabling for their would-be new prophetic poet—is its emergent plot. Fall sick with a glorious, artistically empowering then disempowering, more than Petrarchan love for her, have her die, sing her soul to heaven in a sincerely powerful Christian and musical lyric, and then regain her radiant after-image. It is, of course, a particularly male "solution" (akin to the one portrayed in quite another mode in Robert Browning's "My last Duchess").

In Spenser's case, I believe it allowed him to create or take part in creating an ideologeme so potent that, as Joseph Wittreich has suggested,[15] this first glowing instance of it in the *Calender* contributed to the queen's change of heart, whereby in early 1580 she halted the marriage negotiations, which had seemed all but signed & sealed, and by 1581 dropped them. (The *Calender* would seem to have been taking good or at least acceptable political effect, in the Leicester party's view, since they did not prevent it from being republished in 1581 while she was officially still considering the marriage scheme,[16] even despite the fact that the "March" eclogue had probably left Leicester himself with a red face—see chapter 7.)

The "plot" was to capture the intransigent lady, beautifully lamented, in a lead coffin. It created an ideologeme—let us call it the ideologeme of the captive woman—diagrammed as shown here.

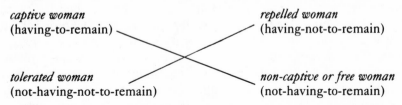

captive woman
(having-to-remain)

repelled woman
(having-not-to-remain)

tolerated woman
(not-having-not-to-remain)

non-captive or free woman
(not-having-to-remain)

The Faerie Queene would generate a luminously erotic, childlike captive woman in the positive term, Amoret, and in its contradictory term (the non-captive or independent woman) her rampant, militant twin Belphoebe, as well as that fictive ancestress of the queen, Britomart; the ideologeme in its contrary term (the anti-captive or repelled woman) is represented there by such exiles or wanderers as Una or Amavia, and in its neg-anti-captive term (the non-repelled or tolerated) by such dependent and morally weak females as Mirabella. Crucial to the early functioning of the ideologeme in *The Faerie Queene*, as Spenser had already begun it by 1580 through imitating Ariosto, particularly his Angelica, was also a doubly modalized figure that we can shortly consider in a some detail, namely Florimell, the utterly 'to-be-captured' woman, whom scarcely any male knight, good or bad, can resist chasing.

Few will doubt that if there was an ideologeme in Elizabethan England, the queen was in the thick of it. I propose that *The Shepheardes Calender* created or contributed to the creation of this ideologeme, out of psychic and cultural-political materials at hand in her own propagated self-image and in the mode of governing she had worked out, as a woman ruler in an overwhelmingly patriarchal society. As has been abundantly studied,[17] through much of her reign she had cultivated the metaphor of herself as Petrarchan and neo-Platonic beloved of her politicians and also, by inverse scriptural analogy (as the Church is the bride of Christ), as bride of her whole people. And turning the force of metaphor upon political practice, she actually demanded unfulfilled erotic devotion from the courtiers, sometimes banishing them from court and from favor when they married. The courtiers, for their part, lived with this tense, divisive-competitive and demoralizing situation by declaring her a prodigy, a phoenix, unique among women, *supra sexum femineum*, and themselves her prodigious devotees.

Spenser's initial terms for the *Calender*, then, were a cultural-political given: Protestant England as a faithful, grieving, incapacitated courtly lover of a heretofore faithful lady now in the process of betraying him. In "January" Colin has, despite the incapacitating blow to his pipe, a remnant of hope that the devastating betrayal may yet be prevented—his motto is *anchora speme*; by the end of "June" the hope is gone (*gia speme spenta*—hope already spent) and it is time to shoot a weedy arrow at the desired lady, though Colin, being presented still in his lyrically impotent state, despairs that he may not hit her. The creation of the ideologeme was the catching of her with a net—alias arrow, alias poem, alias coffin, these being different actorializations of the efficacious instrument—through the threat, the fictive enactment, of a queen's death and removal to heaven. E. K.'s headnote on the "November" elegy for the beloved high lady sends a signal in saying that it has been modeled upon Marot's poem on the death of "the French queen"—Louise of Savoy, but such would Elizabeth also be as d'Alençon's wife. Was such a thing explicitly said anywhere in the *Calender? Mon dieu!*—but of course not, it was *non-dit*, non-said and un-said so potently, so many times, through a thousand declarations of love (but, since "June," poisoned and killing love) that the point could hardly miss, or be missed.

How Things Turn Out in "December"

In a few pages we can sketch something of the ideologeme's socio-political scope and further operation through the rest of the Elizabethan era. But first the account of Colin Clout's and his *Calender*'s ending must be finished, from the perspective of the narrative program we have noted and of the ideologeme—the "imagined solution to a real problem"—that it offered, in its context of intense religio-political strife.

That the climactic "November" elegy seemed as noteworthy to readers as it did to E. K. ("farre passing his [Marot's] reach, and in myne opinion all other the Eglogues of this booke") is suggested by the fact that there is a madrigal setting of two of its stanzas by Thomas Kirby,[18] to my knowledge the only contemporary musical setting of a text from the *Calender*, indeed one of the few such settings of any Spenserian texts (Spenser's lyric verse being usually too verbally and figurally complex for the prevalent musical word-setting styles of his time). The elegy shows the suicide Dido's spirit as Virgil presents it in the Elisian fields of the *Aeneid*:[19] "I see thee blessed soule, I see, /

Walke in *Elisian* fieldes so free." The music builds to its climax on the lines "Dido my deare alas is dead, / Dead and lyeth wrapt in lead," through multiple phrase repetitions in the various voices, rising on an octave leap to a kind of shriek of the uppermost voice on "Dead" (of the second line just given); in the other chosen stanza the climactic phrase comes, again expressively, on the word "walke"— walk in the Elisian fields.

Anthea Hume, in a historically concrete and insightful reading of the *Calender* as a partisan "moderate Puritan" work,[20] points out several features of it that correlate with the structures revealed by the semiotic analysis above: the theme of exploration of young love linking "February" through "April," the summer eclogues symmetrically alternating the poetic and ecclesiastical themes, and the "November" elegy as the climactic point at which Colin recovers competence as prophetic singer, becoming able once again to feed the faithful with his words. The insights of her reading, however, stop with "November," where "the poet, receiving the laurel crown from his companion, contributes his music to the local church's needs." Of "December," after noting that Spenser has intermingled passages on Colin's disabling love with paraphrases of Marot's eclogue on life as a round of the four seasons, she can only conclude that "December" completes the *Calender*'s general "tragicomic presentation of Colin's life-story" as a lovesick poet who "falls back into complaint and ultimate silence because of his mistaken view . . . that love must inevitably destroy his poetic gift."[21] But why should the restored singer of "November" "fall back" in this way? If this is all we can say, "December" is a puzzling anti-climax.

In fact, however, Colin in "December," despite his retrospective imagery of blasted growth, does not reiterate his earlier assertions of poetic incompetence: in pointed contrast to his breaking of his pipe in "January," he now prays intensely, as he had in "January" before breaking the pipe, then hangs up the restored pipe, preserving it for another season; he locks his sheep into their fold to protect them from the "breme Winter" until better days come; he bids both Hobbinol and Rosalind, the loves of his youth, farewell; and he states a projection that "The loser Lasse I cast to please nomore, / One if I please, enough is me therefore." The "one," I propose, is his apotheosized Dido, cleansed by death and reunited with her first husband Sychaeus in Elysium, the queenly muse of a better realm than England can be under Elizabeth after her deadly error. Colin now portrays himself as a disappointed latter-day John the Baptist, going off into the wilderness, to await a time when his recovered competence can be valued, his voice once again heard. Thereby Spenser steps into the position of Jesus in a wry poetic moment, when he said of himself and John the Baptist in their efforts to prophesy for their generation, "It is like children calling out, 'We piped for you, and you would not dance.' We wept to you and you would not lament'" (Matt. 12:15–17).

Just so, Colin says, he piped to his lady love, the power of England, but she would not dance—here we recall the co-occurrence pattern of 'respected lady' with dance in the previous chapter's results. (See also appendix 2, part 4.) For a while indeed then he fell into silent impotence. But not now. The funeral pyre of Dido in the *Aeneid* (who is there sometimes called Elissa—see n. 21) dominates Spenser's imaginative concept in "November"'s elegy to a shepherdess named Dido: it is that of a queen driven to ruin by her effort to marry a foreigner, who instead of helping her to rule deserts her and leaves her to die.[22] Spenser has here translated his queen and muse through death to the Elisian fields of his own interior vision, so fitting for an Elisa Queen of shepherds, where he will hold the image of a cleansed and perfected one who can now be celebrated as a pure image of right queenliness, until some other ruler, in another salvational season or day of the Lord, comes to embody her once more in England. Colin Clout as figure of the English people knows only a seasonal death in this ending, that of winter, which will in due time give way again to a season of renewed prophetic efflorescence.[23]

But the "looser lass" will not see it. This winter will have been her last. By an act of prophetic aggression he has killed her with the burning coals of kind poetry and thereby regained his power to bud again and write poetry in another season. The poetic and political stroke of genius of the *Calender* is that Spenser has played out his beautiful death fantasy so shrewdly and feigningly that he avoided ultimate closure and allowed the queen a chance to step away from the Dido possibility. He took control of the queenly lass with a radically open ending, and perhaps for that reason the missing "December" emblem (a vexed conundrum) was deliberately displaced into the gloss: *merce non mercede*, "favor not payment" I ask—I am piping you one last tune here, he says, will you finally dance?

Once she said "Yes," the whole death fantasy could be re-read as suspended in the blank "November" of a perpetual calendar, the month of the dead, in a heavenly space of the imagination where the queen herself would have been wished off to, had she not relented. The readers from Hamilton to Helgerson who say that the *Calender* is about a poet's acquisition of his poetic competence are right. Those like Louis Montrose who stress the springs of erotic energy as its power source are right. Those like Anthea Hume who see the satiric/political force of the *Calender* as Leicester-party, reformist propoganda are also right. Spenser as young poet drew upon a portrayed experience of erotic rejection (whatever in his own life may have entered into it—see chapter 7 on that point) to present a state of being silenced, disenfranchised, disempowered, of questioning whether it is right to desire heights of power for one's own religious vision and poetry, of demanding on behalf of the Protestant faction that the queen keep faith with them—he did all these things at once, through a poet's covert art of feigning, and left himself a leafy back way out in case his flowers were ill received. Whether or not Leicester and Sidney were in the first instance annoyed by the *Calender*, and whether or not Spenser's being sent to Ireland in 1580 was a punishment (vexed issues of Spensereana that we lack evidence to treat)—in any case Spenser lived to write another day, stayed employed in government service, and would see his poem go through several editions. In getting away with his prophetic effort, he created or helped create a functional desiring machine, an ideologeme that would tick and work for two decades to come.

ECONOMIC INTERESTS AND THE 'CAPTIVE WOMAN' IDEOLOGEME

As a unit of antagonistic class discourse, the 'captive/capturing' woman ideologeme would function as part of the code whereby the emerging entrepreneurial class of international capital sought to solidify and legitimize its gains in political and economic power, and the older, still largely land-based aristocracy sought to retrench. Diverse ways of imaging and thereby appealing to the queen as England's lady-love became, in a new way, everyone's game. Louis A. Montrose has well documented the emphasis on dissimulative courtly play, for example, in Puttenham's imaging of the queen and her court.[24] Puttenham may be said to portray a squirearchist alternative to Colin Clout's earnest entrepreneurial courtship style, packaged by the wily E. K.; in Puttenham, the insider ways of a specific class ultimately define what is both "nature" and "art" as whatever is classy—that which the best people know how to affect[25]—and we shall explore related operations in Lyly, Greene, and Shakespeare in chapter 6.

Before proceeding with direct description of the ideologeme, I must briefly explain the two terms of the dichotomy just proposed. The following account can only be sketchy, and in economic terms inadequate—I would need to be a specialist in economic history to do better. But it seems to me important to offer some suggestion of the ideologeme's very concrete level of economic functioning, in the hope that this dimension of the concept can later be more adequately explored by people with better knowledge. My understanding of 'entrepreneurial' and 'squirearchist' does not assume that the latter people were uninterested in making money—such portrayal of themselves was only a particular fantasy of self-definition (as knights of honor and of duty to land and people, uninterested in mere "pelf"). People of both groups were out to gain wealth by investing in land and ventures. But by 'entrepreneurial' I refer to views and actions in accord with the ideology of merchants' unhindered access to international markets, above all other considerations; such was the clear economic drift of the Leicester party of militant, pan-European Protestants. This is not to question the sincerity of their religious partisanship, only to look at its socio-economic dimensions. By 'squirearchist' in contrast, then, I refer to views and actions reflecting the ideological position that there should be a bounded economic unit co-extensive with the militarily defensible geographic unit, the realm (sometimes termed a mercantilist view), and that its wealth should be controlled primarily by land-owners of long established lineage, though the wealth should not be exclusively agricultural.

To content ourselves with brief illustrations, one concerning woolens and one concerning metalwares, the clothworkers guild could call upon the squirearchist inclinations of William Cecil, Lord Burghley, Elizabeth's treasurer and chief secretary, when they wanted enforcement help against the Merchant Adventurers, who were ignoring the law against export of any more than nine-tenths of England's raw wool output (to be processed into finished cloth more cheaply abroad, sacrificing the clothworkers' wages to the merchants' profit); yet Sir Francis Walsingham (Sir Philip Sidney's father-in-law and perhaps the realm's biggest international investor) in 1579 received a dispensation to violate this supposed one-tenth upper limit, with a shipment of thirty thousand bolts of raw wool above it.[26] Analogously, in metal wares Burghley had been instrumental, in 1565, in splitting off from the original stockholder mining company (founded by certain Germans to mine and export raw iron, tin, and calcite for profitable uses abroad) a second company specifically for English refining and manufacturing use of the metals, namely The Company of Mineral and Battery Works.[27] He stipulated that no more than one-third of the stockholders could be foreigners. In such ways Burghley and the queen characteristically tried to make England an at least partially self-contained economic unit, for relative independence of continental wars and entanglements, while the Leicester party characteristically sought identification with international reformed Protestantism—an identification that positioned them for successful competition amongst the Hanseatic and other trading cities' merchants, and unhindered international profit opportunities. (Through the strategies of Burghley the proto-mercantilist and his bureaucracy, the crown could take a cut of the international profiteering, and the wage-earners and small-scale shop owners (producing pieced goods) could benefit in a small way from the stabilizing of prices and volumes effected by regulation.) Of course entire consistency in this pattern cannot be seen in Burghley, a highly skilled politician whose strategy was typically to stay atop the constituted center between oppositional forces.

The piracy practices of seagoing courtiers like Drake and Raleigh are only the rawer kind of index to the success of the queen's and Burleigh's strategy of profiteering from the international capitalism of the day by siphoning off just so much as would seem to leave it functional (although eventually her own greatest investors, including Walsingham, were bankrupted by conditions beyond their control)— indeed it is an especially telling index, when we recall J. M. Keynes's cheerful calculation that the £40,000 the queen got from Drake as her share of a 1580 expedition's booty, accumulating interest at 3¼% for some three hundred years, amounts to the value of Britain's modern foreign investments.[28]

The close linkage of the Leicester reformist party with international reformed-Protestantism has of course often been noted by scholars not particularly interested in its economic dimensions. M. M. Knappen states, for example, that the queen's project of an emergent prelatical-conservative Anglicanism was thoroughly provincial, while "Protestants with any foreign experience almost always attached themselves to the Puritan party," and notes the close ties of Sir Francis Walsingham with the Cambridge controversialist Thomas Cartwright, author of the famous *Replye* to Archbishop Whitgift of 1573 and brother-in-law of the reformist pamphleteer John Stubbs (see pp. 186 and 261, n. 11); unsafe in England, Cartwright "attached himself, like Tyndale, to the English trading community in the Low Countries [i.e., at Antwerp]," making a career there in marketing.[29] The vitality of the Protestant churches at the center of foreign merchant colonies in trading cities around northern Europe testifies to the internationalist ideological and institutional base of reformed Protestantism.[30] For the English internationalists, the sphere of trade based in ports around northern Europe—and eventually, they foresaw, across the Atlantic—seemed the natural empire England was destined to rule in a new golden age under its queen, the mythic returned Protestant Astraea (see chapter 6). The iconographic form of their usage of the captive woman ideologeme reflects this large economic-ideological unit around which their colonialist thinking naturally shaped itself: Astraea (as non-captive/capturing woman), brandishing her sword above a map of Europe.[31] Thus their ideology programatically obscured any possible conflict between English economic interests and those of international Protestantism—just as the second Isaiah saw no conflict between his vision of a restored, expansionist Davidic kingdom of Judah and his universalist image of Jerusalem as a house of prayer to the one God, for all nations.

To return now to the ideologeme itself, the 'captive woman' construct meets Jameson's criterion of being capable of both narrative and static-semantic or emblematic formulation. As proto-narrative, it is that someone (male) loves/captures or is loved/captured by (or exiles, does not capture, does not exile, etc.) a respected female, who stands for (carries the force of) socio-economic legitimation. Thus we add to the diagram above the term "respected," indicating the figure's loading as carrier of legitimation for hegemony.

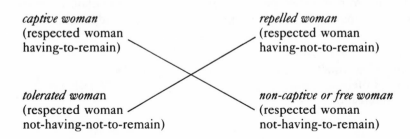

captive woman
(respected woman
having-to-remain)

repelled woman
(respected woman
having-not-to-remain)

*tolerated woma*n
(respected woman
not-having-not-to-remain)

non-captive or free woman
(respected woman
not-having-to-remain)

We may note from this diagram that one could recognize further possible squares, for example by articulating a further opposition on the sememe 'respectedness' rather than on 'having controlling,' thus generating 'unrespectedness' and 'non-respectedness' (the procedure would require semic analysis of 'respectedness'); the result would account for whorish or 'light' figures like Flora and Lettice of "March." But this articulation on having/controlling should be considered central to the ideologeme as such. Recalling the illustrative figures mentioned above, we can see that all the terms of this square are lexicalized in Spenser's work.

The ideologeme as so far formulated would be, in sememic terms

> female
>   respected
>   [having to]
>   remain

Besides this modalization of it, the other one very commonly lexicalized in Elizabeth's reign represents its shadow or nightmare side,
for men of the time, the 'capturing' rather than the 'captive' woman:

> female
>   respected
>   [causing to]
>   male
>   [have to]
>   remain

In semiotic terms, this is the above sememe but governed by a factitive (or in Greimas's preferred terms, manipulative-contractual)[32] modality, that of causing-to-do, with the 'femaleness' seme governing
rather than being governed by the modalization. The semiotic description mirrors the political problematics. Articulated on the
semiotic square, this factitive modalization of the ideologeme is as
follows:[33]

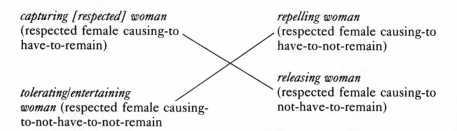

capturing [respected] woman
(respected female causing-to-
have-to-remain)

repelling woman
(respected female causing-to
have-to-not-remain)

releasing woman
(respected female causing-to
not-have-to-remain)

*tolerating/entertaining
woman* (respected female causing-
to-not-have-to-not-remain

The manifestations of an ideologeme will not be limited to the
works of one writer, nor even to writing; as social semiotic patterning they will appear as well in iconographic materials,[34] songs, and
other cultural products made by people of various viewpoints. We
now expand our compass of illustrative examples to the productions of writers such as Sidney, Lyly, Greene, and Shakespeare. Sidney, the *Calender*'s dedicatee, is perhaps the first prominent, near-
contemporaneous source of a set of instances, having written his first

Arcadia draft (of the much desired captive princesses Pamela and Philoclea) at the same time that Spenser was writing and compiling the *Calender*, and partly while in a country retirement that, according to tradition, was brought on by the queen's anger about his letter denouncing her marriage plan. (For discussion of his Arcadian use of the ideologeme see chapter 6.)

Capturing women are the dangerous figures (akin to the witches of popular narratives, but usually unlike them in being property-holders or aristocrats)[35] such as Duessa, Acrasia, Radigund, Sidney's Cecropia, Lyly's Tellus (like Duessa and Radigund a Mary Stuart figure), or a little later Shakespeare's Cleopatra—women who in some way capture men and strip away their masculine *virtus;* the repelling women are fierce defenders of some female domain or status, such as Belphoebe, or Lodge's Harpaste (of *Euphues his Shadowe*) and other Euphuist 'heroines'; the non-repelling are governesses of some house or domain where guests (mostly male) are entertained and nurtured then free to go, such as Alma, Gloriana, or Medina; the releasing woman is, for example, Britomart (rescuing Arthegall—see chapter 6 below).

Returning to the first term of the captive woman, we may add as examples of captive women, besides the *Calender*'s lead-wrapped Dido and the *Arcadia*'s Pamela and Philoclea, Margaret of Robert Greene's *Friar Bacon and Friar Bungay*, and in another vein, the many enticing immured wives of cuckoldry tales, often adapted from Italian novellas.[36] Repelled or exiled women, especially frequent with Shakespeare as we shall see in chapter 6, are aristocratic transmutations of the patient Griselda figure of popular stories, such as Susania of the Euphuist tale *Andrugio*, Erona (of *Arcadia*), Helena (of *All's Well*), Rosalind, Cordelia, Hermione, and Perdita. Non-repelled or tolerated women, other than in Spenser, tend to be comic types of the stage, such as Juliet's nurse, Mrs. Overdone of *Measure for Measure*, or the citizen's gabby Philistine wife in Fletcher's *Knight of the Burning Pestle*. Non-captive women, as free operators, are also the 'releasing' woman figures (of the second modalized square below), representing the only position-overlap of the two squares. Besides Britomart, Belphoebe, and Cynthia (of Lyly's *Endymion*), there are for example the Amazons of court masques. To my knowledge such characters always figure or serve the Queen, who as the prodigy among women, *supra sexum foemineum*, is the only one who can be portrayed as at the same time 'non-captive' and good, and the only figure who can dually lexicalize both squares. (Robert Greene's Mamillia, of the Euphuist tale of that name, is a telling inverse example: the lady leaves home with the expressed aim of independence, but in the end is brought into the fold of marriage.) Let us diagram the overlap just mentioned.

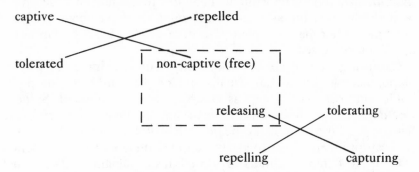

Here we have indeed a politically functioning 'libidinal apparatus' or 'desiring machine' (complete in two interactive Deleuzean partial objects) that served Spenser and numerous other male writers, from 1579 on, as an "imagined solution" to the more general "real problem" addressed by the *Calender:* how to manage the queen. When more of the still unedited texts by women of the age become available,[37] it will be interesting to consider whether and how women as writers used, tried to use, or avoided this ideologeme, obviously defined in itself from a position of male enunciation (see chapter 6 below on the Countess of Pembroke for one example).

The 'captive women' typically have a euphoric loading (they are made good and appealing), usually explicitly erotic—from the dear-lamented, enshrined Dido through Pamela, Philoclea, Stella, Amoret, and Petruchio's gloriously tamed Kate to Romeo's Juliet, dancing from father's house, to husband's arms, to the grave. Characters directly allusive to the queen (such as those listed earlier) are of course also euphoric, except that their eroticism is characteristically renamed by inversion 'chastity.' Tolerator/entertainers too are euphorically loaded, though less strongly so—a dose of sour-sweet medicine seems to come with their ministrations. The capturing women are always dysphoric though often seductive, having as I mentioned the aura, sometimes even the explicit quality of witchcraft. The two positions capable of ambivalent or variant thymic loading, then, are the 're-pelled' and the 'tolerated' woman. The first tends to be appealing but piteous, a sufferer who needs protection (Fawnia of Greene's *Pandosto*). The second, as noted, is often a whore, or a faithless but tolerated wife or other comic type, appealing though having moral/social flaws—tolerated by men as a creature of their own physical and egoistic needs.

As mentioned above, an unusual double modalization of the 'captive woman' is Florimell, one of the figures from Spenser's earliest segments of *The Faerie Queene* when he was writing to redo and outdo Ariosto. Florimell, closely modeled on Ariosto's Angelica, is repeatedly being chased, captured, lost and rechased by men of all sorts and social classes. She is usually in a state of looking over her shoulder in terrified flight. Until her marriage to the liminal knight of the sea shore Marinell finally cancels that defined essence, she can exist in only two alternating states, of flight, or of temporary capture under dire threat of rape; she thus represents the 'ought-to-be-captive' woman.

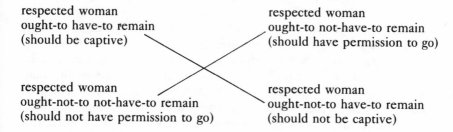

respected woman
ought-to have-to remain
(should be captive)

respected woman
ought-to not-have-to remain
(should have permission to go)

respected woman
ought-not-to not-have-to remain
(should not have permission to go)

respected woman
ought-not-to have-to remain
(should not be captive)

Since 'not being captive' and 'having permission to go' are logically indistinguishable (as are the two left-side terms, top and bottom), the double modalization produces a bipolar semantic category, the odd nature of Florimell: she is always in a state either of temporary quivering capture by an undesired male (by the 'rude foster,' then the Saracen, the witch's son, the lustful fisherman, Proteus the sea god, and finally by Marinell) or of permitted flight—unwillingly permitted by whatever knight is just slightly detained from catching her, namely Red Crosse, Arthur, Satyrane, Braggadocchio, and so on.

HOW THE IDEOLOGEME BEGAN TO TICK AND WORK

To return to the *Calender* to see how the ideologeme began to be used, let us consider what choice its 'libidinal apparatus' posed, from the queen's viewpoint. Would she like to be her Colin/kingdom's captive lady in the form of a corpse most beautifully and elegantly wept to heaven? Or would she prefer to remain his high enshrined lady love alone in her castle, as before? One way or the other, a captive woman she would be. The choice is analogous to that portrayed in Sidney's letter to the queen, which warned of a possible early death in childbirth if she married d'Alençon at her age, but forecast a continuing happy life married to her realm if she remained single. She eventually decided—after great rage at Leicester, Sidney, and others—that she would have the latter, thank you. I am not arguing that any Protestants were at that time literally planning to kill the queen, though such a plot could well have developed, had she gone through with the marriage. The days of John Knox's published attack on queenly rule as a "monstrous regimen of women" allied with the popish antiChrist bade fair to return, in the event of a Catholic alliance (John Aylmer, the *Calender*'s high-living bishop Morrell, had incidentally been one of the young Queen's notable published defenders at that time).

Once her decision in favor of the Leicestrian position was made, the desiring machine could begin to crank out the possibilities latent in it as a semantic and meta-syntactic construct. It would no longer be necessary to figure her, even this close to directly, as the captive and capturing woman she indeed was—those things could now be distinctly 'not said' through her oppositional figurations as the non-captive, entertaining, releasing, or exiled but returning woman (the latter being the exact structure of the Astraea myth, so popular for depicting her in the latter decades of her reign). It also seems clear that this ideologeme did not immediately become defunct upon the queen's death, but as a mental construct people had become accustomed to, it continued 'emitting its bleeps'—anachronistically—into the early years of James's reign.[38]

A good indication that we have here indeed the sort of socio-linguistic image and psychological construct that Jameson means is that it shapes literature written for court, gentry, and city audiences, but does not seem to affect the female figures of Elizabethan folk and popular literature, at least insofar as we can study that literature in its meager and appropriated survivals. If one thinks of such things as the folk tales acted out in George Peele's *Old Wives Tale*, of story collections like *The Cobbler of Canterbury*, of country songs such as those in the music collection *Pamelia*, of Thomas Vautor's song "Mother, I will have a husband," etc., one finds that in folk productions, the female figures are not defined according to the captive/capturing-woman grids outlined above, as are so astonishingly many in 'high' literature. Rather, they are mostly stock female figures of European folk literature generally, such as the necessary helping hag, grandma story-teller, sexually eager bride, or scolding wife. Again, the gender-imaging in broadside ballads—creations tailored to a semi-literate, sometimes upwardly mobile class of small scale producer-marketers, along with busy men and women of shops and work-yards—does not follow the patterns here noted (see the workroom scenes in Thomas Deloney's *Jack of Newbury*). (What ideological gender patterns it does evince would be intriguing to pursue, but beyond the scope of the present study).

THE CLASSEME 'MALENESS-FEMALENESS' WITHIN IDEOLOGEMES

Jameson's definition of the ideologeme as a libidinal apparatus or desiring machine should in itself suggest that gender as a classematic category will characteristically enter into the sememic analyses of ideologemes, in various eras and cultures. Indeed, though he does not seem to notice it, particular concepts of womanhood and manhood are central to the ideologemes he works out in nineteenth-century novels, for example that of potent elegance vs. impotent energy in the post-Napoleonic world of Balzac, and that of Nietzschean *ressentiment* as operable in Gissing. In the first case, the ideologeme's narrative embodiment is construed from the perspective of woman (who is analogous to 'the estate') considering alternative male styles in potential husbands. In the second, its "sentimental" narrative embodiment (as renunciation) is enunciated from the position of the Victorian 'angel of the hearth'; thus Gissingesque "rejection of rejection" and ultimately "rejection of all desire" are definitively linked with a prevalent Victorian concept of femaleness, with its essential element of sexual self-repression.

Classematic oppositions (see the Greimas-Courtés entry "classeme," *Dictionary*) often derive from the features of human perceptual mechanisms, such as height-lowness, heat-cold, or life-death. In terms of the three inclusive kinds of opposition recognized by logicians—the contrary, the contradictory, and the arbitrary or gradual—they are among the third group, which also includes oppositions that may be culture-specific (blonde-brunette).[39] Oppositions of this third sort typically posit a continuum between poles rather than two separated distinct terms, and therefore they cannot themselves be articulated (as the term at issue) on a semiotic square: the square by definition maps the interactions only of the first two kinds of opposition, contradiction and contrariety. Thus a semiotic square cannot be done on maleness-femaleness as a base term.

Nevertheless, such a classematic opposition may be an essential component in the sort of "constructed sememe" we are here spelling out in possible square articulations, when the charting of it is done upon a semantically genuine constituent term or "kernel seme" within the sememe. The classematic term is then carried unchanged—i.e., with its set of local, culturally determined possible

semic contents—from pole to pole, either keeping its original hypotactic position in the posited sememe, or undergoing a hypotactic
shift that changes its position, as we saw with the difference between
female captivity and male captivity by a female. I propose that
'maleness-femaleness' will typically (or perhaps always) be present
as such a constituent classematic element in the sort of construct, at
once a meta-sentence and a set of possible static figures, that can
function as an ideologeme.

In Elizabethan England it would scarcely be surprising to find the
gender concepts within an ideologeme especially problematic and
emotionally prominent. Discontent at being ruled by a woman was
never far beneath the surface of many Englishmen's view of their
case, for all the well documented things they did about it, psychologi-
cally.[40] That their unease did not, as is sometimes assumed, die off
after the first years of Elizabeth's reign is evidenced by the very
patterns we are here examining, and often quite explicitly in political writings.

For example, consider a treatise by the queen's one-time secretary
of state and a major investor in commercial enterprises, Sir Thomas
Smith; Smith was Gabriel Harvey's (Hobbinol's) kinsman and patron,
and his *de Republica Anglorum* is cited in a *Calender* gloss. It was
written in 1565 but entered in the Stationers' Register for publication
in early 1581, while the French marriage was still possible. Well
known to later historians for its assertion of the power of parliament,[41]
the treatise devotes half a chapter to defining the natures of men and
women, and shortly thereafter explains why female rule must be
accepted at times, although it violates the operation of these natures:

> The man [is] to get, to travaile abroad, to defende: the wife, to save that
> which is gotten, to tarrie at home to distribute that which commeth of
> the husbandes labor for nurtriture of the children and family of them
> both, and to keepe all at home neat and cleane. So nature hath forged ech
> part to his office, the man sterne, strong, bould, adventerous, negligent of
> his beautie, and spending. The woman weake, fearefull, faire, curious
> of her bewtie and saving. Eche of them excelling other in wit and wise-
> dome to conduct those thinges which appertaine to their office, and there-
> fore where their wisedome doth excell, therein it is reason that ech
> dothe governe.[42]

To a considerable extent these are commonplaces of the tradition
of marriage manuals and related genres going back to Erasmus' *de
Conjugium* and earlier.[43] But it is striking how in the lexical field of
Smith's political discourse, the gender constructs become invested
with his aggressive entrepreneurial perspective: maleness not only

"goes abroad" to make money and give a due portion of it to the wife while femaleness is receptive and contained in the household (as in the manuals); maleness is also bold, spending, venturesome, and risk-taking, while femaleness is fearful and saving. A few pages after this statement of male and female competences comes a chapter explaining "who can beare rule or jurisdiction over freemen"; it deals with the exception of "absolute queens" in such a way as to stress its exceptionality.

> And in this consideration also we do reject women, as those whom nature hath made to keepe home and to nourish their familie and children, and not to medle with matters abroad, nor to beare office in a citie or common wealth no more than children and infantes: except it be in such cases as the authoritie is annexed to the bloud and progenie, as the crowne, a dutchie, or an erledome for there the blood is respected, not the age nor the sexe. Whereby an absolute Queene, an absolute Dutches or Countesse, those I call absolute, which have that name, not by being maried to a king, duke, or erle, but by being the true, right and next successors in that dignitie, and upon whom by right of the blood that title is descended: These I say have the same authoritie although they be women or children in that kingdome, dutchie or earledome, as they should have had if they had bin men of full age. For the right and honour of the blood, and the quietnes and suertie of the realme, is more to be considered, than either the base age as yet impotent to rule, or the sexe not accustomed (otherwise) to intermeddle with publicke affaires, being by common intendment understood, that such personages never do lacke the counsell of such grave and discreete men as be able to supplie all other defaultes. (Smith, *De republica anglorum*, 64–65)

"Seene and allowed" stands under the title of this book. The queen's own censors found it unobjectionable. Clearly, the male view with which she was surrounded was that a queen, even an "absolute" one, was expected to heed male "counsell."

Jameson's term "strategy of containment" is perfectly applicable here. One common male strategy of containment for woman was to redefine courtly love's high pedestal into a celebrated house of nurturant order—an imagined carefully circumscribed domestic space for female governance—and to celebrate woman glowingly when she stuck to that space. Ben Jonson's near epic praise of Barbara Gammage Sidney for having all her linens and plate ready when the king's hunting party dropped in unexpectedly ("Ode to Penshurst") is a Jacobean example. But to stick to Elizabeth's reign, the taming of the rebellious "fairy queen" Titania in *A Midsummer Night's Dream* illustrates how the queen was surrounded by this strategy.[44]

When Jameson does speak of gender conflict, he terms it merely a "rewriting" of class conflict (*Political Unconscious*, 204), which allows the latter to be presented and explored in another "register" of the veiled and unsaid. But the inadequacy of this view must be apparent if we ask a few pointed questions about the material before us (as it will be also if one gets more thorough than Jameson is about spelling out patterns of oppositions in constructed sememes).[45] A 'libidinal apparatus' or 'desiring machine' must, along with other aspects of its functioning, blank out or put out of force whatever would threaten or prevent stimulation (i.e., displaced sexual stimulation), that is, whatever would cause discomfort or guardedness in the situation of sexually-invested action. What was it that Elizabethan men feared?— whether those inclined to be religiously conservative, fiscally old-fashioned, and devoted to squirearchy, or those inclined to be reformist, entrepreneurial, and oriented toward northern European urban commercial centers. What was the power threat, or what were the power threats, that they feared? Certainly, foreign Catholic powers, certainly at times each other, but also their "own" wives and daughters. The ingenuity and staying power of this particular 'captive woman' libidinal apparatus was that it provided at once a substitute for the old adoration of the Virgin, a successful strategy of containment for the sexual threat of "new-fangled" women, and exactly thereby, an irresistible female image of the socio-economic legitimacy to be contested for by the male-dominated factions. Shakespeare's moneyless but well born Petruchio tames the well-dowered entrepreneur's daughter Kate and thereby wins his "living." About Elizabethan England too much revealing work has been done on changing gender roles and concomitant male retrenchment for us to discount the gender hierarchy in analyzing a possible libidinal apparatus of the political mind of the time.[46]

More generally, a basic assumption of the 'ideologeme' idea, that people in some fashion invest physically sexual energy into political activity and conflict, ensures that their particular gender concepts will be among the mechanisms of such an apparatus. How could they not be? Sir Thomas Smith's definitions of roving entrepreneurial-acquisitive maleness vs. fixed contained femaleness, fencing in the queen who stood in such glaring opposition to them, show why Elizabethan literate culture was compelled to set up an apparatus whereby it would oscillate between and among the poles of the captive woman construct, as outlined above. In the operating of this political desiring machine, he who could joyously capture and be served by woman-power could sign himself the socio-economic victor.

6

The "Captive Woman" at Work

We now examine some texts and other productions by various Elizabethans, so as to note several patterns of usage of the captive woman ideologeme. The instances given above need to be supplemented by more concrete illustration. Recalling what the ideologeme as a metasentence has as installed object-value (i.e., that which its "maker" subject gains control of, namely competence), we should keep in mind that writers, artists, songwriters—all who successfully communicate through the ideologeme—thereby take up, and are taken up by, a unit of socio-political meaning that enables them to speak and be heard at a libidinally vital level. Since the Elizabethan captive woman ideologeme assumes a male enunciator, a concluding issue here will be its bearing on women writers of the age.

Possibly there are genre-specific patterns in the handling of such ideologemes, but that issue must be left for other studies. The following examples will for each genre be too few to offer useful generic evidence; they are taken from verse romance-epic, prose romance, songbook air, comic and romance drama (both prose and verse), illustrated broadside ballad, dialogue verse encomium, and dedicatory verse epistle. I have selected broadly across a range of genres so as to show that these ideologically defined patterns are not limited or local but are culturally comprehensive for the competing class interests noted in chapter 5. Two common usage patterns of the ideologeme will emerge in the following analyses—I have termed them entrepreneurial and squirearchist—and each reflects both narratively and emblematically an ideological component of identity for people who are libidinally invested in its perspective. In the two cases, people's ideological sense of identity makes them favor either swordswinging Protestant internationalism and suppression of Roman Catholicism in Britain, or relative economic and geographical isolationism, conservative episcopal governance, and toleration of private Catholicism. For the fuller definitions of the ideologeme concept and of these groups with their representative court factions see chapter 1

129

and the section "The Captive Woman Ideologeme" in chapter 5; we look now at their characteristic patterns of usage of the ideologeme considered as a socio-linguistic unit.

THE ENTREPRENEURIAL PATTERN IN THE FAERIE QUEENE: BRITOMART VS. RADIGUND, GLORIANA OF THE SHIELD VS. PHILOTIME

In *Faerie Queene*, V, vii, we watch a direct conflict of the capturing woman's positive with her contradictory term: woman herself, temporarily released to be a releaser of men, is made to conquer her reprehensible capturing self, when Britomart rescues her betrothed Arthegall from the imprisoning, emasculating Radigund. This Amazon forces defeated men to submit to her commands, wear women's clothes, and do spinning and weaving. Both the role reversal and the male grief over the supposed need for a "strategy of containment" for such threatening womankind are ironically figured in the image of two stabbing and hacking women spilling their blood as "fruitless seed" of death upon the ground, as if it were semen[1] (for the passage, see p. 133 below). In such unnatural combat, we hear, they are risking "their dainty parts, which nature had created / So faire and tender . . . for other uses, . . . / As if such vse they hated."

As has been agreed since Josephine Bennett's *Evolution of the Faerie Queene* (1942), the story materials from Ariosto that occupy most of books III–IV represent Spenser's earliest work on the epic, begun during the time of the *Shepheardes Calender* (before 1580), even though he did not for some time bring those diffuse narrative strands to some degree of order and closure as book V[2]—not until he had set that material aside while he wrote books I and II, and not until his Irish experiences, in the context of the war against Spain, had supplied him with the basis of the Arthegall/Lord Grey legend of justice for book V. We see then, in the excerpt below, a crucial moment in the working out of *The Faerie Queene's* narrative macrostructure (in the partial and provisional form in which it has survived), namely the climactic episode in the intertwined legends of chastity, friendship, and justice (books III, IV, and V) when Arthegall, knight of justice, as espoused husband the object of Britomart's chastity quest, is set free to carry out his quest and thereby at last to point the long tale of Britomart and her associates in love and friendship toward a projected, though never realized, conclusion. Britomart, one of the epic's several figures for Elizabeth, is the queen as the international militant that the Leicester/ Essex party wished her to be: releaser of others from evil oppression by the Spaniards and their allies. Having published books I–III in 1590, Spenser was writing book V in the early and mid-90s when the English, Dutch, and French war against Spain was in full action, and the costs of war were triggering a peace movement. One dimension, then, of the epic's much discussed incompleteness is the fact that book V, which stands in the penultimate and potentially climactic position for the six books, fails to be climactic because it was functioning as a prophecy of continued Protestant militance that was not to be fulfilled—Elizabeth would soon withdraw from the continental wars, albeit without an official capitulation or peace settlement.

That Britomart beheads an Amazon might seem puzzling when we recall that the queen herself, especially after the Armada year of 1588, could sometimes be depicted as an Amazon.[3] Amazons in the Renaissance, as in classical times, could be either evil or good: they could be wicked oppressors of men, like some of Ariosto's warrior women, or admirable allies of epically praised forces, like Penthesilea with the Trojans, or the Amazonian-attired Camilla with the Italians of the *Aeneid*. Spenser apparently preferred not to use Amazonian elements (half-moon shield, one bared breast, etc.) in any positive portrayal of his warrior queen, but instead to save those for images of evil female militance (held up to Elizabeth as negative *exempla*).

The beheaded Radigund historically images Mary Queen of Scots. Of course another figure, Duessa, does so as well: the latter is condemned to death (as reported event in a subordinate clause) by a tearful Elizabeth as Mercilla in the trial scene of V. ix–x, where no mode of execution is mentioned. Why Spenser included not one but two allegorizations of this execution in book V has puzzled Spenserians. Thomas Cain proposes that Britomart's iron-handed decapitation of Radigund represents what Elizabeth should have done as soon as the captive Mary became an active threat,[4] while the Mercilla episode shows the actual execution after long years of "mercy." Donald Stump similarly argues that Radigund's beheading represents Elizabeth's decree of 1571, after Mary's complicity in the Ridolfi plot, that Mary never be allowed to reclaim her Scottish throne—a decapitation of her body politic—while the Mercilla episode shows the condemnation of her body natural.[5] But while Spenser may well have thought of his two episodes in such a way, in effect the decapitation of Radigund is so vivid and so unmistakably allusive that it was bound to remind listeners (hearing one episode at a time, in the reading mode of the era) of the literal as well as the political beheading of Mary. In effect, Duessa has appeared through most of the books primarily as the Catholic spiritual anti-heroine and thus image of the false church, back-handedly honored for her nobility and original good looks, and even suitable for humorously satirical treatment; as such she can be fittingly condemned with tears, a turning away of the face, and a weakly gestured order to an unmentioned chopping block (much the version Elizabeth herself preferred). The displacement of Mary's image into a second-level and nightmarish figure meets Spenser's need to in glorify a deed the queen did not want to claim. Radigund is a more sheerly demonized Mary, the militant would-be usurper and assassin, whom Elizabeth is portrayed to behead after direct provocation.

On the didactic level Radigund, as do other shadow queens in the epic, also images a negative, to-be-rejected self for Elizabeth, who through this usage of the ideologeme is being enjoined not to become a repugnant Mary *rediviva,* aiding the papist cause (though by default).[6] I suspect that this episode supplied the stroke whereby Spenser at long last saw how to get out of (though not finish) the Britomart story with which he had begun his romance epic. The queen's releasing-woman self is made to kill off a possible capturing-woman self (just as, with enormous male pressure and prodding, Elizabeth had finally indeed beheaded her cousin the supposed "capturer" of men's wits); Elizabeth is thereby portrayed, at the level of the ideological fantasy code, to be restoring woman to her proper subjugated status within male control, freeing at once the male agent of justice within the fiction and the male poet struggling to write justice.

For the pervasive entrepreneurial pattern of usage for the ideologeme, its narrative articulation is a two-stage movement, across a doubly modalized construct illustrated well by the Radigund episode: from the pole of capturing woman to that of releasing woman, then to that of captive woman.

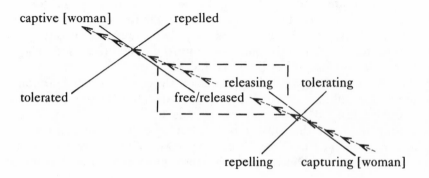

Radigund the capturer succumbs to Britomart the releaser, who then
reinstates male control by releasing and redressing Arthegall, thereby
achieving her own readiness for marital captivity as his wife. Emblematically, this ideologeme usage is the above cited iconographic
figure of Britannia Militant, the English Protestant substitute for the
Blessed Virgin, being enjoined to wave her sword over the map of
Europe for Protestant patriarchy.

Note the deep-running irony of Radigund's "conditions" here as
applied to Britomart, for whom such a switch to female identity is
already her foreseen course of a good life.

> The warlike Amazon [Radigund] out of her bowre did peepe.
> And caused streight a Trumpet loud to shrill, . . .
> But ere they reared hand, the Amazone
> Began the streight conditions to propound
> [for the loser, shaved beards, women's clothes, spinning] . . .
> Which when the other heard, she [Britomart] sternly frownd
> For high disdaine of such indignity,
> And would no lenger treat, but bad them sound [the trumpet] . . .

> But through great fury both their skill forgot,
> And practicke vse in armes: ne spared not
> Their dainty parts, which nature had created
> So faire and tender, without staine or spot,
> For other vses, then they them translated;
> Which they now hackt and hewd, as if such vse they hated . . . .
> So long they fought, that all the grassie flore
> Was fild with bloud, which from their sides did flow,
> And gushed through their armes, that all in gore
> They trode, and on the ground their liues did strow,
> Like fruitles seede, of which vntimely death should grow.

> At last proud *Radigund* with fell despight . . .
> And thus vpbrayding said; This token [a deadly blow] beare
> Vnto the man, whom thou doest loue so deare;
> And tell him for his sake thy life thou gauest. . . .
> That stroke so cruell passage found,
> That glauncing on her shoulder plate, it bit
> Vnto the bone, and made a griesly wound
> . . . yet soone she [Britomart] it requit.
> For hauing force increast through furious paine,
> She her so rudely on the helmet smit,
> That it empierced to the very braine,
> And her proud person low prostrated on the plaine.

Where being layd, the wrothfull Britonesse
Stayd not, till she came to her selfe againe,
But in reuenge both of her loues distresse,
And her late vile reproch, though vaunted vaine,
And also of her wound, which sore did paine,
She with one stroke both head and helmet cleft.

(*Faerie Queene* V, vii, from sts. 24–34)

Queen Elizabeth and her court are here being offered, in this picture of her more-than-justified martial rigor, an image of double import: on the one hand a sanctioning of Mary Stuart's execution and on the other an intense valorization of the entrepreneurial party's desired Irish policy, namely that the queen should be, as she has been in deciding to "free" England from the threat of Mary Stuart, once again the liberating, "releasing" Britonesse—whose action will free iron-clad male justice to operate in Ireland (Arthegall evoking Lord Grey of Wilton, the rigorously suppressive Governor of Ireland and Spenser's employer); she should be a releasing queen rather than the emasculating, capturing Amazon whom the urgers of conciliation in Ireland wanted her to be. The "freeing" of Irena is Arthegall's quest. (From the Irish viewpoint as well as from Mary Stuart's, the extreme irony of this imperial exact inversion of capturing and freeing can be fully appreciated.)

The issue was not settled as Spenser wrote book V: the queen had to be urged to continue both supporting the Dutch wars against popery and permitting Grey's iron policy for Ireland. As the *Calender*'s Dido had seen proposed to her a future self in a coffin if she chose the wrong policy then, so "Radigund" is held up here for the queen's contemplation as an ugly, unnatural, doomed persona which she will be assuming if she prevents her loyal male subjects from enacting justice (i.e., holds them "captive"). Maintenance of a firm power base in Ireland was essential to the entrepreneurial English interests since the Irish periodically allowed continental Catholic powers (in this case Spain, the primary enemy) to use their territory for staging sites; here we see clearly that the ideologeme is a unit of discourse between the expansionist faction and the more isolationist, squire-archist interests, which inclined as much as possible to leave the wild Irish—and the rest of Europe—to their own devices, and were much sooner ready to make peace with Spain, once direct attack on England was no longer threatened.

"How very fortunate," says the fiction to the queen (and to the opposition) "that you have not become and will not become like this ugly, decapitated Radigund!—that you are and will remain the offspring of the ever admirable liberator, Britomart." Thus the poet's fiction becomes a "socially symbolic act," proposing an "imagined solution to a real problem"—in the form of a fictively enacted female killing of an Amazonian queen.[7]

This time, however, the queen was not daunted by the image: she did not permit the completion of Grey's iron policy plans. A point that may already be clear should be stated. Use of the ideologeme to offer and lobby for an "imagined solution" that one wanted the queen and others in power to adopt did not of course guarantee that she or they would accede to the urging. The message might be ignored; one's opponents might be offering a more successful alternative. It may be that the failure of these militant warriors to find favor with Elizabeth, as Una, Gloriana, and Belphoebe earlier had, proved a determinant for the cultural reception history of Spenser's epic: Book V is not included in anthologies, and few Spenserians claim to enjoy it. In any case, whatever the results, an ideologeme construct supplies a unit and mechanism of meaning generation for antagonistic inter-class discourse. The entrepreneurial pattern of handling that unit in this case, shown on p. 132 above, is a motion among the poles of the 'captive' and 'capturing' woman squares, as analyzed in chapter 5: from capturing woman to releasing woman to valorized captive woman. In other words, control moves from a capturing woman to a releasing one, then to one euphorically immured in captivity (usually marriage), thus ultimately returned to male control.

Let us consider another instance in *The Faerie Queene* of a releasing woman saving a male hero from a capturing woman who is defined as her own negative exemplum, an instance that has special bearing on the problematic of power discussed in chapter 1, and much debated among Spenserians since the appearance of Stephen Greenblatt's *Renaissance Self-Fashioning*. Greenblatt proposes that Guyon's destruction of the bower of bliss in *Faerie Queene* II reveals Spenser's love of and thorough implication in oppressive, acquisitive colonial power. But a more direct treatment of that very problematic than the bower episode is an earlier Guyon adventure, that of Mammon's cave (II, vii), where Guyon is tempted by wealth from several perspectives (allegorized as different caverns). Since this episode is both the epic's obligatory instance of a hero's underworld journey and a version of Christ's temptation to power by Satan (complete with angel ministrations to his weakened condition at the end), we should recognize that Spenser is marking it off as one of crucial importance for *The Faerie Queene* as a whole, as well as for Guyon's particular quest.

The first temptation—to miserly running of gold through one's fingers—has no force for Guyon; noting that his joy is in arms, he moves quickly on to the more pertinent temptation of money as something to be sought with fullest effort because it seems essential for procuring the resources of one's calling ("money can thy wantes at will supply / Sheilds, steeds, and armes, and all things for thee meet / It can puruay in twinckling of an eye"—II, vii, 11). Scoring this point and echoing his Satanic model, Mammon quickly expands its reference to the scope of kingdoms ("Do not I kings create, and throw the crowne / To . . . whom I lust?"). To a loftily ambitious person, a kingdom itself is merely a means toward the using of one's talents, the practice of one's calling.

Guyon replies that government viewed as unchecked acquisition of wealth by the powerful (even if seen as supplies for one's proper work) is "wrongfull," therefore highly unstable and productive of sorrow for both ruler and people; as antidote to this temptation, he recommends a dose of golden age simplicity for rulers and courtiers in their personal lives ("But would they thinke, with how small allowaunce / Vntroubled Nature doth her selfe suffise / Such superfluities they would despise"—II, vii, 15). Mammon in turn notes shrewdly that the golden age is long past, and that those "in later times" who want to accomplish anything important "must wage / [their] workes for wealth, and life for gold engage," adding scornfully that Guyon may take or leave the offered wealth, but if he declines, should not afterwards foolishly complain of lacking it.

Guyon then reasserts his claim that he does not want any wealth wrongfully got, "bereaued / From rightfull owner by vnrighteous lot," by such methods as "Castles surprizd, great cities sackt and brent" (II, vii, 13 and 19), whereupon Mammon claims that the wealth he offers comes simply from the earth, not taken from anyone. If Spenser were a simplistic colonialist, the debate might stop here and Guyon might accept Mammon's offer. Certainly Sir Walter Raleigh—as seen in his account of the famous ship fight off the Azores, where he tells of English sailors ashore to forage for whatever supplies "they could by force recover . . . from the land" ("*re*cover"—as if they already owned everything by right)—Raleigh would have been satisfied to question Mammon only thus far, then accept the wealth.[8]

But as Guyon continues resisting, he is led on to another and more absorbing temptation cavern, the throne room of Philotime, whose name means love of honor or of praise. This amazing parody of Queen Elizabeth and her court must have been almost too recognizable; lit by a faint moonlight of "Cynthia," the throne room has a long golden chain stretching from the high dais itself down to "lowest hell," binding all the hierarchies of favor seekers in a fearsome competitive ladder where "euery lincke" is "a step of dignity." By "close shouldring" and thrusting others down, "Those that were vp themselues, kept others low, / Those that were low themselues, held others hard, / Ne suffred them to rise or greater grow"—II, vii, 46–47).[9] Guyon enters this scene with his "glitterand armes" emitting their own bright light to help him through the darkness: on his shining shield is the image of Gloriana the Mayden Queen, Elizabeth herself in her broadest, most comprehensive depiction in the *Faerie Queene*, as sheer glory: Guyon is by definition Gloriana's own knight, on her own quest for the temperance so hard to find when one is "glorious." In emblem fashion, the glittering arms are *pictura* to the subscribed principle he declares at this point as he enters the throne room, which Mammon says is "the fountaine of the worldes good": namely, that he (Guyon) plans "in atchieuements braue / . . . my flitting houres to spend, / And to be Lord of those, that riches haue, / [rather] / Then them to haue my selfe, and be their seruile sclaue" (II, vii, 33).

The bright escutcheon of the liberating maiden Queen Glory meets face to face her darksome counter-exemplum, the deathly and tyrannical Philotime—and the Queen comes out superior to the queen. For it is Guyon's shining armor that saves him from the lure of the dark scene. Here too we recognize the ideologeme pattern of the releasing woman saving a man from the capturing woman; as in the Radigund scene, both are alternative versions of Queen Elizabeth. Guyon can thus finally insult the "Money God" and declare, "all thine idle offers I refuse." Mammon takes him through one last room, a Dantesque suicide garden of subterranean death plants, but Guyon's task here is hermeneutic, to recognize Tantalus and Pilate, the extremes of anarchic rebellion and gubernatorial coldness to one's people, both of course to be avoided. He is then at last released to the upper air, where he faints for weakness after his long effort of resistance. Is the writer of this episode a man who would indulge, in the bower, in an unself-conscious reveling in colonialist acquisitiveness drawn from displaced revulsion for sexuality? More deliberation is needed before we reach such a conclusion. The linkage between sexual arousal and Lucifera's unchecked, prideful wealth is something Spenser himself had portrayed memorably in the Orgoglio episode of book I, where Redcrosse Knight was politically vulnerable because of being "poured out in looseness on the ground." Indeed, aggressional-erotic energy is at work in Guyon's destruction of the bower, but its uses are the very problematic shaping book II's fictions.

After Guyon emerges from the cave, his control of the Mayden emblem, his newly recaptured woman—i.e., of his shield and armor—is in question. For during his unconscious state Pyrochles and

Cymochles try to take it away from him. But Prince Arthur (in each book an intervening agent of divine grace) arrives to defeat them and restore to Guyon his emblematic armor. Thus the second phase of the entrepreneurial usage pattern for the ideologeme is completed: from capturing woman (Philotime) to releasing woman (the shining shield Maiden as held aloft in the throne room) to valorized captive woman (the shield Mayd as restored to Guyon's possession).

In the Radigund and Philotime episodes we recognize two instances of the entrepreneurial articulation of the ideologeme, whereby releasing woman defeats capturing woman, the same conclusion about rightful power for a poet that Spenser had evolved in writing the *Calender:* namely, that it is a matter of keeping a grip on one's own competence, as the key to a measure of independence—so much independence as will permit one to "leave off with the best" when the political structure to which one is subject moves toward some act that seems intolerable. Selling out to Mammon would be to lose that sense of competence—and control of competence—needed in one's self-concept as a writer. Spenser as prophetic writer wants Guyon's power to dictate, through moral authority, to "those that riches haue," and yet to need no riches himself and thus to stand beyond the pale of power's corruptive influence. Whether Spenser succeeded in doing so is of course another matter. He would not have accepted our own usual assumption that colonialism *per se* is an evil. And doubtless in terms of socio-semiotic functioning, if one is the epic poet urging on a colonialist queen, one is *ipso facto* a colonialist. But we should recognize that his romance-epic evinces a concept of moral control for poets that took account of the eroticized condition of political and monetary powers.

THE IDEOLOGEME IN THE *ARCADIA*, OLD AND NEW

Backtracking from *The Faerie Queene*, we return to the year after the *Calender*'s appearance, 1580, for another kind of instance of the ideologeme at work; Sir Philip Sidney (the *Calender*'s dedicatee) was in rustication at his sister's Wilton estate, sent away by, or staying away from, the queen he had so offended with his protests against the French marriage, and completing the first version of his *Arcadia*. After this instance of another Leicester party, entrepreneurial use of the ideologeme, we shall later investigate squirearchist uses of it in Lyly, Greene, Shakespeare, and elsewhere.

In what follows we must several times recall the semiotic square articulation of the unmodalized ideologeme, central to Sidney's initial plot structure and generative of the complications he later builds into the New *Arcadia*.

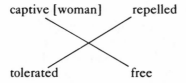

In defining the Arcadian queen and princesses as captives of King Basilius in his state of withdrawal from the exercise of royal power, Sidney shows a king (generically named "king") whose inability to rule is a corollary of the mode of false captivity in which he keeps his women. As for the princesses, they become alternatives within the *vouloir* modalization of the captive woman, i.e., wanting to be free and wanting to stay captive: as the narrator repeatedly stresses, Pamela is strong-minded, assertive, and inclined to independent thinking, while Philoclea is gentle, passive, and submissive. Thus Philoclea has no containment imposed on her beyond that of living in the royal household's protected rural lodge, while Pamela is especially put under the guard of the comical rustic Dametas and his family, a situation she endures only until a chance of escape offers itself—the elopement with Musidorus.

In Pamela's attempt to escape, Musidorus as the agent helping her (the actorialization of another modality governing her action, that of competence) is greatly to be condemned, and Sidney tags his actions of elopement and attempted rape (in the woodland scene, where brigands interrupt him)[10] with strong dysphoria. Thinking to win free from her ignominious captivity under the dimwitted Dametas, Pamela puts herself into the hands of a loving princely rapist, thence falling into the clutches of the brigands, from whom she is happy to be "rescued" by her father's men and carried back to the guarded lodge. So much for the independent-minded woman. On the square as recalled above, her narrative motion is to push from the positive term first of captivity toward the contradictory one of independence, only to be recontained until such time as Musidorus, finally purged of his sin of prematurely attempted capture, can be ready to lead her into the proper and fully euphoric captivity of marriage. Her strong-mindedness will there have its mature value, becoming useful for loyalty and committed wifely effort, because she will then have internalized her captivity.

As for Philoclea, not striving to win free, she finds a quasi-female lover who has won "her" way *into* the princesses' state of captivity so as to court Philoclea—namely, the alleged Amazon Cleophila (in the New *Arcadia* renamed Zelmane), really Prince Pyrocles in female dress. Philoclea's motion, then, is from the positive term to the contrary one, that of repelled woman, which she triply becomes: repellent to Musidorus as the effeminizer of his friend, repellent to herself as (so she thinks) in love with another woman,[11] and repellent to her mother, who, recognizing and sexually craving Prince Pyrocles beneath the Amazon's dress, becomes her own daughter's spiteful rival. From repellence, as Pamela is from independence, Philoclea will be rescued back to captivity—the proper captivity of marriage— once Pyrocles has returned from his temporary state of femaleness.

The queen Gynecia ("Woman"), for her part, swept away by an unworthy passion for a man young enough to be her son (shades of the queen and d'Alençon), tries to escape her husband Basilius for a love night in a cave with Pyrocles, continuing that effort toward independence until her remorse over her seeming accidental killing of her husband (with an over-potent 'love' potion, from which he later revives) brings her back into the proper captivity of loyal marriage (as the real queen should return to her 'husband' England). This love potion, which her own mother had given her to use on Basilius upon the occasion of her marriage, is an actorialization of deadly female desire-to-capture, a modalization of the capturing-woman term otherwise suppressed here or as Jameson would say *non-dit*, but soon to emerge in Cecropia of the revised *Arcadia*.

The political resonances of both Pamela's and Gynecia's attempts at independence, at the court of an exceedingly strong-minded Queen Elizabeth swept away (so it seemed to the Leicester party) with passion for a foreign prince who wanted to carry her off from her proper attachment to her realm into unforeseen dangers—these resonances were left to float uneasily in the air, being tagged with no politically specific topical echoes. In such cautious fashion did Sidney let the ideologeme begin to emit its "bleeps" in the dangerous year of the Old *Arcadia*.

But as he worked on his revision in the next few years—the royal marriage threat safely past—he became bolder, beginning to rewrite the previously 'non-said' political implications into his greatly expanded New *Arcadia*. Space does not suffice here for an inclusive account, but much of the work done in recent decades on the New *Arcadia*'s political implications would accord with the present analysis. To start with an instance from among the entirely new figures imported, the independent Queen Erona, who refusing male counsel and control lets passion govern her and marries badly, thereby ruins her own life and the safety of her realm, spoiling also the happiness of her would-be husband King Plangus. Thus the queen would be doing if she let her passions separate her from her husbanding realm, embodied in Leicester and his faction. Erona is the stable contradictory of all the story's better women, who are eventually led into or returned to the proper captivity of well governed marriage.

Sidney seems intent on actorializing all the possible poles of capturing and captivity (as if defining the socio-semiotic territory for us), but let us focus on the 'captive princess' motif, much expanded in the New *Arcadia*. The elopement and attempted rape are there eliminated in favor of a milder violation, the attempted kiss (III, ch. 1), which earns Musidorus some frowns from Pamela;[12] and the ensuing brigand captivity of the old version, likewise eliminated, is replaced by the far more elaborate and developed captivity of both princesses (along with Zelmane/Pyrocles) in Cecropia's castle. There the Amazon prince learns high philosophical patience in captivity and militant chastity under threat of rape, a far more admirable version of femaleness than he had learned in his womanly wiles of the cave tryst and murder trial episodes in the Old *Arcadia*. I believe Sidney was planning to eliminate the whole cave-tryst and mistaken-murder intrigue, having devised as replacement a more flattering 'test-rescue-marriage' sequence for the two royal young couples, namely in the drawn out conflict with Cecropia and her passion-ruled, mother-dominated son Amphialus.

The fight scenes generated by the captivity afford Sidney opportunity to actorialize the final pole toward which the entrepreneurial pattern tends, namely the valorized female-captivity of proper marriage. The lovely submissive, nurturing wife appears as Parthenia (wife of Argalus) and as Helen (betrothed would-be wife of Amphialus). As a sample of their doings consider the idyllic domestic scene of Argalus and Parthenia, when he receives the order to come fight in the bad cause of Amphialus and Cecropia.

> The messenger found Argalus . . . sitting in a parlour with the fair Parthenia, he reading in a book the stories of Hercules, she by him, as to hear him read; but while his eyes looked on the book, she looked on his eyes, and sometimes staying him with some pretty question, not so much to be resolved of the doubt as to give him occasion to look upon her. A happy couple: he joying in her, she joying in herself, but in herself, because she enjoyed him: both increasing their riches by giving to each other; . . . he ruling, because she would obey, or rather because she would obey, she therein ruling. (501)

In this paradisial scene (which I believe influenced Milton's portrayal of a similar narcissistic Eve hanging upon Adam's words), we

see through Sidney's keen eye for such matters the working of a
general mechanism of domination noted by sociologists, whereby the
dominated person or group appropriates to herself (himself/them-
selves) and internalizes the image of the dominator, thereby embrac-
ing the domination and making it stable. The scene valorizes the
idyllic captivity of woman in patriarchal marriage, the state into which
the falsely captive princesses must be removed, through great blood-
shed. (Argalus himself must be sacrificed and thereby his dear
Parthenia as well.) Parthenia is, then, an instance of the sheerly euphoric, properly devoted and sexually vibrant married woman—
analogous to Amoret as Scudamore takes her by the hand from the
side of pure womanhood in the temple of Venus.

Cecropia the atheistic duchess is an obvious instance of the purely
dysphoric capturing woman we have noted above, from whose
clutches a (supposed) woman warrior must rescue the female pris-
oners. Cecropia's woman-dominated son Amphialus, his reason utterly overruled by his passion, is for all his martial prowess analogous
to Radigund's male captives: his captivity by his mother has made it
appropriate that he should end, severely wounded, by having a
woman, his would-be wife, carry him off. (She knows a good surgeon,
she says.)

We turn in conclusion to the fight between Zelmane-Pyrocles and
Amphialus's last surviving strong ally, Anaxius the misogynist and his
rapist brothers (576). This classematically female victory was the last
scene Sidney managed to do of his revision, and he did not quite
finish it. Having already killed Anaxius's two brothers and having
begun the fight with him, "Zelmane" in a moment of truce for
"breathing" taunts him thus, in his discouragement at having to fight
a woman:

> "What is it," said she, "Anaxius, that thou so deeply musest on? Doth
> thy brothers' example make thee think of thy fault past, or of thy com-
> ing punishment?"
> "I think," said he, "what spiteful god it should be who, envying my
> glory, hath brought me to such a wayward case, that neither thy death
> can be a revenge, nor thy overthrow a victory."
> "Thou dost well indeed," said Zelmane, "to impute thy case to the
> heavenly providence, which will have thy pride find itself, even in that
> whereof thou art most proud, punished by the weak sex which thou
> most contemnest."
> But then having sufficiently rested themselves, they renewed again
> their combat far more terribly than before. (Evans ed., p. 594)

A paragraph later with the fight unfinished, the New *Arcadia* breaks
off. Sidney's last moments with his refurbished and politically ex-

panded romance were Virgilian ones, recasting the dilemma of the
Etruscan Arruns, who achieved a gloryless victory over the warrior
queen Camilla, having vowed to Apollo that he wanted "no spoils /
no trophy of a beaten girl," but only to "wipe out this ignominy"
of his comrades' deaths at a woman's hands (*Aeneid* XI, 1076–78,
Fitzgerald trans.).

The echo, in this scene of gender-specific, appropriate punishment
for misogynists and rapists, shows that Sidney was still taking Pyrocles' femaleness seriously, his captivity in company with the princesses being its natural condition. Presumably this femaleness and
captivity would have been left behind at the end of the fight, for
with Cecropia and her last strong ally Anaxius dead and Amphialus
in his swoon, the way was fully prepared for a victorious return of
princes and princesses to the royal lodge. That Pyrocles-Zelmane by
the female virtues of patience and militant chastity wins clear of
captivity to independence means that 'she' has gone through femaleness as a pathway back to a male self. As Britomart would later free
Arthegall, Pyrocles/Zelmane's chastened and patient female self has
acted as releasing-woman to the proper male self about to reemerge,
ready to become the proper capturing husband to a beloved princess.

The pattern so far noted in the *Faerie Queene* and the *Arcadia* represents the most notable and prevalent reformist-entrepreneurial way
of handling the ideologeme: to make woman militant herself, as admirable rescuer, defeat a reprehensible capturing woman figure (Radigund, Cecropia), thus making possible a released male's proper
marital captivity of a desired female—at once wife and valorized
fortune. As was noted above in the Radigund analysis, diagrammatically the narrative movement goes from the pole of capturing to that
of releasing to that of valorized captivity. Offering aristocratic woman
a certain exercise of power (within the constraint of always eventually
returning to captivity), it was calculated to please assertive women
as well as sanguine men and apparently often did so. On this score
it contrasts markedly with the squirearchist pattern, as our next instances will show, by moving through the poles of more active rather
than more passive female "doings."

"SWEET CYNTHIA, HOW WOULDST THOU BE POSSESSED?"
—LYLY, DOWLAND, AND THE SQUIREARCHIST PATTERN

The prevalent squirearchist way of handling the ideologeme was,
instead, a movement first from the contrary to the negated contrary
pole: i.e., either from repelling to tolerating or from repelled to tolerated (possibly both, for either they can be correlative as the same

instance seen from the male and the female viewpoints, or a plot and sub-plot can introduce both in one text). In truncated versions of the pattern, toleration can be accepted as the close-enough substitute for a lost pure captivity. More commonly, however, an additional action or "narrative program" would carry the tolerated woman on into the full captivity of marriage, whether it became euphoric or was left non-euphoric. Thus the prevalent squirearchist pattern, like the entrepreneurial one, consists of a two-stage narrative motion, but across different positions. The first stage, from repugnance to toleration, might be visually imagined as a sort of cavalier wave of the bonnet, as if to say, "My lady, take this defined seat of arbitrary, capricious, and circumscribed power, and let us agree to call it yours while your admirers officially dance around you." An important aspect of it was the aristocratic notion that a husband should not jealously guard, spy on, or confine his wife—she might or might not be whorish, but at least he thus kept her in the place of wifehood, contained in a circumscribed realm of limited female control, and avoided any obsession with jealousy. This pattern of aloofness was calculated to please some explicit misogynists as well as the general conservatives of the time and usually did so. With the queen it appears to have succeeded more often than one might at first expect (she operated at times through a male self-concept), though it could offend her if enacted too baldly, as we shall see. As mentioned earlier, it has already been recognized in connection with Puttenham, in terms relatable to my own, in Louis Montrose's essay "Eliza Queen of Shepherds and the Pastoral of Power."

It could have two correlative articulations, both sometimes occurring, as noted, in one text.

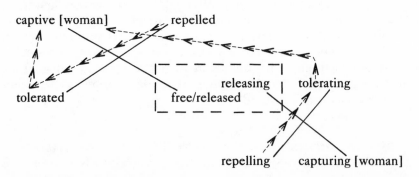

Comparing this diagram with the one on p. 132 for the entrepreneurial pattern, we recognize that in terms of historical process, this is a suitable pattern of a party gradually losing ground: its path of action bypasses the Queen (released/releaser, the only position overlap of the two squares), while the action path in the entrepreneurial pattern tracks directly through the released and releasing queen. That more successful pattern reflects the entrepreneurial party's rising hegemony in the general tendencies of English and European economic history.

My first sample texts will be *Endymion* and *The Woman in the Moone* (ca. 1585–86 and 1591–92) by John Lyly, the misogynist writer of *Euphues* (1579) and *Euphues and his England* (1580), who was brought to court as director of the Earl of Oxford's players and protegé of Burghley, and later was a partisan of the bishops in the Marprelate controversy (cf. his *Pappe with an Hatchett*). As a writer-courtier seeking the lucrative post of Master of the Revels (which he never got,[13] rising only to the assistant directorship of the boy-players, an appointment celebrated by *Endymion*), Lyly was out to flatter the queen and anyone in her favor, yet also to shape court situations ideologically into fictions adapted to his perspective. In studying the squirearchist use of the ideologeme, we will not confine ourselves entirely to works thus directly addressing the court, but they make a good starting point.

Cynthia of Lyly's *Endymion* has long been analyzed as a figure of the queen, even through times of greatest formalist distaste for topical study.[14] I see no reason to doubt the identifications offered by Lyly's 1902 editor R. W. Bond: Endymion as Leicester, the queen's long-time favorite, who in 1585 had just been restored to favor (after the estrangement over his secret marriage and his stand against the queen's French marriage—Cynthia's kiss emblematizes Elizabeth's reacceptance of him); and Tellus as Mary Queen of Scots, the prisoner whose very existence remained a threat to Elizabeth's crown, and whose hand in marriage had been sought by Leicester some years earlier (whether he really wanted to marry her may be doubted).

Lyly's plot is an inversion of the classical Endymion myth, whereby Cynthia, the moon, was infatuated with a cold youth, put him into an extended sleep, and enjoyed him at will. Lyly by contrast makes Endymion so infatuated with cold Cynthia that he wastes away his youth in a decades-long adoring sleep on a bank of "lunary" herbs. Adapting this inverted representation of Elizabeth as psychosexual exploiter of her devotee, Lyly could introduce Tellus as a capturing woman operating by witchcraft, and transfer onto her the guilt of the real capturer. Briefly, the plot is that the envious Tellus (the earth), realizing Endymion will only love Cynthia (the moon) not herself, has a witch put him to sleep; he is roused only after twenty years when his dear friend Eumenides, at a magic well given only one

wish, chooses to put Endymion's welfare above his own quest for a
lady, Semele (with attendant Euphuistic celebration of male friendship over love for fickle woman). Eumenides learns that a kiss from
Cynthia will break the charm, as it then does, and Tellus is denounced but allowed to marry her noble admirer in the country.

In Tellus's rivalry with Cynthia for Endymion's love, in her con-
signment to house arrest with a guardian nobleman in the wilderness
(evoking the Earl of Shrewesbury, Mary's guardian), and in Cynthia's
merciful treatment of her even after her attempted treachery, Tellus
in 1585–86 could not fail to be recognized as a figure for Mary Stuart.
(Note how this squirearchist faction continued to plead for merciful
marital containment for Mary, rather than execution.) But the inversions are almost mathematical in neatness. Elizabeth, in the court's
perception actually the twenty-year capturer of Leicester (and secondarily other "admirers"), who refused to marry him or anyone yet
rebuked him whenever he took up with another woman—Elizabeth/
Cynthia can become the releasing woman through a merciful kiss on
his sleeping face; Mary, actually the captive (within two years to be
executed) can appear as the hateful capturer, who in frustrated love of
him has employed a witch to cast him into the bonds of mythic sleep.

Through the agency of the scintillating kiss, the repelling woman
Cynthia (whose chastity was such that Endymion had never dared
express his longing) becomes the tolerating woman: she recognizes
and tolerates, though she will not accede to, his love.

> *Endimion*. The time was Madam, and is, and euer shall be, that I hon-
> oured your highnesse aboue all the world; but to stretch it so far as to
> call it loue, I neuer durst. . . . Such a difference hath the Gods sette
> between our states. . . . Onlie wishing of impossibilities: with imagina-
> tion of which, I will spende my spirits, to my selfe that no creature may
> heare, [I will] softlie call it loue. . . . From this sweet contemplation if I
> be not driuen, I shall liue of al men the most content . . .
> *Cynthia*. *Endimion*, this honorable respect of thine, shalbe christned loue
> in thee, & my reward for it fauor. (*Endymion*, Bond ed., III, 76)

This enacts the first and definitive motion in the squirearchist pattern, either from repelling to tolerating, or seen from the other side,
from repelled to tolerated. As noted above, the two modalizations
can also appear as separate plot strands, likewise the case with *Endymion*. Then the guilt of the capturing woman is installed in a second
figure (often in such plots a sister, cousin, or other status-correlate of
the primary figure—as Tellus and Cynthia are here). Exposed and
condemned as capturer, Tellus/Mary is thus a repelled woman, exiled
to "desert" house arrest. After the move from repugnance to tolera-

tion comes that from toleration to marital captivity. In the completion of this plot's enactment of the pattern, the repelled woman is forgiven (tolerated) and handed over as bride to Corsites, her jailor-guardian, who has been longing to marry her. Thus through Tellus and the other originally repellent women married off in the ending—namely Eumenides' shrewish Semele, the haggish witch's assistant Bagoa,[15] and the witch herself, returned to her estranged husband Geron— through these comic marriages as well as that of Tellus, it becomes possible for Lyly, while leaving Cynthia in glorious isolation and transferring guilt from her to Tellus, to complete the squirearchist pattern: from repugnance to tolerableness to proper marital captivity.

The instance is a politically successful one from the squirearchist viewpoint partly because, by having Cynthia release Endymion from sleep, it allows the queen to seem to exercise the releasing woman role that so often appealed to her sense of power in instances structured by the entrepreneurial pattern. Of course, it is only the captivity of sleep from which she is releasing him, not from his sexual captivity to her. He remains in the end her devoted, wifeless captive. The impetus toward recontainment of woman in marital captivity must be carried by the circle of other characters (four marriages being enough for the ending of any comedy), leaving Endymion and the queen as it were hypostatized in their state of unfulfilled beautiful longing.

In the multi-marriage completion of his comic plot Lyly left his referent situation behind (the Earl of Shrewesbury had of course no desire nor opportunity for marriage to Mary) for, in Jameson's terms, a "socially symbolic act" designed to offer an "imaginary solution" to a "real problem": while the entrepreneurial party wanted Mary executed, the squirearchist faction (whose horror at the thought of any assassination of a monarch was intensely shared by Elizabeth herself) wanted instead to see her married off into the containing arms of some religiously tolerant but loyal English nobleman, who would ostensibly forestall the plots that periodically coalesced around her as Catholic claimant to the throne. The next year when Sidney's father-in-law Walsingham, by permitting her mail privileges and then intercepting her mail, trapped her at last into putting a treacherous complicity with the Babington plot into writing, the Leicester party won that debate (in which, incidentally, Burghley was on their side). Elizabeth, after further months of delay, finally sent the execution order in early 1587.

By the time Lyly again dealt with courtly moon allegory some six years later, in *The Woman in the Moone* (ca. 1591–93), his own situation and that of the court were entirely different. Mary Stuart was gone, the Armada defeated, Leicester and Sidney dead, Burghley and his son greatly in the ascendant, and the younger Essex leading the entrepreneurial faction, which was no longer so religiously and ideologically unified as it had been in the two earlier decades. The "Paul's boys," Lyly's major source of income, had been shut down (why we do not know), and as Lyly's later, surprisingly bold and plaintive yet still unsuccessful petitions to the queen for money indicate, he personally was enjoying little if any royal favor. The play's eventual printed title page says it was performed for the queen, but not when nor by whom; and what impact it had we cannot say, except that neither it nor any other of Lyly's efforts to regain royal acceptance succeeded. The fact that Blount, reprinting Lyly's plays in 1632, omitted this one may indicate that it had not been well received. I suggest that it represented an enactment of the squirearchist narrative pattern that was too crass for the queen to tolerate.

The plot is that the shepherds of Utopia, having asked Dame Nature for a woman to propagate issue and to "comfort our sole estate," are given the archetypal ill-fated woman Pandora; despite being blessed with every gift of supposed good womanliness, she succumbs to the baleful influence of each of the planets in succession (being a while melancholy and cross under Saturn, arrogant under Jupiter, promiscuous under Venus, changeable under the moon, and so on). Having chosen one of the four shepherds, Stesias, as her husband, she betrays him by flirting with all the others and with her servant Gunophilus ('woman-lover'), proving so impossible to live with that her husband in the end wishes her sent off to anywhere far away from him. Hearing that Nature will remove Pandora to one of the planets, Cynthia (i.e., Luna—both names are used) claims the chance to change places with her and come live in the earthly woods (i.e., as Diana), letting Pandora in her stead manage the sphere of the waxing and waning moon as the appropriate place for one of such changeable essence; perversely, Nature orders Stesias to accompany her there as slave. Staying forever behind her wielding a scratchy hawthorn bush (who is her metamorphosed "man" Gunophilus) to prevent her from looking back, Stesias becomes the man in the moon, giving the mythic tale an aetiological conclusion. (Such an aristocratic containment of a wife and her affair with a personal secretary would have called to mind echoes from both gossip and fictional narrative— from Mary Stuart's David Rizzio to the maligned secretary of Gascoigne's "Adventures of Master F. J.")

That Lyly should have thought he could please the queen with this amalgam of stock misogynist motifs seems astonishing, although the name Pandora ("All gifts") did have a court history of positive usages (e.g., George Turberville's "Tymetes to Pyndara" sonnets to Elizabeth's chief lady in waiting, Anne Russell, Countess of Warwick, John Soowthern's *Pandora* sonnets to the Queen of 1584, and the Pandora in William Warner's *Albion's England*). She could not have avoided seeing herself at least in Luna/Cynthia (the moon being her all pervasive symbol), one of the planets balefully influencing Pandora and ultimately identified with her despicable changeableness through Pandora's elevation to "woman in the moon." And Pandora's actions throughout the play of capriciously toying with all her male devotees' affections would have been easily recognized as a parody of the queen's management of her court. Bond, while declaring the suggestion of such a satirical intent almost unthinkable, recognizes that someone had thought of it before him.[16]

Perhaps Lyly staged the play with Luna loftily apart from the scene, maintaining her otherness even in the concluding exchange of places with Pandora (which ostensibly leaves her as simply the well admired Cynthia of long fame); and perhaps he supposed that this distance would be sufficient to prevent the satirical implications from being too direct and thus offensive. Perhaps the strategy was to urge her not to behave like this Pandora image, as Spenser was urging her not to be Radigund. If so, the strategy seems to have backfired, as flattery and as activism.

In terms of the captive woman ideologeme, Pandora through most of the play is a repelling woman, playing with every man on the scene and giving loyalty and satisfaction to none. The ending moves her to the pole of tolerating and tolerated figure only by moving her from a human to a mythic status on high. But the marital captivity into which it thereby settles her—with a vindictive pursuing husband and prickly metamorphosed ex-lover eternally at her back—is a debased squirearchist parody of marriage. Lyly ends the play with a misogynist tirade, in the form of a commission to Pandora spoken by Mother Nature:

Now rule, *Pandora*, in fayre *Cynthias* steede,
And make the moone inconstant like thy selfe;
Raigne thou at womens nuptials, and their birth;
Let them be mutable in all their loues,
Fantasticall, childish, and folish, in their desires,
Demaunding toyes:
And starke madde when they cannot haue their will. . . .
Stesias. O that they [the other planets] had my roome! [i.e., place
  with her]

Nature. I charge thee follow her, but hurt her not.
FINIS

(Bond ed., III, 288)

It is as if Lyly has blown the ideologeme's cover. Nothing is *non-dit* any more. So bald and utterly dysphoric an enactment of it can scarcely have brought him any result but settled disfavor from the queen, not because she harbored proto-feminist views, but because the poet has forgotten to "cleanly cover what cannot be cured" (as Hobbinol put the matter). Perhaps it speaks for the discomfort of squirearchist men (that faction being the one in process of losing hegemony) that they sometimes produced this overly blatant version of their ideologeme pattern: reality bearing too remorsely down, the woman is shoved with too great and obvious effort from repugnance to the state of being tolerable, and on to the state of marital captivity.

The squirearchist pattern had from the start been amenable to Lyly's thinking, being similar to the plot shape of his matched pair of courtly fictions in prose *Euphues* (1578, just before the year of the *Calender*) and *Euphues and his England* (1580), both of which gained him fame at court. Euphues the misogynist, to whom women are in the main repellent, is superseded as hero in the sequel by his marrying friend Philautus, who manages to make his lady first tolerable, then a wife (a pattern reiterated, incidentally, in Thomas Lodge's *Euphues his Shadow*).[17] In *The Woman in the Moone*, a frustrated Lyly seems to have trapped himself in the pattern he had managed, through diversionary scintillation, to use successfully in *Endymion*.

An enactment of the ideologeme strikingly similar to that of *Woman in the Moone* is a song of the late 1590s by the Catholic composer John Dowland, obviously attempting to flatter the queen, though in that effort he apparently succeeded no better than Lyly had. (Dowland ended up going to Denmark for patronage.) Ever since *Endymion's* success at flattering the queen through the moon imagery of a goddess immutable in her constant mutability, this notion had been fair game for men seeking the queen's favor. But in "Say, Love, if ever thou didst find," as Lyly did in *Woman*, Dowland tips his frustration from the *non-dit* rather too far into the obvious.

On the emphatically foreshortened third line of each stanza, stressing an admired "queen's" singularity, the music comes to a complete stop, while on the like-meaning penultimate line (containing even twice as many *shes* as Fellowes bothered to print in the text below), the singularity is again stressed but by the very opposite strategy, of almost humorous extreme lengthening. This musical witticism of extremes of short and long is perhaps delicate enough in the first and last stanzas, but note the over-strong ironic effect of it in the second and third, where under the commanding royal eye the queenly mouth "mocks desire with endless No."

> Say, Love, if ever thou didst find
> A woman with a constant mind?
> > None but one.
> And what should that rare mirror be?
> Some goddess or some queen is she?
> > She, she, she, and only she,
> She only Queen of love and beauty.
>
> But could thy fiery poisoned dart
> At no time touch her spotless heart,
> > Nor come near?
> She is not subject to Love's bow;
> Her eye commands, her heart saith No.
> > No, no, no, and only no!
> One No another still doth follow.
>
> How might I that fair wonder know
> That mocks desire with endless no?
> > See the moon
> That ever in one change doth grow
> Yet still the same; and she is so;
> > So, so, so, and only so.
> From heaven her virtues she doth borrow.
>
> To her then yield thy shafts and bow,
> That can command affections so.
> > Love is free;
> So are her thoughts that vanquish thee.
> There is no Queen of love but she,
> > She, she, she, and only she,
> She only Queen of love and beauty.
> > (*The Third and Last Booke of Songs or Aires*, 1603)[18]

SHREW-TAMING, *PANDOSTO*, AND SHAKESPEARE'S REWRITING OF THE WOMAN RECAPTURED

Shakespeare's *Taming of the Shrew* (ca. 1590–94) is so obvious a handling of the squirearchist pattern that we can consider it rather briefly. The incorrigibly repellent, well-dowered Kate, who carries Petruchio's proper but lost "living" (income) as a gentleman, is through his clever strategems maneuvered into the status of a tolerable bride (she just does get through the wedding ceremony), thence in act V to become a glowingly managed captive wife, solid winner in a wife-obedience contest against her sweet sister and another bride. So successful has Shakespeare's euphoric rendering of the ideologeme pattern been, even with many modern respondents, that the play's editor Anne Barton, for example, declares it "poles apart from the mere vindictive savagery of ['The Curst Wife Lapped in Morel's Skin'"] and lauds Kate in the following terms:

> Heartily sick of a single life, not to mention all the adulation showered on Bianca, she [Katharina] is really more than ready to give herself to a man but, imprisoned within a set of aggressive attitudes which have become habitual, has not the faintest idea how to do so. Petruchio's strategy is perceptively designed to make her abandon a shrew's role originally adopted as a defense, not intrinsic in her nature, and to permit her to escape into freedom and love within the bonds of marriage.[19]

The popularity of the shrew theme is indicated by the appearance of the said "Curst Wife Lapped in Morel's Skin" (a tale of a husband's sadistic torture of his unfaithful wife into submission) among the books of a well-to-do craftsman, a list cited for its illustrative character in a study of Elizabethan middle-class culture[20] (craftsmen, from their economic position, could hold the squirearchist ideology—see the definitions, p. 117). The theme's popularity is also shown by the amusing anonymous broadside ballad with woodcuts reproduced by Barton, entitled "The Taming of a Shrew: or The onely way to make a Bad Wife Good: At least, To keep her quiet, be she bad or good." An admonishing father stands to the left of the ballad text, pointing his finger across to a formally dressed and stiff young wedded couple on the right of it, superscripted as follows:

> As the Old man saith, so let it be,
> And thou and I, shall wedded be.

The groom, looking straight ahead with a faint bland smile, has a victim look about him while the bride, her mouth a wry straight line, looks slightly askance.

The look of them and the line "keep her quiet, be she bad or good" carry a strong message overriding the tame sentiments of the text:

> Of all the mischiefs I have known,
> there is none like home-bred strife,

> When the House peace is overthrown,
> > between the man and wife.
> I see how women suffer wrong,
> > by men that are unkind,
> I can no longer hold my tongue,
> > but must declare my mind . . .
> The duty of the man i'le shew,
> > if he observe it well,
> His wife will be no shrew,
> > but friendly with him dwell. . . .

As in Shakespeare's play, the repellent woman is by enlightened good management to be brought to a state of at least tolerable if not delighted wifely captivity.

But to conclude the present treatment of the squirearchist pattern of handling the ideologeme, I turn to a comparison of Robert Greene's *Pandosto* with Shakespeare's use and revision of Greene's story in *The Winter's Tale*. Greene's opening paragraph, expatiating on the evil effects of husbands' jealousy, sets up the thematic framework soon to define Pandosto's Bellaria as a repelled wife: "whoso is pained with this restless torment [male jealousy] . . . has that wherein consisteth all his joy to be the breeder of his misery."[21]

If Shakespeare's *Taming* is the most cheerfully exuberant embodiment of the squirearchist pattern, Greene's *Pandosto* may be the gloomiest. This Bohemian king with his famous sea coast could move his wife from the status of repelled (he was "so inflamed with rage and infected with jealousy, as he would not vouchsafe to hear her nor admit any just excuse"—Salzman ed., 164) to tolerated to captive only by having her live in prison until he could consult the Delphic oracle about her supposed guilt, then when she had died of grief, by cherishing her in the encapsulation of a marble tomb through daily penitential visits.

Significantly, his jealousy is not, as in Shakespeare's rehandling, unfounded: Bellaria, though physically innocent of adultery, has indeed formed an absorbing attachment to his friend.

Bellaria . . . used him [Egistus] so familiarly that her countenance bewrayed how her mind was affected towards him, oftentimes coming herself into his bedchamber to see that nothing should be amiss to mislike him. . . . For Bellaria, noting in Egistus a princely and bountiful mind . . . and Egistus, finding in her a virtuous and courteous disposition, there grew such a secret uniting of their affections that the one could not well be without the company of the other; insomuch that when Pandosto was busied . . . Bellaria would walk with him [Egistus] into the garden,

where they two in private and pleasant devices would pass away the time
to both their contents. (157)

Yet Pandosto is, from the squirearchist point of view, a thoroughly
negative *exemplum:* having failed to be tolerant of his wife's indiscreet
though not evil conduct, he simply loses her. And with the wife's
echo image, the long-lost daughter Fawnia whom he undeservedly
gets restored to him after her shepherdish upbringing abroad, he
succeeds no better: again, by trying to capture and clutch her through
sheer intolerant force, he destroys his chance for possessing a woman
at any level. That is, with the daughter having returned to his court
still unidentified, he falls into such a passion for her that to win her
consent for sex with him he tries coercive threats (against her young
husband Dorastus) and is about to resort to sheer rape when her
identity is finally revealed; he is then so devastated over the thought
of having lusted for his own daughter that he kills himself.

Many dire pages of Euphuist hortatory exposition have set forth
Pandosto's evil efforts to get poor Fawnia as a mistress; following
thereupon, the sudden redefinition of his passion at the moment
when he embraces the newly identified daughter Fawnia is recounted
in a sentence of piercing and most unsettling irony: "Fawnia was not
more joyful that she had found such a father than Dorastus was glad
he should get such a wife" (203). What sort of father? What sort of
wife? The literal sense is of course, 'a royal one, such that Prince
Dorastus can now acceptably marry her.' But after what Pandosto has
done, no one could be glad to have such a father as he in any other
sense. The effect is a striking devaluation of the father and thereby
also a questioning of the much-longed-for daughter's value. It is not
the result of Greene's having absent-mindedly cranked out one too
many Euphuistic parisons, but is deliberate; its point is confirmed
by the immediately ensuing ending, which very briefly has Pandosto
see to the wedding, then kill himself.

Greene finishes off the man and the story in such a hugger-mugger
fashion that it is as if he could no longer bear to work with them.
Thus I interpret the ambivalent final sentence, which has sometimes
been taken to mean that Fawnia also soon afterwards died, in some
unspecified way,[22] because of the puzzling "they" in the penultimate clause:

> . . . and to close up the comedy with a tragical stratagem, he [Pandosto]
> slew himself; whose death being many days bewailed of Fawnia, Doras-
> tus, and his dear friend Egistus, Dorastus, taking leave of his father, went

with his wife and the dead corpse into Bohemia where, after they were sumptuously entombed, Dorastus ended his days in contented quiet. (204)

Perhaps the "they" was meant to refer to Pandosto and Egistus, the latter having been named just above in the sentence (i.e., the other old king soon thereafter also dying, Dorastus afterwards ruled both kingdoms in peace), or else "they were" should have been "it was," either way a case of careless pronoun usage. But I believe rather that Greene meant to write "after they sumptuously entombed it" (the corpse) instead of "after they were sumptuously entombed," and we have a mere slip of the pen as this prolific professional writer hurried to finish off his manuscript. After the glowing presentation of Dorastus's joyous and successful courtship of Fawnia, it would have been mere nonsense for Greene to say that she thereupon died right after the wedding, not even to say how she died, and to note that Dorastus accepted the event with "contented quiet."

Even with a charitable view of the ending, *Pandosto* is an extremely negative instance of the squirearchist pattern of using the ideologeme: it moves from repellence to a toleration Pandosto can achieve only by putting his wife and daughter at great distance from himself (prison and exile), to the useless forms of captivity he achieves for them in death and would-be incest. Greene's concluding "tragical stratagem" of suicide for him is entirely appropriate, though inelegantly recounted.

That Shakespeare revised this dread instance cannot be surprising. When one thinks of how many of his plays centrally feature a repelled woman of some sort (from *Love's Labors Lost* and *All's Well* to *Lear* and *Cymbeline*) who is redeemed into acceptance or even euphoric marriage, his rewriting of *Pandosto* into *The Winter's Tale* appears quite in accord with his habits, indeed is even a schematization of one of his most characteristic dramatic patterns. First, he redefines Leontes' jealousy into an entirely unfounded, almost abstract obsessive force, so as to clarify his absolute guilt—as if by distillation to get a pure sample: Hermione shows Polixenes only innocent, uncommitted courtesy. This is in keeping with the first impulse of the squirearchist pattern, toward toleration of woman, as a kind of loose and thus viable containment (giving her a long leash, so to speak). Within her permitted terrain, only discretion is required (Hermione, unlike her predecessor Bellaria, does not even violate that)—chastity must be seen as possible and praise-worthy for her, but not to be forced or demanded. Leontes, even more purely than his predecessor Pandosto, is to be a clear negative instance. The more crucial and sweeping revision, though, is to give Leontes female help in his effort to tolerate, then to capture and contain woman without crushing both her and thereby himself: a fairy godmother or *dea ex machina*, in the form of that very strange directress, that female version of Prospero, Paulina, who is named after the moralist Seneca's wife. (*The Winter's Tale* and *The Tempest* were produced, respectively, in May and November of 1611.) As a figure from fairy-tale as well as moral-sententious traditions, Paulina occupies the position of the entertaining woman (such as Alma or Medina in *The Faerie Queene*, in whose house one can stay as long as one spiritually and emotionally needs to be there). Hidden away in Paulina's "safe house" for a battered woman, Hermione will be kept tolerable for Leontes during his sixteen-year penitence for his violence. Here we see, as was noted in chapter 1, that this Elizabethan ideologeme could continue "bleeping and ticking" through the opening years of the next reign, as Shakespeare revisited the ideological impulses of his youth.

Probably thinking of Greene's other Euphuist tale *Mamillia. a Mirror for the Ladies of England*, Shakespeare renames the young prince (Garinter) Mamillius. He is strictly a function of his mother: when she is disgraced, he is smitten ill; when she swoons into her seeming death he dies. He is the only member of the royal family who will not ultimately be saved from his father's cruelty—a kind of first-born male sacrificial victim. Along with Paulina's husband Antigonus, eaten by the bear, and along with his father's tears in the daily graveside penitential rites supervised by Paulina for all the years of Perdita's youth, he pays the sufficient male penalty.

The point is to save the wife. For what would be the good of getting and keeping her if, to do so, one had to kill her and become a monster in the process? Viewing the play from the perspective of the captive woman ideologeme, we understand why Shakespeare could not give Leontes a restored daughter only, and revise to a happy ending in that direction. The restoration of a libidinally invested captive daughter is merely incest. It drove Pandosto to suicide and would have done the same for Leontes. Above all, in this family romance, the cruelly repelled wife must be restored.

The linkage just noted surfaces in Paulina's rebuke to Leontes when he looks erotically at the shepherdess Perdita, not yet identified as his daughter, while she and Florizell are asking for his help to get them married before Florizell's father Polixenes can arrive to separate them. Unlike Pandosto, instead of yielding to his attraction for his daughter, he controls it and consents to help them.

Florizell. . . . Beseech you, sir,
"Remember since you ow'd no more to time
Than I do now. With thought of such affections,
Step forth mine advocate. At your request
My father will grant precious things as trifles.
Leontes. Would he do so, I'ld beg your precious mistress,
Which he counts but a trifle.
Paulina. Sir, my liege,
Your eye hath too much youth in't. Not a month
'Fore your queen died, she was more worth such gazes
Than what you look on now.
Leontes. I thought of her,
Even in these looks I made. [*To Florizel.*] But your petition
Is yet unanswer'd. I will to your father.

(Winter's Tale, V.i.218–29)

This is the toleration, the willingness to give breathing space, to let live and let be, that he should have shown before to Hermione, even if he were unable to be sure of possessing her entirely. Now able to show it, he is ripe to receive the restored wife, even from the grave (we are here on the border between romance and mythic fable). Paulina is an actorialization of the necessarily permitted female governance—governance within a circumscribed female realm surrounded by male control—that sometimes libidinally enables the squirearchist pattern to be euphoric, rather than dysphoric as in *Pandosto*. (It also suggests why the moon is the prevalent squirearchist image for the Queen, seen as a nurturing though virginal mother.) The statue scene labels this managed female power a sort of white magic.

Paulina. I'll make the statue move indeed, descend,
And take you by the hand; but then you'll think
(Which I protest against) I am assisted
By wicked powers.
Leontes. What you can make her do,
I am content to look on; . . .
Paulina. It is requir'd
You do awake your faith. Then, all stand still. . . .
Leontes. Proceed;
No foot shall stir. . . .
Paulina. . . . [to the statue] Come;
I'll fill your grave up. Stir; nay, come away;
Bequeath to death your numbness; for from him
Dear life redeems you. You perceive she stirs.

[*Hermione comes down.*] . . .
Leontes. O, she's warm!
If this be magic, let it be an art
Lawful as eating.

(V.iii.88–111)

Note that it is necessary for Leontes three times to state his approval, to give his authorization for the proceedings, and even to "awake his faith" and believe in the magic. Thus at the same time as he is enabled to become thoroughly invested in the resurrection of a redefined wife, complete with a contained female sphere of operations, his broader, encompassing male control is reaffirmed.

Through the years while he was dogged by guilt over his bullying violence, we must suppose his control over his goods and kingdom to have been quite limited, through his diminished capacity for action and the diminished respect his people held for him. The recovery of the lost wife restores him to full manliness or male socio-political and economic functioning, as well as to emotional health. Thus Shakespeare rewrote poor Pandosto, by putting him and his wronged wife into a sort of psychic suspended animation while his guilt could be unloaded under matronly supervision. As Lyly had for once done in the ingenious device of Cynthia's awakening kiss, Shakespeare finds a way to give woman some apparent say about her case, while retaining ultimate male circumscription and control around her sphere of power. He had discovered that strategy much earlier, in the *Taming of the Shrew:* it was Kate who in the end rode the high horse over which Petruchio had tossed her; into her mouth was put the ringing masculinist manifesto which so delightfully cowed the upstart wives into submission and inspired the whole company to belt out a concluding Psalm.

ENTREPRENEURIAL SATIRE IN *WILLOBIE HIS AVISA*

An ideologeme will not be at work only in an era's most famous pieces of literature and art but also in other productions of many kinds. Nor will its usages always derive from some sophisticated or nationally important political intention; but they will have in them something of the *animus* of a writer or artist identifying with some group or influential personage and/or disidentifying with some other such. To conclude by broadening our picture of such operations, let us look at *Willobie His Avisa* (1594), a supposed verse encomium in several dialogues of a militantly chaste country inn-keeper's wife, ostensibly written by one Henry Willoughby.

Terms like supposed, alleged, and ostensible usually besprinkle discussions of the *Avisa,* which because of its references to "H. W." and his "player" friend "W. S." (among other initialed apparent figures of London and courtly circles) has been searched for a bearing on Shakespeare's sonnets. That issue will not concern us here, nor need we decide for certain who the writer and the satiric targets, under the portrayed wooers of Avisa, were. G. B. Harrison made a quite credible case that it was written by someone in the circle of Sir Walter Raleigh (perhaps Matthew Roydon), as a riposte to a legal proceeding of early 1594 against Raleigh and some of his associates that had charged them with "atheism";[23] *Avisa* in that view lampooned members of the group held responsible for the atheism charge, probably the Southampton circle with its affiliates and patronized figures. Henry Wriothesley, Earl of Southampton, and William Shakespeare (by then a well-known dramatist) would seem indeed to be likely referents of young "H. W." and his "player friend W. S." in the climactic set of dialogues, though it is not necessary to my case here to assume so.

My interest is in the means of satiric attack, for it works with the entrepreneurial pattern of the captive woman ideologeme in its emblematic manifestation, namely the figure of the militant woman campaigner for chastity. Furthermore, what began as a spoof of the womanizing of certain London notables—some of whom (or their associates) had perhaps dared to attack another group as insufficiently religious—what began thus unseriously lived on to enjoy the unforeseen popularity of a straight reading. That is, the author had for a satiric purpose portrayed a supposed vehemently chaste inn-keeper's wife learnedly and puritanically rejecting the advances of London notables, who were sent away with tails dragging; but he warmed so well to his task that he produced a spirited, free-spoken female advocate of militant chastity who could be admired by moralistic bourgeois readers for over three decades, through six editions of *Avisa.* For it is not likely that anyone in 1609, much less in 1632, was taking enough interest in the original controversy to buy the book on that account.[24]

Two possible situations would explain what gave rise to this parodic but rather too good female encomium, and for my purpose it does not matter which was the case. Either the ale-wife behind the Avisa figure was a notable loose woman frequented by the targets of the spoof (proponents of her as Shakespeare's dark lady take this line) and it worked ironically by directly inverting her character, or perhaps there were indeed some such incidents with an attractive but high-toned west country ale-wife, propositioned by a couple of the target personages, who rebuffed them and sent them packing. Other members of the circle could then be lampooned as having done the same thing, even if they had not. Either way, the situation would be good material for a satire of them as womanizing fools, cast in the safe format of moralistic dialogues between a solidly chaste country woman and various unsuccessful courtly seducers, evoked only by initials. (Harrison proposes that the inn in question was the George of Sherbourne, Dorsetshire, an estate then newly granted to Raleigh by the queen, the inn being a stopping point on the London-Plymouth road and thus well known to traveling Londoners.)

Among many uncertain matters concerning the *Avisa* one is certain: the playfulness of the ostensible publisher, calling himself Hadrian Dorrell. In his first edition preface, dedicating his labors to the honor of England's chaste women and identifying "Avisa" as an acronym for *Amans vxor inviolata semper amanda* (a loving inviolate wife, always beloved—Harrison ed., 6), he says that his author's manuscript mentioned "one in the west of England, in whome the substaunce of all this hath been verified,"[25] and that in his opinion "there is something vnder these fained names and showes that hath been done truely" (9). But in a complete reversal, his second edition "Apologie" (1596) declares that Avisa stands for no actual woman but only for the idea of "chastity itself," further that the work was written thirty-five years ago, and that the name is to be deciphered as *a visa* or "not seen," meaning "Such a woman as was neuer seene" (240–43)—i.e., there is no chaste woman. He also jibes at the bastard-fathering of certain respondents to the first-edition *Avisa*, who have claimed that its author "eternized his folly" by glancing at Avisa's "betters" in print. No such intent had entered the author's thoughts, Dorrell avers: "None can eternize their folly in things which they never thought of: but I pray God some other haue not eternized their follies, more wayes then one" (240). Enough said.

Willobie His Avisa works, satirically, through the pattern of the militant releasing woman, with weapons and barbed words freeing herself from would be seducer-captors into the right and euphoric captivity of marriage. (She is a chaste maid in the first dialogue, a chaste wife thereafter, often proclaiming her devotion to her husband.) Dorrell's "Apologie" spells out the basic image of combat that crops up again and again in the verse dialogues, once even quite literally when she pulls a knife to fend off her first "Nobleman" tempter (49).

[The author] chose out two of the most approued Captaines of bothe the Campes [i.e. of vice and virtue], . . . *Luxuriam*, Lecherie, and *Castitatem*, Chastitie, a souldier rarely seene (in these dayes) . . . . The souldiers which hee drawes forth to fight vnder the banner of this Captaine Lecherie, are all estates and degrees . . . to raze the walls of besieged Chastity. Vnder whose banner he sendeth forth onely one poore woman, of a fayned name . . . to resist so many fighting with such forcible weapons. (240–41)

The men defeated by this Chastity Militant in the form of a lower-bourgeois fighting female "of a fayned name" are all the more disgraced than was poor Anaxius up against Zelmane in the *Arcadia*—they are all the more radically diminished—because Avisa is low-born. The entrepreneurial pattern is being used to hit certain courtiers and city men with an action of *déclassement*. They are mocked by and thus set beneath a finger-wagging, over-"precise" country ale-wife. It is not surprising that the copies of a third edition (1599) were recalled, first having been on a list of books to be burned (Harrison ed., 185).

What sort of figure does Avisa cut? She listens carefully and frames her ringing replies intelligently, according to what particular smooth line the given seducer has used. With the Frenchman bandying Petrarchan desperation extremes she parodies the lingo, answering "My hap is hard, and ouer bad, / To be misdeemd of euery man. . . ." Reminded that David and Solomon did not refrain from taking many women, even if sometimes adulterously, she replies that they were for their pains "plagu'd . . . With mightie plagues of each degree," showing herself knowledgeable in Scripture.[26] Told by "Caveilero" that wives in such a position as hers cannot be so high-toned, she returns a rebuke that would have delighted someone recently troubled by an atheism charge:

> Thou wicked wretch, what [,] dost not thinke
> There is a God that doth behold
> This sinnefull waies, this Sodoms sinke?
> O wretched earth that art so bold,
>   To iest at God, and at his word,
>   Looke for his iust reuenging sword.
>
> Saint Paul commands vs not to eate,
> With him that leads a wicked life;
> Or shall be found to lie in waite,
> To seeke to spoyle his neighbours wife,
>   Such wicked soules God doth forsake,
>   And dings them downe to fierie lake. (64)

The ideologeme pattern underlying the satiric strategy becomes unmistakable when we note that several of the pitiful love pleas of

"H. W." end with emblem phrases from *The Shepheardes Calender*, given in the satiric context a piercing thrust.[27] Ending some verses on how his hope has been "turned to dispaire" by Avisa's utter rejection of him and letting "the teares trill downe his cheekes," H. W. is commented upon by Cuddie's motto from the "August" eclogue (which in the *Calender* applies also to Colin, whose sestina Cuddie has just sung). There it refers primarily to competence in poetry-making: *Felice chi puo*—happy he who can (is able, is competent). The context here makes the suggestion satirically sexual, and H. W. then a ludicrous figure who "cannot." Two pages later H. W. takes Colin's "June" motto expressing despair of the hard-hearted Rosalind's love, *Gia speme spenta*, hope already spent; again this shows H. W.'s erotic subjugation to the rigorous ale-wife. And a few pages later he is tagged with the "September" emblem drawn from Ovid, *Inopem me copia fecit*, my riches make me poor, which in this context glances at the literal riches and supposed sexual poverty of the target nobleman—he cannot even buy a piece of the action with Avisa. This witty linkage between Spenser's cruel Rosalind (always rejecting Colin) and the hard-hearted, militant Avisa is thus explicitly indicated by *Calender* mottoes, and the ideological bent of the satirizing group is also signalled. The author finishes off the allusive signals by taking as motto for his own concluding verses (thus ostensibly for the whole *Avisa*) *Agitante calescimus illo*—We grow warm [with inspiration] when that god stirs [us] up, Cuddie's "October" motto for the debate on the vaticinal nature of inspiration.

Besides in this tagged *déclassement* of the militant chaste woman and thus of her satirized wooers, the fact that the author is using specifically the entrepreneurial ideologeme pattern of militant female chastity is clear in another way, namely from the reply that was published in 1596, *Penelope's Complaint Or A Mirrour for wanton Minions Taken out of Homer's Odissea*, by Peter Colse. Portraying himself learnedly reading the *Odyssey* in Greek, Colse in his dedication of the piece to Lady Edith, wife of Sir Ralph Horsey of Dorsetshire (one of the chief movers in the atheism proceeding against Raleigh), proposes that the right image of wifely honor is not this Avisa of a "late published pamphlet," a country woman slandering her "superiors," but is the aristocratic Penelope, showing her wifely loyalty by weaving and unweaving a blanket while waiting for her husband.

In the *Avisa* by contrast, not Penelope but Lucretia and similar ideal women (Dorrell names more in his Preface)[28] had been the proper antique models for the entrepreneurial figure of Chastity Militant because they represent woman conquering or suppressing her own aggressiveness, sexuality, and very life in order to reconcile male guilt with a male ideal. Sidney analyzes this interior structure of the figure succinctly in the *Apology for Poetry* when he says that Lucretia, the noble Roman rape victim who killed herself for shame, is the perfect model of female chastity because she denounced rape by "punishing in herself another's fault."[29]

In the entrepreneurial usage then, Britannia Militant as an aggressively chaste Protestant lady warrior, conquering other images of femaleness and/or the male figures who promote such other images (e.g., Grantorto—Spain), is a revised substitute for the Penelope ideal. Penelope fits the squirearchist ideal of the tolerated wife in her contained space of home and nurture, defining and holding it through wifely tasks such as weaving and unweaving, until the morally free-wheeling husband as aggressive protector returns. Thus Peter Colse attempts to restore Penelope to the place usurped by the knife-wielding Avisa.

The *Avisa* parodied a certain squirearchist-invested group through having the image of Chastity Militant at a lower-bourgeois level defeat them;[30] it also achieved something quite telling in its later fame in the straight reading of tradesmen (and perhaps of some of their wives as well). As Lyly's *Woman in the Moone* does for the squirearchist pattern, the *Avisa* shows the capacity of the ideologeme in its entrepreneurial pattern to carry some form of its characteristic sociopolitical loading whether a user's intent is satiric, hortatory, epideictic, or whatever it may be. If someone of Raleigh's circle used the entrepreneurial pattern of the ideologeme satirically in his behalf, he himself could use it quite straightforwardly just afterwards: in his *Discouerie of Guiana* (1596), wanting to urge the queen to send forces to conquer and colonize that territory, he drew upon the tales of an Amazonian land in South America (from which the Amazon River was named) to urge that the queen should be a valiant "conquering virgin" to rid the land of "these women" with their perverse practices of ruling men.

BRITOMART VS. PENELOPE

To return to Spenser for an impression that can pull together the images of the squirearchist and entrepreneurial usages of the ideologeme, we note that he too, like the Peter Colse who replied to the *Avisa*, contrasts Britannia Militant with Penelope as alternative female ideals; but Spenser exalts the lady warrior over the home-bound wife. As if replacing the Homeric landowner feudal hero Odysseus with a new model of maleness, he very oddly equates the mobile and victorious Odysseus of the homecoming with the captive Arthegall. We return to the episode with which the present chapter began, but now a few stanzas after Britomart's victory over Radigund, as she is releasing captive knights from the dungeons.

> At last when as to her owne Loue she came,
> Whom like disguize no lesse deformed had,
> At sight thereof abasht with secrete shame,
> She turnd her head aside, as nothing glad,
> To haue beheld a spectacle so bad . . .
> [And] sought with ruth to salue his sad misfortunes sore.
>
> Not so great wonder and astonishment,
> Did the most chast *Penelope* possesse,
> To see her Lord, that was reported drent, . . .
> Come home to her in piteous wretchednesse,
> That she knew not his fauours likelynesse,
> For many scarres and many hoary heares,
> But stood long staring on him, mongst vncertaine feares.
>
> Ah my deare Lord, what sight is this (quoth she)
> What May-game hath misfortune made of you?
> Where is that dreadfull manly looke? where be
> Those mighty palmes, the which ye wont t'embrew
> In bloud of Kings? . . . .
> Thenceforth she streight into a bowre him brought,
> And caused him those vncomely weedes vndight;
> And in their steede for other rayment sought, . . .
> In which when as she him anew had clad,
> She was reuiu'd, and ioyd much in his semblance glad.
>
> (*Faerie Queene*, V, vii, 38–41)

The comparison of Britomart-Arthegall to Penelope-Odysseus is so precisely inverse in its aptness (Odysseus was rescuing the captive Penelope), that the passage in effect substitutes Britomart for Penelope as womanly ideal and proclaims that men must be men with the queen's help and permission.

My conclusions about the configurations of the entrepreneurial and squirearchist patterns of speaking through the captive woman ideologeme find a partial correlation in Louis A. Montrose's article on gender and power in Elizabethan England, which identifies in Shakespeare's *Midsummer Night's Dream* something quite similar to the squirearchist pattern I have observed. Speaking of Titania's beloved changeling boy and of Oberon's ultimately successful claim to be lord of them both, he says:

A fantasy of male dependency upon woman is expressed and contained within a fantasy of male control over woman; the social reality of the player's dependency upon a Queen is inscribed within the imaginative reality of the dramatist's control over a Queen [i.e., Titania, the fairy queen].[31]

This analysis reveals a central portion of the same narrative enactment of the squirearchist pattern for the ideologeme noted above: woman is given a space for female rule, contained or circumscribed by a broader and controlling male rule (cf. above on *Endymion, Woman in the Moon, Shrew, Pandosto, Winter's Tale*), which allows her to be captured and controlled as carrier of cultural validation. As Montrose recognizes, "The female body is a supreme form of property and a locus for the contestation of authority" (38). He has also sensed the entrepreneurial articulation of the ideologeme, for example in noting the Raleigh strategy in the *Discoverie of Guiana*, cited above. Thus turning up part of each pattern, he refers to them as "two archetypes of Elizabethan culture: The engulfing Amazon and the nurturing Virgin" (47).

I have here proposed that they should be analyzed as something more culture-specific than archetypes if we are to uncover their full figurations, recognize their specific relation to each other, and explore the extent of their functioning in Elizabethan ideology and culture. That is, they should be seen as the two most common usage patterns of the captive woman ideologeme, the entrepreneurial and the squirearchist, each capable of both static/emblematic and narrative formulations: they are respectively Britannia Militant (the chaste woman warrior subduing aggressive, "capturing" womanhood so as to subjugate womanhood itself to male control), and the glowing, actively submissive tamed wife within her patriarchally contained female space (the initially repelled and/or repelling woman brought first to tolerability, thence to valorized marital captivity). Each construct works libidinally—when it does work—by allowing woman either a temporary or a partial exercise of power, while giving man the ultimate and fuller exercise of power. It works socio-politically by imaging a central ideological fantasy of each faction, with woman as the carrier of legitimation and hegemony: that is, for the entrepreneurially inclined, the pattern renders a nascent colonialist free-market expansionism as the lady warrior Britannia or Chastity militant, ruling Europe by suppressing her own femaleness; for the squirearchist, it renders geographical containment of the desired locus of economic control as a male-circumscribed female realm under the round moon, with the queen as wifely and motherly English

Penelope, nurturing her male subjects while also submitting to their husbandry (obviously she herself participated actively in both these iconographic/ideological patterns). Finally, to reiterate a point made earlier when the two patterns were diagrammed, the entrepreneurial one gives woman the more active roles (capturer and releaser) while the squirearchist one gives her, relatively, the more secondary or passive ones (repeller and tolerater), before each moves her on into euphoric captivity. That the first, in this budding time of modern capitalism, was the more successful faction's ideological way with women—giving them more scope for limited action—appears to represent a stage, in the ideologically articulated history of changing gender concepts, from which seventeenth-century Puritanism would soon retreat.

Tinkering with the Ideologeme?
A Countess Tries to Speak

An important issue not yet raised here is what happened if a woman—who in semiotic terms might try creating textual enunciative positions with the wrong gender seme, for use of the captive woman ideologeme—had occasion to use it. For clearly it implies a male enunciator. Probably it and other such socio-linguistic structures comprised yet another reason (besides lack of educational opportunity, lack of public status, male suppression of particular efforts, etc.) why relatively few women of the time managed to write original texts for more than private use. Much work is recently appearing on those who did write something that has survived,[32] sometimes within the marginal paratextual spheres of translation and dedicatory verse. Among them was Sidney's sister Mary Herbert, Countess of Pembroke, of whose surviving original poems two addressed to the court and the queen are noteworthy here: her "Dialogue betweene two shepheards, *Thenot* and *Piers,* in praise of *Astrea,*" and one of the two dedicatory poems for her manuscript of Psalm paraphrases, apparently prepared as a gift for the queen, "Even now that Care which on thy Crowne attends."[33] At this concluding stage in a lengthy chapter, I am going to concentrate mainly on "Even now that Care," with only subsidiary reference to the "Dialogue."

During the 1590s the countess prepared for a visit of the queen that apparently never came off, perhaps partly because of the earl's worsening health;[34] the "Dialogue" title says it has been "made by the . . . Countess of Pembroke at the Queenes Maiesties being at her house at Anno 15   ."[35] The spaces indicate that the place and time of the anticipated visit were yet to be determined when the manuscript was copied. The "Dialogue . . . in praise of *Astrea*" and the two dedicatory pieces, "Even now that Care" and "To the Angell spirit of Sir Philip Sidney," complement each other very well for this context, the "Dialogue" seeming to be a conventional public pastoral suitable to be declaimed or sung during a dignitary's visit, while the other two pieces are written only for the eyes of the queen and a select few readers (it seems that other copies were made—see Waller ed., 44). As will be explained, the Astrea dialogue with its witty handling of the impossibility topos (none can praise her truthfully or adequately) argues that defining the queen's virtues and powers must mean taking care at each point to say enough yet not too much; the more particularized "Even now that Care" makes that Renaissance concept of adequation concrete in a telling political meditation on Elizabeth as a Davidic monarch. While the "Dialogue" seems purely conventional on the surface, when we consider it as an entertainment to be viewed while one skims the more personal and original meditative poems on the flyleaves of the gift book just received, we realize that it had various political implications.

Among other effects, it accomplishes a blanking out of gender in the poet's representation of the queen: it repeatedly poses elements of the mythic Astrea figure as virgin of the golden age (springtime floweriness, fairness of nature, "maiden bay"), but each time cancels the evoked feature, calling in the end for "silence" as the only adequate praise of the queen. In terms of the captive woman ideologeme's patterns, the mythic Astraea would have fit very readily into the slot of the exiled or repelled and later returning woman: a golden age goddess of justice, Astraea was said to have fled human kind when they became cruel and corrupt, becoming the constellation Virgo in heaven; as in its French Protestant uses for the reign of Henri of Navarre and pageantry initially associated with him, the appropriation was that Astraea/justice is now returned to earth under a monarch restoring true religion.[36] The Astraea figure suited England even better than it did France because of the monarch's gender, just as the David figure suited France better for the same reason—in international Protestant mythography, they were perhaps of roughly equivalent status, as the most laudatory figures one could evoke to compliment a monarch.[37] But surprisingly, the countess does very little with this mythic Astraea figure except in every stanza to blank her out, as a wholly inadequate representation, while exalting the queen into a being beyond gender; at the same time, in the companion poem "Even now that Care," she thoroughly develops the David comparison. (Of course, the long-standing concept that as regnant

"prince of the blood" the queen was legally male would permit this
strategy, as long as it were not too concretely pursued.)[38] The countess revives and rehandles a masculine metaphor from Protestant po-
lemic pre-dating the period we have been considering (the 1580s and
90s), thus predating *The Shepheardes Calender* and the emergence (as
I have argued) of the captive woman ideologeme. In "Even now that
Care" the queen as David figure of victorious, prophetic Protestant
rule[39] is imagined as uniting in a kind of political comradeship or
androgynous marriage of minds with Henri IV, the French David:[40]
"a King should onely to a Queene bee sent." Of course the literal
sense of this metaphor is that the biblical King David in book form—
the book of his Psalms—is being sent to the queen.

One difficulty in this overall metaphoric construct is that the countess wants to have David two ways: the queen is to *be* a Davidic figure
("rivall still to Judas faithful King") yet also to marry in spirit, or at
any rate to *embrace* a David—namely Henri/his cause, sent via King
David's Psalms. This latter idea evokes yet at the same time lays to
rest all the long marriage negotions of Elizabeth's earlier years, when
she inclined to flirt with strategically useful Catholic alliances while
the Protestant internationalists wanted a firm Protestant suitor or none
at all. Now in the 1590s, it is as if the countess invites the aging
queen to embrace a king, but only spiritually, politically, androgy-
nously—one who is at once an ancient king coming to her in a book
of God's holy word, and a modern French one whose cause she is
being urged to continue supporting.

One must see the countess's planned entertainment of the court
and gift of Psalms in their literary and political context of the 1590s.[41]
Her brother had done the first forty-four, in a range of experimental
stanza forms drawing upon contemporary verse for music, and she,
ongoing patroness of musicians and song poets, had finished the project in the same vein, as part of her efforts to complete and preserve
his writings and through them to publicize him as the great martyr
of the internationalist Protestant cause. Nor was she alone as a woman
in this activism: Penelope Devereux Rich, Sidney's Stella, was Essex's politically active sister—he later would blame her for instigating
his rebellion—and Frances Walsingham, Sidney's widow, was now
Essex's wife: Sidney's three favorite women, his sister, widow, and
beloved Stella, were at this point still part of his on-going cause. The
countess may have planned for the desired visit a number of times,
revising her poems each time (evidence for this point will emerge
shortly). In addressing the queen and the privy council, she displays
a different attitude from that of her brother and his associates in the
early 1580s. They had undergone a crisis of confidence in Elizabeth's

judgement and survivability, while for the countess in the 1590s, even though Catholic enemies continue to be intensely denounced, the awe of the Armada victory is upon her. The queen must be doing something right, it seems, to enjoy such palpable divine favor. The countess does not want to pose any challenge against her, but to encourage her to do even more in the war against Spain (this is the time when Spenser's Grantorto as King Philip was conceived, with his monster Gerioneo portraying the cruel inquisition).

> Thus hand in hand with him [David] thy glories walke:
> but who can trace them where alone they goe?
> Of thee two hemispheres on honor talke,
> and hands and seas thy Trophees iointly showe.
> The very windes did on thy partie blowe,
> and rocks in armes thy foe men eft defie:
> But soft my muse, Thy pitch is earthly lowe;
> forbeare this heau'n, where onely Eagles flie.

> Kings on a Queene enforst their states to lay;
> Main-lands for Empire waiting on an Ile;
> Men drawne by worth a woman to obay;
> one moving all, herselfe unmou'd the while:
> Truthes restitution, uanitie[s] exile,
> wealth sprung of want, warr held without annoye,
> Let subject bee of some inspired stile,
> Till then the object of her subjects ioye.

> Thy utmost can but offer to hir sight
> Her handmaids taske, which most her will endeeres;
> and pray unto thy paines life from that light
> which lively light some, Court, and kingdome cheeres,
> what wish [i.e. a wish that] shee may (farre past hir living Peeres
> and rivall still to Iudas Faithfull King)
> In more than hee and more triumphant yeares,
> Sing what God doth, and doo What men may sing.

In the stanza asserting that Elizabeth's glories have gone beyond those of David, I believe the countess is thinking of the Armada portrait, already famous in various copies.[42] There the queen sits resplendently centered in a space flanked on either side, behind her, by two open windows (or pictures in frames?), each showing a seascape of the armada, the one with fireships being blown into it, the other with it being battered by dark rocks that evoke the shape of a massive earth giant, with pounding fist extended (the very winds and rocks fight on the English side); thus the two portrayed seascapes have become trophies of her victory. Also her two hands, at the front of the picture, display trophies: an elaborately worked crown on the stem end of the fan in her left hand (echoing the larger imperial crown on the table behind her), and a globe on which her right hand rests, covering all of Europe. ("Hands and seas thy trophies jointly show.") The two hemispheres that speak of her honor are the old world of Europe and the recently colonized Americas, together making the globe under her hand.

As for the second of the stanzas cited, the rulers of France and the Netherlands through the 1590s were indeed looking to Elizabeth as their best stay against Spanish conquest, and she was spending tens of thousands of pounds per year supporting troops abroad. In the early nineties the Dutch and French constantly called for more help, and the English parliament of spring, 1593, granted the queen and Burghley all the military money they requested[43] (it was up to that point a "war held without annoy," without any significant dissent at home). Yet after early 1593 the queen, fearing excessive strain on her treasury and people, declined to increase her contributions further.[44] Later in the spring of that year the English court learned that Henri IV was considering converting to Catholicism, and as his decision still hung in the balance, Essex tried to mount a new relief expedition while Burghley slowed down the effort. In May Henri indeed converted,[45] an act represented by Spenser as Bourbon changing his shield, and a definitive one for the history of Europe.

It may well be that in this alarming spring and summer Mary Herbert, working to finish her Psalms, first tried to plan a royal visit affording a chance for support of the Huguenot effort. Her phrase "war held without annoy" certainly suggests the climate of the early nineties rather than of later years, when the merits of continuing the war became highly debatable in England. We have an early draft of the second dedicatory poem for the Psalms (of which the later draft is dated 1599), "To the Angell spirit of the most excellent Sir Philip Sidney" (Waller ed., 190–92); and we know that the countess had a complete draft of her Psalms done by 1594.[46] She might well also have drafted her poem to Elizabeth ("Even now that Care") this early, although the only surviving copy is dated 1599. Further, the fact that, as Leicester Bradner notes, the queen in 1593 boasted of how quickly and easily she had done a verse translation of Boethius[47] suggests that court flattery of that year and shortly thereafter would have picked up on her pride in displaying poetic skill ("Even now that Care" ends by equating her with David not only in doing what men sing but in singing what men do). Thus from 1594 on, possibly even from mid-1593, the Countess may well have been trying to arrange a royal visit and thereby to support the Essex faction's aggressive war efforts. After Henri's conversion in mid-1593, their hope was still for increased aid to him, so that even if he could not be reclaimed for the faith, France could at least be persuaded to remain among the allies against Spain rather than making a separate peace (as eventually it did)—the first reports of that feared possibility reached England in September, 1594.[48]

The mid- and later 1590s brought further Essex expeditions (the most successful capturing Cadiz in June 1596) and further crucial moments when the countess could have tried again to make her case for the Protestant cause, perhaps most notably after the sailing of the second great armada, ninety vessels that left Spain in October 1596, only once again to founder in the British weather. If she revised her poem after that news came in early 1597, it may reflect a renewed impression of England's favor with the God of storms. But it seems to capture especially well the national sense of astonished reverence and awe after the 1588 Armada storm, as celebrated in the Armada portrait: after the loud winds and rocks have been fighting for England, "soft my Muse," this matter is too high for you. When in July, 1598, the French signed the Treaty of Vervins making formal peace with Spain, the English faced the choice of also making peace or fighting on with only the war-torn Dutch as allies, and the issue was fiercely debated. Burghley had died the previous summer, having advocated peace in his last months. Essex was adamantly opposed to peace, and the queen acquiesced in the war party's wishes, at least to the extent that she never did officially make peace with Spain. Such was the state of affairs in 1598–99 when the countess tried (I suggest, was trying again) to arrange a royal visit to Wilton. The 'J' MS. of the Psalms, with the revised version of "To the Angell spirit," is dated 1599. The queen finally did visit the countess's brother Sir Robert Sidney at Penshurst in 1599, but by then she could not be there as her husband was too ill.

The metaphorics of "Even now that Care" show a woman poet doing something unusual with the biblical tropes that had earlier been common for addressing the queen. In the 1560s and 70s, when it came to biblical comparisons, the chosen figures had been the female war leaders Judith and Deborah (see Elkin Wilson's chapters on each);[49] if the queen was compared with male Old Testament leaders, writers briefly mentioned a list of several such, concentrating on their notable functions rather than on them as persons: as Moses and Joshua had, she led her people from slavery, as Solomon had, she built a temple of true faith or attracted admiration for her wisdom, as Hezekiah or Josiah had, she reformed a corrupt religion; and so forth.[50] David was sometimes included in such a list, his youthful imprisonment and later royal success being compared with hers (as in the case of Edmund Bunny—see n. 39 on Hannay). But writers stopped short of direct, unmediated comparisons between the queen and male figures: Fulke Greville, looking back on her reign, calls her not "a David" but "a she-David."[51] Thomas Bentley's *Monument of matrones: conteining seuen seuerall Lamps of Virginitie* (1582), a late instance of the kind, offered proper reformist prayers that she is imagined to speak "with Dauids spirit" (320); Bentley portrays God addressing her as "thou Virgin mine, the *Kings* Daughter" (i.e., a daughter of David), to whom the Lord speaks just as he did to David, "Thou art my Daughter in deede, this daie haue I begotten thee" (307). But she is not said to *be* David, or even "a David," but his daughter, which sets her beneath him in status.

The countess developes her Protestant empress figure by evoking such metaphorics of the 1560s and 70s and works out something original—and something quite different from the Cynthia, Diana, Idea, Astraea, Belphoebe, Britomart sorts of figures prevalent in male representation of the queen in the 1580s and 90s. We must now go back to the stanzas of the poem preceding those quoted above (which are its ending). The countess's persona mixes two metaphors, speaking of herself and her brother together weaving their psalms (like cloth), and expecting them to be "sung . . . to thy [the queen's] musicke," i.e., spoken by her in devotional reading:

> . . . wee thought the Psalmist King
> Now English denizend, though Hebrue borne,
> woold to thy musicke undispleased sing,
> Oft having worse, without repining worne;
>
> And I the Cloth in both our names present,
> A liuerie robe to be bestowed by thee: . . .
> enough to cause our neighbours see
> we will our best, though scanted in our will:
> and those nighe feelds where sow'n thy favors bee
> Unwalthy doo, not elce unworthie till.

These last two lines introduce a third metaphor (besides cloth and songs): the brother and sister poets have tilled some fields where Elizabeth is or was to sow seeds of favor; they have had little wealth (i.e., royal support) for their tilling, but have nevertheless shown themselves worthy and devoted to the task. This is a quite bold and self-assured call for more support for the reformist cause.

The countess next compares the queen's breast to a cabinet where

Muses hang their trophies, calling it the place where all trophies of
divine wit and art are most fitly housed, then returns to her David
trope in earnest.

> Which [the "best cabinet" image] if men did not (as they doe)
>   confesse,
> and wronging worlds woold otherwise consent:
> Yet here who mynds so meet a Patrones
> for Authors state or writings argument?
> A King should onely to a Queene bee sent.
> Gods loued choise unto his chosen love:
> Deuotion to Deuotions President:
> What all applaud, to her whom none reprove.
>
> And who sees ought, but sees how justly square
> his haughtie Ditties to thy glorious daies?
> How well beseeming thee his Triumphs are?
> his hope, his zeale, his praier, plaint, and praise,
> Needles thy person to their height to raise:
> Lesse need to bend them downe to thy degree:
> Theise holy garments each good soule assaies,
> some sorting all, all sort to none but thee.

What is already conventional within the habits of address to Elizabeth as Davidic ruler is that her religious status and her military
victories are comparable to David's, and in the following stanza, the
point that her foes the papists are as pernicious as David's foes the
Philistines. But some elements here amount to a step by step extension of the earlier mediated comparisons. For one thing, she is compared not to David's daughter but to his spouse, companion, or equal:
only a king should be sent to a queen. Second, she is claimed to be,
in human terms of royal elevation, of equal status with him, and in
terms of manifest divine favor (the Armada victory), blessed "with
greater conquest" than even his. Finally, she is celebrated in the
international constellation of Christendom—most amazing claim—as
an unmoved mover ("one moving all, herselfe unmou'd the while"),
a scholastic definition of God. We take up quoting from where we
left off just above:

> For eu'n thy Rule is painted in his Raigne:
> both cleere in right: both nigh by wrong opprest:
> And each at length (man crossing God in uaine)
> Possesst of place, and each in peace possest.
> Proud Philistines did interrupt his rest,
> The foes of heau'n no lesse have beene thy foes;

Hee with great conquest, thou with greater blest;
Thou sure to winn, and hee secure to lose.

Thus hand in hand with him thy glories walke:
but who can trace them where alone they goe?
Of thee two hemispheres on honor talke,
and hands and seas thy Trophees iointly showe.
The very windes did on thy partie blowe,
and rocks in armes thy foe men eft defie:
But soft my muse, Thy pitch is earthly lowe;
forbeare this heau'n, where onely Eagles flie.

Kings on a Queene enforst their states to lay;
Main-lands for Enpire waiting on an Ile;
Men drawne by worth a woman to obay;
one moving all, herselfe unmou'd the while.

(We have come to the Armada passage once more, this time through
the stanzas before it.)

All this still does not make what would be metaphorically the most
direct claim, that Elizabeth *is* England's David. It is as if the gender
disjunction is so strong that the countess, unable to call her David,
moves on to claim that she is greater than David and indeed moves
on to explore the very concepts of 'likeness' and 'difference.' Several
shrewdly applied logical distinctions—three of them ending successive stanzas just quoted, to make a kind of rhythmic recurrence of
oppositional logic—are put to work to image difference in likeness,
and to develop the theme set forth by the rigorous truth-lover in
the "Dialogue":

Sufficeth not no more to name,
But being no lesse, the like, the same,
Else lawes of truth be broken.

In other words, in posing a metaphor, it does not suffice only to avoid
overstating the similarity between tenor and vehicle, one must also
state enough similarity to substantiate the claim of 'likeness' or, if
one is going even further, 'sameness' (of course a complete sameness
would result in tautology rather than metaphor). The distinctions are
that "all applaud" David while "none reprove" Elizabeth; all people
can find some Psalms that particularly fit them while only the queen
finds all the Psalms to fit her; and she is "sure to win" militarily while
David was "secure to lose" (i.e., secure from losing, sure not to lose).

Further, her status need not be rhetorically raised (*amplificatio*) nor that of his glories lowered (*diminutio*) because they already match— an ingenious *praeteritio*, since the statement in saying this achieves exactly the amplification that it claims is unneeded. And finally, while David was God's "loved choice,"[52] she is His "chosen love"; the countess turns the biblical strong sanction of David as the "man after God's own heart" into a chiasmic rhetorical figure that sets the queen certainly as high as David, perhaps even higher, as God's "chosen love."

In each case, the phrase or concept for the queen would at first seem to be synonymous with its Davidic correlate but is not. Having no one reprove you is not the same as having all applaud you: the latter implies the former, but not vice versa. Among other opposition figures of sound and sense here exploring difference in likeness, the countess has in effect noted the principle of one-way presupposition that defines the relation between term and sub-term on the semiotic square, i.e. between a term and the contradictory of its contrary (see chapter 2, p. 56 on the semiotic square): winning is not identical to "not losing": though winning implies not losing, not losing (a concept including stalemate) does not necessarily imply winning. Subtly such contrasts make the point that Elizabeth is militarily more powerful than David (sure to win while he only 'did not lose'), but not necessarily sure to enjoy the approbation that he has (none reprove her now, but will "all" applaud—will history applaud her?). That would depend on her present actions. And if all the Psalms fit her (though otherwise only 'some' of them fit 'all' people), then those fitting for her include Psalms of penitence, of confession of wrong, and of pleading for divine guidance.

Despite these subtle questionings, because the poet claims that Elizabeth outdoes David in power and divine favor, there is in the hierarchy of statuses here being posed to her no human being—male or female—who stands between her and the triune God. She is invited to look, not mediately but immediately, to the divine nature and to obey God's will for achieving the great Protestant victory. Far from imaging her as any sort of captive, capturing, or releasing woman, the countess has construed for her an ungendered, supporting cosmic identity ("one moving all," a kind of power incarnate), beyond all human maleness, beneath only God. Yet at the very moment of concluding this process of definition she suddenly remembers that the queen is after all a woman ("Men drawn by worth a woman to obey")—and enjoys the fact. What of the countess herself in relation to this exalted persona? She is only a handmaid to, as it were, her lady of service, offering a piece of woven work—but one that if donned by the royal recipient might have weighed heavier than the robe of state she had already worn for four decades.

Could the countess have successfully addressed the queen and court while strategically circumventing or doing without the captive woman ideologeme, in the manner we have observed here? Unfortunately, since she never got a chance to present her planned entertainment, the question is moot. But my guess is that, for all the political commitment, logical ingenuity, and poetic skill displayed in the pieces we have considered, she would not have managed to make a memorable impression with this original development of a Protestant metaphorics from earlier in the reign.

CAPTURING AND LIBERATING: WHAT THE QUEEN SAID

Did the queen stolidly endure all the imaging of her as captive, capturing, or releasing woman? Did she only nod, smile, or frown like some silent Stella, always talked to but almost never talking except to give brief commands? Even Stella finally got in a word once, in a song. The countess's celebration of Elizabeth as comparable to David not only in glorious monarchy but also in lofty poetry may make us wonder whether the queen wrote more poetry than has survived; we do have verse translations of hers of Boethius (1593—mentioned above) and selections from Plutarch and Horace (1598), as well as several original poems of undoubted authorship and a set that Leicester Bradner calls doubtful pieces.[53]

One of these latter was published in *Mele sive Odae . . . Epigrammata* (Nuremburg, 1580) by the imperial poet laureate Paul Melissus Schede, who had earlier sent flattering poems to Elizabeth, perhaps for the occasion of the Emperor Maximillian II's honorary induction into the order of the Garter in 1576.[54] In the 1580 book Melissus included an epigram he had sent the queen, along with an answer to it, *Reginae Responsum*.[55] Since the issue in these two epigrams is whether Melissus will be a "slave" to the queen, they are of interest here. At the same time that Spenser was writing *The Shepheardes Calender* with its lady-queen-shepherdess so many ways captured, Melissus was writing of his longing to be captured by this queen, and she, it appears, was elegantly responding.[56] Whether or not she actually wrote this poem, she sent it in her name. First his poem.

Ad Elisabetham Angliae, Franciae, Hiberniae Reginam

Non solum, Regina, meos tibi sacro libellos,
    Iam quibus imposita est ultima calce manus:
Sive Poesis erit, seu cantio Musica, sive
    Nescio quid melici; scilicet omne tuum est.
Non solos, inquam, tibi dono [sic] sacroque libellos:
    Ipsum me Genio dedico Diva tuo;
Germanumque hominem Francaque propagine cretum
    Regia me dedo sub juga servitii.
Utere me servo domina; ingenuoque ministro
    Sis hera, qui laudes incinat usque tuas.
Eccui libertas tanti sit, ut esse recuset
    Tantae patronae nobile mancipium?

[To Elizabeth, Queen of England, France, and Ireland

O Queen, not only do I offer you my works,
    On which the final polishing is finished:
Whether they be poems, songs, or whatever sort
    Of lyrics, I know not what, they are surely yours.
Nor do I give my books alone to you,
    Goddess: my genius and myself I consecrate;
A German born of Frankish stock I place
    Myself beneath the yoke of your royal service.
Employ me as a slave, Lady; be mistress
    To a free-born servant who always sounds your praises.
Is freedom worth so much that any would
    Decline to be noble slave to such a patroness?]

The queen's reply is as follows.

Reginae Responsum

Grata Camena tua est, gratissima dona, Melisse:
    Gratior est animi dulcis imago tui
At quae tanta movet te causa, quis impetus urget,
    Ex homine ingenuo servus ut esse vellis [sic]?
Haud nostrum est arctis vates includere septis,
    Aut vel tantillum deminuisse caput.
Tu potius liber fieres, laxante patrona
    Vincula, si famula conditione fores.
Sed vatum es princeps; ego vati subdita, dum me
    Materiam celsi carminis ipse legis.

Quem Regum pudeat tantum coluisse Poetam,
Nos ex semideis qui facit esse deos?

[The Queen's Reply

Your song is welcome, your gift most welcome, Melissus:
    Yet more welcome is your soul's sweet image.
But what inclines you thus, what could impell you,
    A freeborn man, to wish to be a slave?
To put poets in confinement is certainly not
    Our custom, nor to diminish their scope at all.
Rather, you would be set free if you were of servile
    Status, the patroness loosening your bonds.
But you are prince of poets, I subject to a poet, when
    You choose me as matter of this lofty poem;
What ruler would it shame to have nurtured such
    A poet, who makes us into gods from demi-gods?]

Melissus in Heidelberg, comfortably supported by the Elector Pala-
tine, may not have realized what chord his hyperbolic gesture of
figurative slave captivity would strike in England. But the queen, it
seems, was quite as much aware of the political potential in the
metaphorics of the 'capturing-releasing' woman as was any writer,
musician, artist, or courtier. Indeed this would have to be the case,
given the back and forth communication between her and her subjects that the ideologeme enabled. In her view, she was not capturing
anyone, but rather herself living as a subject to the poets' and courtiers' many fantasies. The ideologeme here tracked was a major socio-
linguistic mechanism for this functioning.

7

Compositional Order and Colin's Framing of Male and Female Loves in *The Shepheardes Calender*

In this chapter we move on from a discourse analysis of the *Calender* and various socio-semiotic implications of it to a concluding discussion taking cues from the field of discourse pragmatics—i.e., sociolinguistic study of the modes of interaction among discourses, their writers, and their readers/listeners. (This is the American sense of the term that developed from the work of Charles W. Morris—for Greimas's comment on it see his *Dictionary*'s "pragmatics" entry.) In chapter 2, while illustrating the Greimassian concept of the actant, I discussed the *Calender*'s perspectival and deictic framing through describing its "communication actants"—i.e., sender-receiver positions appearing as a series of narrator-narratee pairs, terms which are part of Greimas's preferred way of discussing such matters, as part of the "cognitive dimension" of discourses. We recognized there "Immerito" (the first authorial pseudonym introduced) and his addressed "book" ("Go, little book . . . ") as initial narrator-narratee pair (Philip Sidney being inscribed through them as secondary narratee—a structure of indirection), then "E. K." and "Master Gabriel Harvey," dedicatee of the apparatus, as the next narrator-narratee pair, then the unnamed introducer/concluder voice of "January"–"December" with a defined, socially up-scale "you" as primary narratee[1] (we ourselves being the secondary one there, thus indirectly situated), then Colin Clout and the "gods that pity lovers" within "January," and lastly the interlocutor-interlocutee pair of each middle eclogue. We recognized further that each of these sender-receiver positions functions as a kind of Chinese box containing the more centered ones inside it. And each has different deictic functions, with respect both to the implied textual center inside it and to those perspectival layers outside it; through these functions the surface diegesis of the ec-

179

logues takes on political coloration and complex referentiality. In the present, concluding chapter we will consider these layers of framing not in their text-internal relations but in the functioning of some of their utterances as paratexts, namely texts constructed to define, condition, and shape an ideologically desired readership for the *Calender*.

Gerard Genette in *Seuils* has defined the paratextual as a sphere existing between the framed or centered text and the social world of its potential reception: the paratextual is a threshold or vestibule, a permeable zone of transaction, where the writer or parties allied therewith try to attract and fashion a desired ideologically pertinent readership or readerships.[2] Having thoroughly taxonomized such paratexts according to grids of their various possible relations to the writer, readers, and framed text—dedications, footnotes, promotional interviews, and many more—Genette in conclusion notes that still more kinds of productions, such as translations and illustrations, have "undeniable paratextual pertinence" (372), although he has omitted them so as to define the outward boundaries of the paratextual conservatively, and not end up saying that "all is paratext" (374). If the border on that outward side of the paratextual is hard to define (with affairs like illustrations, which are not even textual, widening it to a blended zone), the border to its inward side, that between paratext and text *per se* (centered or framed text), cannot be considered clear cut either; texts of famous writers, for example, may eventually absorb their original and sometimes even later paratexts, so that what has been originally presented as paratext becomes text (370). Something that was ostensibly a "private epitext" or materially separate paratext sent to a particular person (by Genette's sub-categories), namely Spenser's letter to Raleigh about *The Faerie Queene*, eventually becomes part of what editors consider the text, surrounding it in turn with notes and commentary.

When preparing his *Shepheardes Calender*, Spenser understood such matters so well that he incorporated with his eclogues a pseudo-extrinsic editorial apparatus that from the start would be both text and paratext, essential to readers'—and his own—interactions with the eclogues and their political intimations.[3] To push the proposition a step further, I believe it was through the co-creation of the *Calender*'s E. K paratexts along with his close friend Gabriel Harvey (see my essay "Spenser's 'E. K.'") that Spenser resolved certain personal and political difficulties in the task of publicly setting forth his calendric eclogues, and thereby came to the ordering of them that we now see. Paratexts are not necessarily *ex post facto* and extrinsic to the presentationally centered text they frame: in many cases, as with the *Calender* I propose, the production of them is intrinsic to the writing process.

In adopting a complexly strategic use of paratextual conventions, including woodcut illustrations integral to the eclogues' dealings with readers, the *Calender* invited its readers—including us—to play a special kind of game with its text-paratext combination, and it also provided more distinct indications of Spenser's ideological maneuvering than are typically given by texts regarded as poetic. For paratexts, Genette says, take sides with the writer, to serve his or her interests and purposes for the text (375).[4] Their ideology is the rightness of the text's and the writer's viewpoint (however complex or indeterminate that may be), just as an ethnologist's is the rightness of a cultural belief or practice being studied; the view of "a certain formalism" that the text has no implicit sense, or that of a certain "psychologism" that it does have one and the writer cannot know it—these are alike irrelevant to paratextual practice (375). While thus having a typical "ideological" character, paratexts can yet function in a great variety of ways, with respect to centered texts and to readerships.

Richard Halpern's neo-Marxist chapter on the *Calender,* drawing a distinction from Lyotard's *Post-Modern Condition,* views the difference between its eclogues and their framing E. K. apparatus as that between a "narrative pragmatics" (a discourse mode like that of the almanac *Kalender of Shepherds,* where the truth of statements is validated by their being actively functional within a rural society and its accepted traditions, however inconsistent or illogical these may be) and a "scientific pragmatics" (a discourse mode that defines itself as making truth claims independent of social functioning, that are justified by "formal criteria"). The E. K. apparatus, says Halpern, amounts to a humanist, self-conflicted and also self-amused or parodic version of such a scientific-pragmatic discourse, which is "folded back into" the fictions of the eclogues through its multiple ways of relating to and conditioning them. Since the poems as archaically anglicized pastorals represent "an imaginary version of a society governed by narrative pragmatics," while the apparatus through its self-parodic scientific pragmatics depicts a "nostalgia of the outside for the inside," the *Calender* was able to function "as a transitional work," juxtaposing a pre-capitalist native English rural sensibility with a foreign, rhetorically suave, humanist poetic that was assimilable (though not "directly reducible") to the interests and perspectives of emerging capitalism.[5] Halpern's proposal is promising and seems to deserve more study; at any rate I certainly agree with, and as mentioned will here elaborate upon, his brief suggestion that the *Calender* poses a "humanist game of interpretation"; he adds that the game "turns solemn when transposed to religious and political contexts" (202), and that in addressing the Alençon marriage negotiations through an anonymous publication, it became a risky one "of interpretation and concealment. The more paradigmatic questions of knowledge and interpretation raised by E. K.'s commentary thus provide a general context for more specific and sensitive interventions into the political and religious spheres" (203).

Thus as I do here, Halpern sees the interaction of eclogues and paratextual apparatus as having, among other functions, that of setting in motion a game of response and feedback with readers, which operates to effect the book's desired political impact. I would suggest also that, on the basis of the marked secondary narratee position noted in chapter 2 above, where actual readers find a position within the text as shadows of the socially up-scale "you" addressed by "January"'s introducer voice, the *Calender* posits a screened court-insider identity for its carefully positioned desired readers. This position could have a double ideological loading, namely of affiliation either with the Leicester party or with the French-sympathizer party; but clicking into the one or the other option-versions of it would make a difference in how one read and responded—whether one chuckled at "February" and skipped several heartbeats in "March," or vice versa (see p. 191 below). In other words, Spenser wanted his eclogues, particularly the opening one, to draw into his game both his enemies and his ideological fellow travelers; this intent I believe explains the often noted, allegedly apolitical and urbane balancing of conflicted viewpoints in the *Calender*'s eclogue debates. To pursue this strategy, he had not only to compose debates where no one clearly wins or loses but also to make his E. K. apparatus interact subtly with those eclogues, to do the job of ideological formation of readerships. At one end of the range of this subtlety—i.e., not very subtle—is the E. K. argument for "July" unmistakably signaling the eclogue's critique of the prelatical conservative Bishop John Aylmer (although within it "Morrell" will be allowed to make some convincing points): "This Aeglogue is made in the honour and commendation of good shepeheardes, and to the shame and disprayse of proude and ambitious Pastours. Such as Morrell is here imagined to bee." At the other end of the scale is "February"'s argument beginning "This aeglogue is rather morall and generall, then bent to any secrete or particular purpose," a claim which the woodcut just above it preveniently belies (see pp. 188–190 below).

Of course, in moving from description of readily identifiable textual structures, as in chapter 2 on actants, to the sphere of relations between text and possible readerships—i.e., that of discourse pragmatics—I have betaken myself to a more speculative realm, indeed in this case one where speculation is the name of the game. My primary effort here will not be to arrive at definitive conclusions on all the topical issues raised, but to specify, so to speak, the rules of a game: the game which Spenser's eclogues and paratexts invite readers to play—in his own time possibly for very high stakes.[6]

The *Calender*'s glossator persona E. K., while serving Spenser's ideological interests, lets us know that we cannot take everything he says at face value. By signals of several kinds the *Calender* invites readers to sort E. K.'s statements into categories of the straightforward footnoting, the teasing and obfuscating, and the tongue-in-cheek disinformational. The lack of such sorting, in the history of Spenser scholarship, has caused a fog of unknowing to arise around the *Calender*, wherein scholars have sometimes declared that no one can say what the eclogues referred to in their socio-political context, nor what interests they tended to serve. But let us do some of the indicated sorting and see what emerges. Some further results here, along with an account of the text-readership game, will be a theory of the order in which Spenser wrote the eclogues, why what used to be "February" became "November,"[7] and how Spenser in the "January"–"June"–"December" frame portrays himself as the object of competing male and female loves, a portrayal that I believe allowed the final organization of the eclogues to fall into place for him.

THE EASY MOVES IN THE *CALENDER* GAME OF WHO'S WHO: THE CLEAR IDENTITIES

Consider first the explicit links that the eclogues and E. K. state between characters and actual persons. These are long known identifications; but their clear bases must be recalled here because we are going to distinguish them from the beclouded evocations of further people, look at the explicitly signaled ones as a group, and study Spenser's textual strategies for achieving both clear and beclouded evocations.

Colin Clout, E. K.'s introduction says, stands for "the Author selfe" or as we now know, Spenser (he had only signed himself "Immerito"—the Undeserving One). The name Colin Clout had been used by John Skelton for a character who satirized abuses in the English church, and Clement Marot at the French court had also used "Colin," for the shepherd depicting himself as poet. Thus Colin is Spenser's self-image as engaged churchman and court poet. The shepherd Hobbinol, we are explicitly told in the "September" gloss, is Gabriel Harvey. Besides being Spenser's best friend, Harvey had been his tutor and rhetoric lecturer at Pembroke Hall, Cambridge. The E. K. apparatus is dedicated to him although the whole book is dedicated to the Earl of Leicester's nephew and staunch ally Sir Philip Sidney—it was quite unusual to have a separate dedicatee for an apparatus, so the fact supports my point above that the apparatus is textual as well as paratextual. Featured at the quarterly spaced intervals of "January," "April," "June," and "September," Harvey in the eclogues is presented as the new university poet's warmly affectionate and supportive mentor (though he was only a few years older than Spenser), while in E. K.'s paratexts, the credits to and reflections of Harvey and his learning are in their effects more various, even sometimes bantering and teasing (see my "Spenser's E. K."). We know a good bit about Spenser's and Harvey's activities in 1578–79 when the *Calender* was being prepared, through the E. K. apparatus, the letters they published the next year (*Three Proper and wittie, familiar Letters*, 1580), and other surviving writings of Harvey's. Both were seeking posts among Leicester's faction; Harvey failed to get one, Spenser got a secretaryship, first with John Young, Bishop of Rochester (former Master of Pembroke Hall), then with Leicester himself—at least he worked for Leicester in some capacity, perhaps only minor, as in the *Letters* he portrays himself having friendly conversations with Sidney and others at Leicester House.[8]

Besides Harvey, Spenser, and the dedicatee Sidney, five other people are unmistakably evoked: Eliza the Queen in "April," one courtier, and three bishops. Of the last, Spenser's employer Young is seen—through his Latin title as Bishop of Rochester, Archepiscopus Hroffensis—as the good shepherd Roffy of the "September" fable, who tries to guard against wolves (Catholic agents—see n. 16) in his diocese though his operatives sometimes fail him. The shepherd Algrind, described in "July" as having been stunned by a shellfish dropped by a she-eagle, cannot but call to mind through inverted syllables Archbishop Edmund Grindal, recently suspended from his functions ("sequestered") by the queen for refusing to ban reformist theological meetings ("prophesyings"); his fate is lamented though the eagle-queen is not directly criticized. And one of their opponents, the prelatical conservative John Aylmer (or Elmore), Bishop of London, is likewise by inverted syllables shown in Morrell of "July." He appears as a high-living, Catholic-tolerating bishop of the sort that the Leicester party and their clerical allies denounced, bishops who allegedly lined their own and relatives' pockets with church incomes, leaving many parishes without resident ministers, and failed to uphold high standards of education for parish ministers. Having been so bold as to risk a clear identification of one of the reformist party's chief opponents, Spenser gives them persuasive, genial voices and lets them have their say, but he subtly sets the terms of each debate so that the reformist view sounds more straightforward and accordant with gospel teachings. (As with the clearly tagged Morrell vs. Thomalin debate of "July," Palinode vs. Piers in "May" present a conservative-reformist encounter, where Palinode, though himself educated, approves of the ignorant, Catholic-style village clergyman Sir John, who "little can say" in the pulpit, prefers to read out official sermons supplied to him, and spends his time a-Maying.)[9] Furthermore as noted above, Spenser will at times use his paratextual resources to undermine the position of the conservative-prelatical "fox" in each debate, for example through the very naming of Palinode, a shepherd always ready to retract his earlier views with each political wind-shift.

The one clearly identified courtier shepherd is Lobbin of "November," Robert Dudley, Earl of Leicester—so called because of his court nickname 'my Lord Robin'. ("Lobbin" is by further details unmistakably tagged in *Colin Clout's Come Home Again*.) Donald Cheney, noting the Leicester evocation in Lobbin, adds as caveat that "the moment that suggests this application quickly passes."[10] Indeed, we will not expect Spenser to keep hitting us with repeated tags, as in the constantly reiterated correspondence of mystery-play allegory—no, such an application will be foregrounded only for a brief stretch of text or gloss. "They who have eyes to see, let them see"—the clue will soon pass. But it is a definite evocation nonetheless, in the sense that scarcely any but the dullest intended reader of the time would have missed it. In other words, any who would miss such obvious signals might select themselves out of the desired readership, through boredom.

"November" features a funeral elegy, composed and sung by Colin Clout in his first return to live performance since he sadly broke his pipe in "January," for a maiden called Dido whom "Lobbin" has loved and now intensely laments. Just before "November" begins, namely in the gloss on Leicester's well known heraldic image in the "October" eclogue (a white bear at the stake), Leicester has been actually named, as the "worthy" whom Eliza loves best (in earlier years he had enjoyed enormous favor and close intimacy with her, had for a time even seemed likely to marry her, and had continued to proclaim himself her devoted admirer). This version of the identification is softened by a displacement across a short stretch of text. In other words, there is a tactical slight offset between this explicit gloss after "October," naming Leicester as Eliza's beloved, and the ensuing Lobbin who has deeply loved the lamented maiden, Dido-Elissa, of "November." (Despite this aggrandizement of him—or probably the aggrandizement was trying to help redress exactly this state of affairs—Leicester in late 1579 when the *Calender* appeared was suffering severe disfavor from the queen, not only because he opposed her marriage plan but because of his own marriage to the widowed Lettice Knollys, Countess of Essex.)

Through these definite references to the queen and Leicester, to Leicester's gallant, strong-minded nephew Sidney as dedicatee, to the reformist bishops Grindal and Young and their conservative opponent Aylmer, and to Gabriel Harvey as an endorsing, at this time respected Cambridge academic (he only later became a target of satire), Spenser clearly tagged the *Calender* as the work of a career-seeking university poet, in some way addressing the court and church leadership on the subject of the Leicester faction's efforts to implement further church reform. His publishing of the *Calender* at that moment of national alarm over the queen's marriage plan was bold, for all his glowing praise of her in "April." (John Stubbs had also, only weeks before the *Calender*'s appearance, lifted his hat and shouted "Long live the Queen" just after his right hand was cut off for writing a pamphlet criticizing the marriage plan, printed by the same printer who would do the *Calender,* Hugh Singleton.)[11] Spenser must have believed that these seven definite identifications, plus his own occupational identity as university-trained secretary, were necessary if his work was to be understood by his desired readers.

E. K.'s recurrent paratextual strategy with these identities was to gloss them cheerfully and casually, trying to 'put a spin' of harmlessness on each by offering some trivial scholarly comment—as, on the name Algrind, that Algrind's fate with the shellfish was drawn from a story about Aeschylus, who was supposedly brained in that manner.[12] So much for the easy moves of the Spenser/ E. K. riddle game—the readers able to play win a clear concept of who is being addressed and on what general theme: the queen, court, and bishops on the reformist agenda. As noted above, these identifications are nothing new for us; they are in the *Variorum.* But so is a great deal else, and thus Spenserians have not always kept in mind that these evocations of particular people are not tentative.[13] This does not mean of course that the ecloguic characters should be seen as rounded or personal portrayals of their referent people, but only that for the great majority of readers who were anticipated—and were being pertinently formed—by Spenser and his associates producing the *Calen-*

der, these personages would have been clearly called to mind by the combined strategies of the text and paratexts.

THE TRICKIER MOVES OF THE GAME: THE BECLOUDED IDENTITIES

Around the further identifications beyond those just listed, fog has arisen because scholars, as doubtless were the original readers, have to their peril been drawn into trying also the trickier moves of the Spenser/ E. K. political game, namely those with the category of the teasing, obfuscating, or directly inverse references. For to indicate topical references beyond those listed above, Spenser devised shrewdly veiled, sometimes tactically general, officially self-canceling, or even inverse allusions, such as he could deny if necessary; and again, not only the E. K. apparatus but the woodcuts too are integral to their workings. Scholars have long recognized in the *Calender* "elusive hints and seemingly contradictory leads," evoking real people but in such a way that the author could not be prosecuted.[14] The technique necessarily generates riddles because any effort at conclusively tracking certain allusions is up against Spenser's own ingenuity at purposely beclouding them, just enough for safety, even while evoking them.

Here is where text linguistics and discourse pragmatics may be helpful. We could, as has been done often enough, throw up our hands (or hats) in an *O altitudo* of reverence before the mystery of poetry or the murkiness of scholarship; but another possibility is to identify the particular textual tags, moves, markings, or strategies whereby such evoking-with-beclouding was accomplished (again, for further instances see my "Spenser's 'E. K.'" article). As has been reiterated by recent scholars (e.g., Cheney, in "The Circular Argument," 155), we may still be left unable to settle upon an incontrovertible "identity" for certain characters—Spenser has perhaps beat us at some of those trickier moves—but at least we can identify the particular rhetorical means by which he took his readers as far as he pleased along the road to evocation with certain references.

It was more dangerous to criticize politician/courtiers than clergy— the former had more powers of retaliation. While besides the incontrovertible Grindal, Young, and Aylmer we can also with high probability recognize, of academics and clerics, Palinode as Perne, Thomalin as Cooper, Diggon Davie as Davies, and Piers as Pierce,[15] of courtiers only the admired and celebrated Leicester is tagged at all clearly, and he only in a context where no particular action of his can be recognized. (As we shall see, he is probably also evoked in a criticized and more concealed identity in "March"). The *Calender* figure who has regularly been considered to stand for some enemy of the Leicester party is the young Briar of "February"'s fable of the Oak and the Briar, but his identity has remained debatable. He has most often been argued to be either William Cecil, Lord Burghley, the queen's chief secretary (unmistakably and dangerously satirized by Spenser in another work of this period, *Prosopopoia or Mother Hubberds Tale*, not published until 1591), or Burghley's short, Italianate and fancy-dressing, at the time Catholic son-in-law Edward de Vere, Earl of Oxford, a strong supporter of the queen's marriage plan, and in style and youth certainly like the Briar, as Burghley was not. The two of them would epitomize, from Spenser's viewpoint, the older and younger generations of the enemy faction, as Leicester and Sidney do for the party being supported. The "February" fable is Spenser's most biting satire in the *Calender*, featuring a prettily decorated, arrogant, treacherous, finally self-destructive courtier. That point in itself would have indicated to readers of the time to take the "Argument"'s claim that it is only "morall and generall" as ironic. But there is more to the paratextual signaling.

The fact that Oxford had married Burghley's daughter Anne in December, 1571, just when Burghley was solidifying the case for beheading Oxford's older first cousin the Duke of Norfolk—for whom the fable's chopped off Oak is always said to stand when Spenserians identify him—makes Oxford the highly likely person to have been evoked for most readers by the defamed Briar, who is shown betraying the tree under which it has grown. In this view, Spenser was following the widespread though ill-informed impression that Oxford had somehow contributed to the case against the popular and putatively Protestant Norfolk, betraying him to the block in order to get Burghley's consent for a lucrative marriage to daughter Anne (apparently in fact Oxford married Burghley's daughter partly in the hope of getting help for his cousin Norfolk, then his expectation was crossed).[16] In the context of supporting the queen's marriage plan and under the eyes of the French diplomats, Oxford direly insulted Sidney in the notorious tennis court encounter of August 1579, a few months before the *Calender*'s appearance.[17] Through such a figure as the Briar, he, his father-in-law Burghley, and all who favored or tolerated the French marriage plan could be denounced, without the risk of any specific reference. Harvey for his part also satirized Oxford (for Italianate affectation) in his poem "Speculum Tuscanismi" (published in the *Letters*, 1580), where the barb hit so well that he was confronted and obliged to deny to Oxford that the Earl had been the target.[18]

Let us consider "February" a bit further to see just how text and quasi-paratexts together achieve its effects. Some scholars have swallowed the E. K. "Argument"'s opening declaration that the eclogue is not topical but "rather morall and generall, then bent to any secrete or particular purpose." But this I propose is one of the marked, directly disinformational statements. The immediate clue for its irony ends the paragraph where it occurs: "the olde man telleth a tale of the Oake and the Bryer, so liuely and so feelingly, as if the thing were set forth in some Picture before our eyes, more plainly could not appeare." This remark signals readers to look carefully at the woodcut immediately before their eyes, which then leaves them in no doubt that the eclogue will indeed be "bent to some particular purpose" rather than only "morall and generall": the broad-hipped, becoifed, distinctly female form of the chopping "husbandman," holding the axe in so effeminately wrong-handed a way, supplies a witty and safely nonverbal clue to the coming fable's reference to the queen's execution of Norfolk, now widely recognized (see Ronald Bond, "Supplantation"). Picture and text together work in the well known manner of an emblem *pictura* and *subscriptio*, interactively creating an import that neither alone would carry. As Halpern notes, it is amusing and telling that in the woodcut, "the characters in the fable occupy the same representational space as Cuddie and Thenot [the debate interlocutors, one of whom tells it]—one of Cuddie's cattle even munches on the briar!" (193).

The Catholic associations given to the besprinkled Oak in lines 207–12, and reinforced by E. K.'s note that "popish priests" in olden times thus used to "sprinckle and hallowe the trees," tag the fable as shadowing some affair in which a powerful, Catholic-allied nobleman was defamed by someone among his own Catholic-sympathizer faction and was then executed, leaving the traitor himself without protection. If a survey could be done of *Calender* readers of the 1580s, it is most unlikely that any would be found for whom the lopped off Oak did not call to mind the Duke of Norfolk, popular and declaredly Protestant but with Catholic background, family, and political ties, beheaded in 1572 on a charge of conspiring to marry Mary Queen of Scots and put her on the English throne. Apparently many reformist Protestants in the 1570s had disbelieved the conspiracy charge and saw him as a victim of Burghley's thirst for power, though state papers now public do indicate his guilt.[19] (Harvey owned a copy of the published letter of 1572, anonymous but by Burghley, justifying Norfolk's arrest [see Stern, *Gabriel Harvey*].) While the Oak is thus shown as admirable but unfortunate for having been caught up with the doings of popery, his botanical cousin and younger protege the Briar is the satiric target, eventually trampled by cattle in the dirt—his downfall can be something desirously prophesied, rather than representing a depicted past occurrence. As Louis Montrose has noted, the fable is wrapped in three layers of contrasting perspectives:[20] old Thenot as the direct narrator of it states his sympathy with the betrayed 'old' Oak; yet as a second perspective, both before and after Thenot's framing comments, young Cuddie's debunking of the tale undermines Thenot's view (he calls it a tedious affair that left his britches stuck to the ground); and finally, as outermost layer of framing, the gloss's concluding moral generalizations on the eclogue's undecidable potboiler debate topic—age vs. youth imaged as winter vs. summer—add a further buffer around the fable's thrust.[21]

In sum, Spenser's text and paratext working together have kept this vitriolic attack safe or at least unprosecutable by three techniques: by a buffering of it through layered perspectives that sets the uncontroversial school-boy debate theme into the eclogue's diegetic foreground; by irony-signaling effected through the *pictura/subscriptio* functioning of the woodcut and "Argument" as well as through the contrast between the fable's ferocity and the bland editorial claim that it has no "secrete purpose"; and third, by a referential displacement or metonymy making it not the briar but the sympathetic (and safely dead) oak who is unmistakably recognizable. This much of Spenser's political skill with the paratextual can be seen immediately in the "February" text, paratexts, and surrounding realm of political reference; we will come later to what I consider the particular triggering event for composition of this "February," and why his organization developed as it did (as several scholars have argued, I believe he had earlier meant to fill that slot with the present "November"—see n. 7).

Playing the trickier moves of the Spenser/ E. K. game does not always mean that one will encounter the ploys just noted; there can be others, including some within the centered text. Certain details of a passage may remind readers of a given personage and situation, yet for safety's sake two or three other points may be included that are distinctly not parallel to the evoked situation, and may even make the fiction a bit like something else in particular, to which the writer could appeal if necessary as the supposed meaning. This might be called the red herring move. For example, if the dead and beautifully lamented Dido of "November" did for many readers prophetically evoke a possible married Queen Elizabeth of the future, like Queen Dido of Virgil's *Aeneid* dying and then being beautifully lamented after a disastrous attempt to gain a husband to help rule her kingdom, then Dido could also, if somewhere an explanation became necessary, be claimed to refer to poor Ambrosia Sidney, Leicester's niece who had died a few years before; Spenser includes in the eclogue a mention of "ambrosia" in heaven.

Another such precautionary ploy was offered by the Renaissance habit of generating writing by closely imitating or paraphrastically translating famous writers. A passage likely to be suspected of giving offense might be so written that one could say no such reference was intended, one was only fittingly imitating the great so-and-so: thus if someone should mislike a possible reference to Ambrosia Sidney, well, Spenser was only paraphrasing eclogues of Clement Marot, and the word ambrosia is there—the reminiscence was purely accidental. Topical reference was a game of enormous ingenuity, and the only ground rules were *Hony soit qui mal y pense* and "If the shoe fits, don't wear it." Powerful parties hit by such glancing references—as in the Harvey-Oxford instance noted above—often found it best, if they even raised the issue with the writer, to accept denials of referential intention. Insistence and punishment would only make the dart stick.

As a final instance among these unprovable or beclouded evocations, we now take up one from "March," where a Leicester tag equivalent to the white bear at the stake of "October," namely his plant badge the hawthorne, is used; but here it is so neatly integrated into the eclogue's botanic scenery and thematics that, instead of being highlighted for topicality with deictic marking signals (as is the named and glossed white bear), its presentation more resembles a round of "find the concealed boy in the intricate picture." That is, diegetically the hawthorn bud is simply one blooming botanical detail amidst the lovers' landscape, rather than being named as a badge or highlighted by a gloss.

Even so, Thomalin the love-struck shepherd of "March," through this hint and others, probably took on an alarming topical import for at least one too many readers. The shepherdess on whom he and his interlocutor Willye dote is given the name Lettice, a quite uncommon one in real England of the time and not well known in pastoral conventions either, but the name of Leicester's lady-love Lettice Knollys, with whom he had had an affair and was in 1578 secretly married. Spenser while drafting "March" may not have known with certainty of the marriage, but if not may have sensed it coming, especially when Lettice Knollys became pregnant. A convincing proposal going back to Charles Mounts and reiterated by Helena Shire and Richard Rambuss (also asserted in the Yale *Shorter Poems* edition)[22] is that Thomalin's love wound in the heel while he and Willye wish for Lettice warns against Leicester's secret marriage (or impending marriage), which as we have noted was to ruin Leicester's standing with the queen just when he especially needed to be in her favor to combat the French marriage plan. Besides the other clues noted, there is Thomalin's ewe injured in a fall, which recalls the death of Leicester's first wife Amy Robsart after an injury in a fall. If this application was perceived, it must have been highly offensive. It would be a piece of attempted meddling if it was circulated before the fact of Leicester's marriage (or before Spenser's knowledge of it) and a smug "I told you so" afterwards, portraying his affair as a boyish though understandable compulsion apt to bring trouble, as indeed it did.

As with the other liminally evoked identities, the E. K. glosses play their interactive part for "March," through warning that the boy shooting at Love should "beware of mischiefe to come," and through Thomalin's emblem, that love has more gall than honey. Also, the gloss states about the eclogue's glancing-eyed Lettice (a phrase mock-heroically translating the Homeric epithet for the girl Briseis said to have caused all the trouble amongst the Greek captains) that to "wax light" with her means to find a "loose" girl for casual love-making. E. K.'s "March" glosses saying that "breaking Love's slumber" means exercising the delights of love, i.e. making love, and suggestively calling attention to Love's "winges of purple," contribute to the general debate-theme of the eclogue, the physical actions of eroticism. The four substantive notes taken together (on 'Flora,' 'Swaine,' 'In the heele,' and 'Embleme') comprise a mini-treatise on the psychology and supposed physiology of sex as a force at once unpredictable, troublesome, compelling, and procreative. Especially E. K.'s gloss on Thomalin's honey and gall emblem must have carried an unwelcome message to someone in Leicester's situation:

Hereby is meant, that all the delights of Loue, wherein wanton youth walloweth, be but follye mixt with bitternesse, and sorow sawced with repentaunce. For besides that the very affection of Loue it selfe tormenteth the mynde, and vexeth the body many wayes, with vnrestfulnesse all night, and wearines all day, seeking for that we can not haue, & fynding that we would not haue: even the selfe things which best before vs lyked, in course of time and chaung of ryper yeares, whiche also therewithall chaungeth our wonted lyking and former fantasies, will then seeme lothsome and breede vs annoyaunce, when yougthes flowre is withered, and we fynde our bodyes and wits aunswere not to suche vayne iollitie and lustfull pleasaunce.

What a high risk you are taking for this pleasure, when soon you will be too old to enjoy it—this was a message not likely to be welcomed! The effort to prevent the Leicester allusion from being too obvious—the beclouding practice—may explain why Spenser reused for "March" the name Thomalin from the earlier written "July," there a clerical character who in that eclogue could not be taken for the Earl,[23] though he was a reformist cleric such as Leicester supported. But it appears that in this case Spenser may have become carried away with the pleasure of his own wittiness in piling on hints, no one of them telling in itself, and may have generated too little fog for covering them. Immerito makes a costly move and loses ground in the game. Harvey mentions in his *Letter-book* (101) in a passage of 1579 or 1580 that Immerito is in trouble for some indiscretion, and Spenser himself later (in *Virgils Gnat*) refers to some offense taken against him by Leicester (see n. 24). If this was it or part of it, then we have a case where the beclouding ploys, while perhaps producing adequate fog for some of the court readership, left too much clarity in the mind of a crucial player. As the *Calender*'s structure turned out, "February" and "March," tucked just inside the "January"–"December" frame story of Colin's sad love affair and seeming on the surface to be so "moral and generall" and harmless, together amounted to a two-edged sword: it struck not only with denunciation for the enemy party (in the Briar fable) but also with moral correction for the admired leader of the poet's own faction.

GROUPINGS AMONG THE ECLOGUES AND THEIR ORDER OF COMPOSITION

To return for another purpose to the case of "February," its particular reference to the court scene accords with a theory I now want to present about the order in which Spenser wrote the eclogues, and how a Spenserian self-concept portrayed in "January," "June," "November," and "December" solidified the organization that fell into place for him in the late summer or fall of 1579. Again we will see that examining the interactive functioning of text and paratexts—on the assumption that Spenser's writing process included co-production of many of the latter—allows us to discern more of the inner workings of these eclogues than we otherwise could do. Because of the strong indications that the "February" fable was a shrewd attack on the Catholic-sympathizer faction through its dashing and anciently aristocratic luminary the seventeenth Earl of Oxford, I believe that "February" as we have it was written at some point soon after the notorious

August quarrel over tennis court time, when Oxford called Sidney a puppy, Sidney challenged him to a duel, and the queen intervened, infuriatingly reminding the *Calender*'s dedicatee of Oxford's social superiority to him.[24] I propose that Spenser at that point changed his earlier plan for "February," making room for the new fable of the briar. We have indications that such was the case.

Scholars long ago observed that Spenser did not write the twelve eclogues in their present order. He apparently started with the Mantuanesque middle eclogues critiquing churchmen (most of "May" through "September") in 1578 when he was secretary to the Bishop of Rochester, and their issues of churchmanship would have been often on his mind. The E. K. introduction sets forth a scheme that sorts the twelve eclogues into three thematic categories: those on "plaining" (Colin's plaints about himself as thwarted poet), on "the recreative" or "matter of love" and "commendation of personages," and on things "moral . . . mixed with satirical bitterness" (religion-politics): that is, the three interweaving themes of the *Calender*, namely the difficulties of poetizing, erotic love and praise, and morality/politics. Most of the eclogues relate to all three but focus centrally on one. A few focus on more than one theme; thus we could cross-list at least "August" and "October" under the plaintive, "January" and "December" under the recreative, and "September" under the moral. (Incidentally, the "E. K." listing of "March" under 'love and praise' not under moral/political satire may comprise one more veiling ploy to protect the "March" implication.) E. K. lists:

"the plaintive" (on thwarted poetizing)	"the recreative" (on erotic love and praise)	"the moral" (on morals/satire)
"January"	"March"	"February"
"June"	"April"	"May"
"November"	"August"	"July"
"December"	"September"	
	"October"	

Notice how this scheme defines "January," "June," "November," and "December" as a distinct grouping.[25] Analyzing that group for formal patterns, we can note further points that will, together with the clue of a zodiac error, suggest an order in which Spenser wrote the eclogues. "January" is closely linked to both "June" and "December"[26] in several formal as well as thematic ways that enable these three, as beginning, middle, and end, to frame the whole set. "January" and "June" together portray the relationship between Colin and Hobbinol (Spenser and Harvey) as an idyllic, passionate friendship of scholar-poets that has been disrupted by Colin's lady-love Rosalind (see p. 199 below on Virgil), and the two eclogues are also linked through the correlated mottos assigned to Colin in each: *anchora speme* for "January" ('hope my anchor/ still [there is] hope' [a pun]), and *gia speme spente* for "June" ('hope already spent'). This marked pairing implies a development—E. K. ended the "January" gloss by saying that Colin, "leaning on hope, is somewhat recomforted"; but between January and June Colin has lost his hope that Rosalind will relent. As we noted in chapter 4, he even says in "June" that his poetry, if he could make it potent, would now serve as a sharpened arrow shot at her heart, to make her feel the harm she is doing. As well as "January" and "June," "January" and "December" are also strongly linked: both are meditative laments of Colin comprised in large part of prayers to the shepherds' god Pan (not the case elsewhere), they have the same stanza form, and, as we examined in chapter 2, only they have passages spoken by an unidentified 'introducer-concluder' voice (who speaks about Colin as central figure and is himself not named at all). This introducer-voice begins "January" by saying that Colin is a mere "shepherd's boy" (a minor employee of a bishop—"no better do him call") but in "December" praises him as a worthy successor of Chaucer. Again a development is implied: the mere shepherd's boy has over the course of the year become an accomplished poet. It seems, then, that "January" and "December," as we now have them, were among the last eclogues completed, in the fall of 1579 after Spenser had worked out his concept of the *Calender*'s overall structure, and that "January" and the perhaps already drafted "June" were at that point carefully coordinated in their shared treatment of the tale of Colin's progressing misfortune in love for Rosalind.

Now for the zodiac clue. Although "November's" woodcut correctly pictures the 'Archer' zodiac sign, I believe as earlier scholars have (for example, Renwick, *The Shepherd's Calendar*, 226) that the eclogue shows itself to have been planned originally as "February": it says it is under the sign of Pisces, when the sun is in the "fishes haske." The sensible explanation is that Spenser originally meant this November Dido funeral lament to be "February," and when he moved it, either he or the printer neglected the needed correction of the internal zodiac reference (see n. 7).

This alteration, together with the second introduction to the whole *Calender* (offering a scholarly defense of its use of the Gregorian January-to-December calendar), constitutes a distinct clue to the *Calender*'s compositional process. England until the eighteenth century continued following, as its legal calendar, the older March-to-

February scheme (often called the Julian calendar, though that term does not necessarily mean a March-to-February calendar);[27] in 1579 Pope Gregory XIII had recently published the new calendar of our era for study, and it must have been of much interest to calendric experts like Gabriel Harvey. Assuming that Spenser at first planned a more traditionally English March-February calendar, the present elegiac "November" eclogue would under that scheme have been fitting for "February," the death of the old year in the end of winter; but if he decided to change plans and follow the "January-December" calendar, then he might have wanted the calendric essay to justify his choice of the Gregorian calendar—even if one believes that Parmenter overstated her claim that a January-December calendar would seem popish, Spenser did think it appropriate to include a defense of his choice, entitled the "Generall Argument." And given his statement in a letter of October 1579, thanking Harvey for his fine new "addition" to the work about to appear, it is highly probable that Harvey drafted that extra introduction for him.

Why would he have switched calendars? And if he did, why did he not make the former "February" into "December"? (The equivalent for the former twelfth month February would have been December, not November.) The present "November" and "December" are closely related in diction,[28] in elegiac tone, and in their shared paraphrastic imitation of eclogues by Clement Marot, centering as E. K. notes on the theme of complaint about the challenges of writing poetry at a court. As Spenser began the lament now placed as "November," based on Marot's elegy for the queen mother Louise of Savoy (Marot, Mayer ed. 321ff.), I believe he meant to end it by giving Colin a brief meditative farewell passage, glancing back over his life as a blossoming but then failing lover-poet. The model for this continuation passage was to be part of Marot's *Eclogue au Roy* (to Francis I), where Marot's "Colin" portrays himself as aging, reflects on his past poetic career, and prays to god Pan (Mayer ed. 343ff.). But as more and more of Marot's eclogue proved irresistible for imitation, the passage outgrew its planned scope and became a separate eclogue, a meditation of the new, prophetic-revisionist Colin upon his own career to this point (see Patterson, "Re-opening").

The problem then would be what to do with this new one, that had sprung from the end of the Dido lament and had to follow it. He could not simply move each eclogue back one. slot because the Dido funeral dirge would not do at all for January with its feasting and Roman New Year. But "November" is the month of the dead in the church year, with All Saints' and All Souls' days, and so is just right for a funeral dirge. Spenser must have seen that he could conclude with this powerful elegiac pair as "November" and "December"—and could also leave himself a slot for something new in "February"—if he would switch to the January-to-December calendar. As I have proposed above, recent events had given him something to work in, namely the fable of the Oak and the Briar. Spenser uses as its narrator "November"'s (the former "February"'s) Thenot, a shepherd from Marot, but as a directly contrastive figure to his (now later) "November" role of approving admirer of a young poet, making him in "February" a gruff denouncer of a young shepherd/poet. The reconstruction is of course only speculative, but in some such fashion he came to recast a formerly planned "February" as "November."

To put the sequence together, Spenser had first (starting in 1578 or perhaps earlier) written most of the ecclesiastical and political eclogues of the middle months, "March" through "September," plus a lament, now the "October" eclogue, for the hard lot of poets in such spiritually corrupt times.[29] Also, taking a cue from one of Harvey's rhetoric lectures on love and poetic inspiration (see my "Spenser's E. K."), he had written the "April" glowing praise of the queen, as antidote to the sting of his carefully couched attack on the conservative-prelatical clergy and to appeal for more support for church reform. Since he was imitating Virgil and Mantuan, each of whose eclogues number ten, perhaps he originally planned that many, only later deciding on a calendar format of twelve, to follow the English year pattern of March through February. Then in the late summer of 1579 when, because of the queen's planned marriage, he began to see himself as the thwarted advocate of a desperately endangered Protestant cause, he wrote what he first planned as his conclusion eclogue, the would-be "February" (but now "November"), namely the lament for 'Dido,' whose namesake in Virgil's *Aeneid* had lost her kingdom and very life through a misguided effort to get a husband. When that eclogue became long enough for two, he switched calendars, made the new elegiac pair "November" and "December," wrote or adapted the new "February," wrote or rewrote "January" to portray himself as a silenced, castrated singer, and revised "June" to relate it to "January." Thus the sequence fell into place, with the politically barbed new "February" protectively tucked inside the framing story of Colin's failed love affair with Rosalind, anxiously watched and regretted by the affectionate Hobbinol. The woodcuts must have been done at the end of the compositional process: the "November" picture has the correct zodiac sign despite the confusion in the text; and the "February" picture, as we have noted, works in subtle synchronization with the apparatus, narrative framing layers, and fable.

As adjustments accordant with the now clarified overall concept—of Colin breaking his pipe in "January" and not regaining a voice till "November"—Spenser took the "April" lay of Eliza from the now silenced Colin and made Hobbinol speak it; and likewise, he removed Colin from the earlier completed 'singing match' of "August" (assigning the original Colin song to Perigot) and added after it Colin's solitary sestina of rejected love, importing Cuddie to perform it and adding a hint (in an "October" gloss) that the Cuddie of "August" may stand for "the author self."

Through this process whereby he came to use the Gregorian calendar for his declaredly English, Chaucerian, and Protestant eclogues, Spenser became able to write, as L. Staley Johnson says he did, about a "disjointed time": he "used his *Calender* to thrust himself and England into the future, for he embeds within a medieval calendar a modern, Elizabethan one, a calendar of revolutionary time."[30] I would apply this to my general thesis here, that in finding a way to speak prophetically to the crisis moment of a particular calendar year, he created, or significantly contributed to creation of, an ideologeme for the rest of Elizabeth's reign.

COLIN'S TWO LOVES

In concluding this analysis of the eclogues' composition and organization as a writing process interweaving text and paratext, we have one further point to consider. That Spenser in the fall of 1579, in a moment of national crisis, should have been able to work out the concept of himself as poet that the *Calender* presents is, as we have noted, partly a matter of his modeling himself on Marot's presentation of a court poet's dilemma in being dependent on the powerful people he would like prophetically to admonish (see Patterson, "Reopening"). It was also very much a matter of something from his reading and absorption of Virgil's eclogues that I believe found a resolution for him at this point. Thus in conclusion to this view of his compositional process with the *Calender*, we consider something that shows itself to have been essential to his creation of the self-reflexive frame of a love poet's tale of loss ("January"–"June"–"December"), which he needed to build—as container and containment—around his book's dangerous import. This last step in our examination will show how the sphere of the paratextual, especially in such a complexly framed production as the *Calender*, serves, through a kind of negotiation of poetic self with textual possibilities, to align the framed or centered text not only with the social world of its desired reception but also with the inner libidinal world of the writer in process of working on it, including certain personally valued reading that the writer will treat revisionistically.

"January" draws on Virgil's second eclogue (as so often, with E. K. explicitly citing the relevant passage for us), where the speaker—the shepherd Corydon—laments his hopeless love for a beautiful young man "cruel Alexis," who has rejected his gifts; the hurt Corydon threatens to give them to his less desired girlfriend instead. Of course topically and dramatically speaking, Virgil does not represent himself in Corydon (he is elsewhere in the eclogues 'Tityrus' or some other shepherd), but this homoerotic Eclogue II is clearly the center of his treatment of the theme of poetic self-imaging or self-reference: in a later eclogue Virgil characterizes himself as that poet who was able to create "Corydon loved fair Alexis." In "January," Colin Clout takes a famous passage of Eclogue II to depict himself and his beloved friend Hobbinol (Harvey), whom he portrays as trying through gifts to woo his love back again from his lady Rosalind, just as Virgil's Corydon tried to woo Alexis with gifts: the gloss gives the Latin, "rusticus es, Corydon; nec munera curat Alexis" [Corydon, you're a country rustic; Alexis does not care for the gifts]. Spenser is evoking the intense male affection from Eclogue II to characterize his friendship with Harvey and its empowering force for him as poet: he is the man who could write 'Hobbinol loved poor Colin Clout.' But while reproducing that Virgilian love triangle of two men and a woman, he shifts the roles in it (reversing the enunciative and denotative positions, in Kristevan terms of intertextuality as revisionist transpositioning), so as to counter any implication of a physical homosexual relationship between himself and Harvey; at the same time a fiercely vehement E. K. disclaimer gloss to the passage (drafted I have argued by Harvey), works in tandem with this strategy by saying that not physical but spiritual "pederasty" is meant.[31] The shift is that Colin the poet-speaker takes the role of pursued Alexis rather than of pursuer Corydon, who was the poet-speaker in Virgil.[32] Colin then, as coy neo-Alexis, can refrain from directly rebuffing Corydon-Hobbinol by refusing his gifts, and instead can say more mildly that he is receiving but passing them on, to *his* lady-love Rosalind.[33]

In other words, while in Virgil we have a triangle of pursuer-poet, beloved young man, and pursuer's secondarily loved mistress (as also in Shakespeare's sonnets—"Two loves I have"—and in the reformer Theodore Beze's youthful neo-Latin poem weighing his affection for a male friend Audebert above that for his young lady),[34] in Spenser we have instead pursuer, beloved young man-poet, and young man's primarily loved mistress.[35] The affection between Colin and Hobbinol is through this inversion and the gloss reinforcement made safe for poetic processing and public consumption.[36] Thus their affection can later, in "June," be acceptably portrayed as a powerful, supportive nurturing ground suffused with unthreatened pastoral maleness, and central to the emergence of young Colin-Spenser's poetic powers. I believe it was Spenser's working out of a way to treat this matter through his ingenious interlockings of text and paratext, to make it acceptable, and to set its presentation into the framing eclogue pair "January" and "June" that made the keystone of the arch for him, and allowed the reorganization and completion of the eclogues that I have here described to fall into place in the autumn of 1579.

From the political perspective of 1579—that crucial turning-point year when Elizabeth was at last forced to define herself fully as Protestant blessed Virgin and to leave behind her attempts at arrangements with foreign Catholics (see chapter 1 above)—Spenser was able to make his *Calender* not only for all time but also for the course of the year just finishing.[37] Early in the year Spenser's party had learned of the queen's threatened 'betrayal' through the proposed Catholic marriage and were much distressed but hoped still to dissuade her ("January"—*anchora speme*); in the summer, after the envoy Simier's spring months of well received overtures, they began to feel extremely alarmed ("June"—*gia speme spente*); in the fall, after Anjou's August visit, Elizabeth's increased promoting of the marriage, and the chopping off of the anti-marriage pamphleteer Stubbes's hand in November, they lamented the impending death of the Protestant English church, the queen's own possible death in childbirth or by assassination, and as they feared, the death of all English Protestant expression and poetizing as they had known it ("November"—*la mort ny mord*—they turned their eyes to heaven). "December" ends with a motto, displaced to the gloss conclusion as Colin is perhaps to be thought already in his winter death/sleep, posthumously sending one last desperate plea to the queen for relenting: *merce non mercede*, favor not payment.

Spenser as poet of the *Calender* had found, through a highly intricate deployment of paratextual framing around and between his poems, a way to take imaginative control of that intensely threatening moment in his personal and political life, and to open his publishing career with a culturally definitive book. He was thereby an agent in the generating of an ideologeme, the 'captive woman' as here described, that would in Jameson's phrase "tick and work," for decades to come. For when the queen gave up on her possible marriage, she did not thereby put herself in the pocket of the Leicester (or their later successors the Essex) party of internationalists. But she did agree to conduct much of her future dancing among political options to the tune of "Sweet Cynthia, how wouldst thou be possessed," in whatever variation, at a given moment, a particular piper might play that could gain her favor.

Appendix 1.
Algorithm or Description Proceedures Used

(Terms are from A.-J. Greimas and J. Courtés, *Semiotics and Language: An Analytical Dictionary*, 1982. The ordering of the procedures is mine.)

[Prefatory note:
I agree with Jonathan Culler that this model of textual analysis does not constitute a scientific poetics, nor can it generate accounts of "correct meanings" of texts because meanings are located not in the text itself but in the processes of reading, and with Fredric Jameson that both writer and reader value investments are always politically conditioned elements of ongoing cultural processes.[1] However, the structurated scan-profile of a text that one obtains by applying the following algorithm is still a piece of information of considerable potential interest. The matter of 'what have you got when you've got this' needs further study, but perhaps it approximates what H. R. Jauss calls the *Sinnpotential* of the text at the moment and place of the algorithmic application—a particularly sequenced selection of semantically and syntactically describable units. Although Greimas would not, I assume, endorse the present tentative algorithm since it includes concepts that, as he often notes, need further research, the analytical concepts are here regarded as developed enough to suggest procedures (which I propose for further refinement) for tentatively displaying a text's particularizations of the rudimentary patterns of discourse generation.]

I. Objectification of the text as enunciation: this retraces and brackets out the initial stage of discoursivization, the projection of a not-I, not-here, not-now by the implied enunciator.
A. Transcribe the outer-level category of person: for pronouns or nouns referring to the whole-text speaker/addressee substitute the terms enunciator/enunciatee.
B. Eliminate all time indications "relative to the now" of the whole enunciation (though keeping indicators of internal time systems).
C. Eliminate all enunciation-level deixes except the spatial 'here/elsewhere' (e.g. all enunciator appreciations).
D. Eliminate all enunciation-level phatic elements (attention gestures to any particular reader or readers).
II. Segmentation: hypothetical analysis of the text into sequences (each one possibly but not necessarily correlatable with a narrative syntagm, i.e.,

"set of utterances that presuppose each other," comprising e.g. a 'test,' or argumentative point). These sequences as such are "textual" not "discursive" units—i.e., they are segments of the textual surface.

A. Search for demarcators such as "but" or other transition signals that indicate a "frontier between two sequences," and on the other hand for grammatical anaphora or other continuity signals indicating sequence continuation.

B. "Recognize categorical disjunctions," such as the spatial (here/elsewhere), temporal (before/after), thymic (euphoria/dysphoria), topical (same/other), actorial (I/he or she), logical (causing/caused, or other), referential (dialogue/narrative). [Note: "The degree of certitude of the operation rises with the number of concomitant disjunctions," though these will not always be located at precisely the same place; i.e., between two sequences there may be an area of proximate disjunctions, analogous to the proximate isoglosses defining the dialectal zone boundaries in a language.]

C. List the resulting hypothetical semio-narrative sequences and leave results aside until step V.D. below.

III. Extraction of terms for a corpus: identification of a set of isotopically indicative lexemes (extraction from the whole text, rather than elimination of non-selected sequences, has been chosen as the method here). The procedures outlined in this section are a combination of statistical sampling and saturation of the model: that is, at each inventory stage, a selection of 'most frequently occurring' lexemes is made, and then the whole-line co-occurring lexemes, i.e. "qualification variables" (those found along with each occurrence of each of these "frequent" ones in the computer defined line where it appears) are exhaustively inventoried, generating in turn the source list for the next selection of most-frequent-lexemes for another inventory stage. The base hypothesis is that the most frequently occurring lexemes will, after processing, yield the "general semantic isotopy of the text."

A. Make a concordance of the complete text, each occurrence of each word being shown in whole-line context (of computer-generated, arbitrary lines of equal length). Coalesce variant inflective forms into a single occurrence count for the whole text, for each lexeme.

[The wat.con concordance program, run on the complete 1579 text of the *Calender*, with spelling modernized, has in the present study produced this initial data of total word frequencies and word occurrences, in whole line context.]

B. Scan the concordance for the most frequently occurring open-class lexemes. (The instances of each particular word will have fallen together in the alphabetizing sort.) I.e., do not include words with only grammatical semes, such as articles, conjunctions, etc.; also eliminate from consideration, along with the grammatical or closed-class lexemes, three further categories of lexemes:

1. euphoria/dysphoria tags (e.g. 'good,' 'wicked,' 'delightful,' 'drearisome')

2. qualifiers/quantifiers (e.g. 'specially,' 'often,' 'more,' 'part')

3. general purpose lexemes that rely for much of their contextual semantic import on combinatory partners (e.g. 'cause,' 'take,' 'say,' 'set,' 'man,'
'tend'); do not include them in the inventory lists unless in combination
with separable-verb components, e.g. 'set forth'. [This third step is my
proposal, not so far as I know suggested by Greimas/Courtés.]).
Record the word counts, and in a numerically decreasing list, beside each
number show the list of words found to have occurred that many times.
C. Make the first-extraction (first-stage) inventory of the most frequently
occurring lexemes. To choose the lexemes for the first inventory, look from
the top-most frequency level down the list to find a frequency drop-off
point: a point where there begin to be much longer lists of words of that
many occurrences.
[As for the determination of "most frequent," in *The Shepheardes Calender,*
a clear frequency drop-off point proved to be that between 26 and 25
occurrences: thus all words of from 41 down through 26 occurrences (that
were not categorically eliminated above) are included in the first-
extraction inventory. Section III,D,1 below will have a further principle
for determining the 'most frequent' range for a given inventory-stage,
after this first one.]
1. Make a chart for each lexeme chosen as "frequent"; for each of its
occurrences, record the co-occurring words (again observing the above
four exclusions); show each of these linked with its line number [in the
above concordance, arbitrary computer-assigned line divisions] and linked
with the word from whose context it is being inventoried. Thus each
entry in the resulting second and subsequent lists will have a word, a
number, and another word (see pp. 213ff.).
Note two adjustments I made in this process of word-selections from each
computer-designated line:
  a. Wherever the extraction base-word occurs within the first or last
  three words of the whole-line unit, extend the line unit to cover the
  next words preceding (or following) the base-word, to first grammatical
  closure point [my suggestion, not from Greimas/Courtés].
  b. Include classemes (e.g. 'high'-'low,' 'life-death') in the inventories
  as supplying information of potential subsidiary interest, but do not
  select them as lexemes for each new (succeeding) inventory stage, as
  the goal here is to recognize indicators of isotopic kernel semes.
2. Alphabetize the complete list of co-occurring context lexemes (qualification variables) derived from these first inventory ones.
D. Conduct the next extraction and inventory.
1. Decide upon the frequency level (in the just completed list) to consider determinate for the next extraction, then extract the most frequently
occurring of these derived lexemes, and make them the basis for another
extraction inventory, in turn from their phrasal contexts.
  [For *The Shepheardes Calender* I used in the first-stage inventory the level
  of 6 or more occurrences of a given lexeme to consider significant.
  The number must be adjusted, according to the length of the text and

consequent length of the inventory, and should represent that frequency level which will result in the reselection, from inventory to
inventory, of most of the already selected lexemes, with a few additional ones emerging each time—this last is my proposal, not to my
knowledge suggested by Greimas/Courtés.]

2. In drawing up this and each further new extraction word list for the
succeeding inventory, exclude, along with those less frequent than the
determined frequency level, two further categories of lexemes:

a. Lexemes already inventoried.

b. Any not 'thematized' as one among a set of synonymous or para-
synonymous lexemes occurring in the given inventory being examined.
I.e., at each stage as one extracts the lexemes for the next inventory,
consider for each lexeme that meets the frequency criterion whether
there are in the same list two or more synonyms of it (and other semi-
cally related lexemes): if few or none can be found, exclude it from
the extraction [this is my proposal, not to my knowledge suggested by
Greimas/Courtés]. (In practice, one is thus at each stage in preliminary
fashion beginning the task of sememic structuration—see IV below.)

E. In this manner continue successive extractions and inventories until new
qualification-variables stop appearing. The progressive expansion and modi-
fication of the lexeme list and observation of lexeme collocations will allow
one to determine which are the isotopically indicative and linked ones
among the frequent lexemes, out of which the structuration into sememes
can then follow.[2]

F. List the lexemes that have emerged, hypothesizing that they comprise
the suitable corpus for analysis, i.e. that they are the surface indicators of
the text's semantic isotopy (see p. 213).

IV. Structuration: the sememic description of the semantic isotopy.

A. Make a semic inventory for each of the lexemes of the hypothesized
semantic isotopy, with both kernel seme indicators and contextual semes
(including classemes or classematic opposition categories, e.g. verticality-
horizontality, sound-silence, plant-animal, youth-age.) A descriptive meta-
language for the semes and subordinate sememes must be devised.[3]

B. Recognize and formulate the recurrent sememes (combinations of
semes, often hypotactic) in the isotopically indicative lexemes identified by
the inventory process.

C. Carry out the dual operation of reduction/homologation.

1. Reduction: "transforming an inventory of sememic occurrences, para-
synonymous in nature, into a constructed class or 'constructed sememe'
joining together many occurrences of a sememe dispersed throughout a
discourse and belonging to different lexemes."

2. Homologation: recognizing, with respect to the sememic category
being constructed, whatever occurrent contradictory and contrary terms
belong to the structure, the description of which is being sought (i.e.,
projecting the constructed sememe onto the semiotic square, to relate
terms and their contradictory and contrary opposites). [In the present

application, homologation was provisionally already done in part at the stage of the initial complete word-list (III, A).]

D. Divide the constructed sememes into actants and predicates, the latter in turn into those of doing and those of state.

E. Attribute substantive form (i.e. with -ing,-age,-tion, etc.) to all sememes; then transcribe and sort them into "semantic messages," using the following notation:

Function: F (for predicates)

Subject: S (for actants)

Object: O (for actants)

['Sender' and 'Receiver' as actants of narration are also being used in this study, but not in the present set of procedures, which aim to produce the text's instance of the "base narrative program" formula; it contains only 'subject'-'object' actants.]

conjunction: $^\wedge$

disjunction: U

Function of doing (redundant for 'F'): ->

conventional order of transcription: for utterances of state, either $F(S \wedge O)$ or $F(S \cup O)$; for utterances of doing, $F (S \rightarrow O)$].

[Note: Greimas no longer uses the concept of "qualification" to characterize the relation of terms in utterances of state. Thus he has abandoned his earlier F/Q notation.]

V. Identification of the discourse's "base narrative program," correlation/superposition of the semantic/thematic isotopy with the actorial isotopy, and thereby the locating of the "instrumental narrative programs."

A. Using the constructed sememes as indicators, identify the discourse's pre-thematized value or values, and their thematizations (which will be middle-level abstractions, e.g. "freedom" thematized to "spatial escape" and "temporal escape"—later to be figurativized as a trip to faraway seas and a return to childhood).

B. Determine the figurative isotopy by tracing the two phases of figurativization from the above determined themes:

1. "conversion of themes into figures"

2. iconization ("endowing [these figures] with particularizing investments").

C. Again using the constructed sememes and sorted "semantic messages" as indicators,

1. Identify the (thematized) "subject actant" behind the various actors carrying out the base NP.

2. Apply the notation of the NP as "an utterance of doing governing an utterance of state":

$NP = F: S_1 \rightarrow (S_2 \wedge O_v)$ or $NP = F: S_1 \rightarrow (S_2 \cup O_v)$.

D. To the sequences hypothesized in 'II' above, apply the thematic and figurative isotopies evident for the constructed sememes, so as to relate the "instrumental narrative programs" to them, using the 'NP' equation notation, and thereby localize sequences. [Sequence boundaries can be corrected at this stage, if need be, with information from correlation of semantic and actorial isotopies.]

1. Use the "reference system" of the "utterative time" within the discourse to begin to "localize" the instrumental NPs.

2. Once the base narrative program has been identified, use it also to localize instrumental NPs by beginning at a proposed sequence boundary and scanning until the identified NP formula, through actorializations of each of its elements, can once again be completely rewritten in positive (not contrary or contradictory) terms, with either disjunction or conjunction of S_2 and O_v [This is my own proposal, not so far as I know, suggested by Greimas/Courtés.]

E. List the formula instance for the base narrative program in terms of its thematized actants, and likewise list the instrumental NPs, indicating their locations within sequence boundaries.

Appendix 2.
Data of the Algorithm's Application

Part I.

The constructed sememes with their indicator lexemes (from the completed list) after 5 inventory stages, substantive form attributed:

[pastoral maker of artistic/prophetic expression]

boy
poet
shepherd
swain

[canine—incompetent or parody 'maker' of auditory art/prophecy]

wolf

[plant—vegetal maker of excrescence, figuratively, 'maker' of artistic/prophetic expression]

oat
grass
reed
tree
woods

[product of artistic/prophetic expression]

aeglogue
complaint/plaint
emblem
music
poem/poetry/poesie
rhyming
singing
verse

[organic excrescence/growth—figuratively, product of artistic/prophetic expression]

blossom
flower

[product of partial artistic/prophetic 'making']

dance

[activity of artistic/prophetic expression]

feigning
framing
making [crafting]
tuning
working

[covering—secrecy (being/non-seeming, veridictory modalization, figuratively as activity of 'making')]

mantle
shade

[uncovering—truth (being/seeming, another veridictory modalization of pastoral 'making')]

call [call out]
feign [paint out]
show
spring [spring forth]

[repose—not doing (negation of artistic/prophetic 'making']

home
sleep

[*pouvoir* modalization of artistic/ prophetic expression (being-able-to pastorally 'make'/prophetize)]

can/conne/couth/conning
learning [knowledge]
skill
studies

[figurativization of being-able-to 'make'/prophetize]

pipe
reed

[competition—activity of actualizing competence]

leading
playing
warring

[recognition—valorization of competition]

commendation
fame
honor
praise
scorn [as contrary]

[recognition—figuratively]

gift

[herd animal—figuratively, *materielle* of pastoral 'making']

flock
lamb
sheep

[reception/consumption of 'making']

god [subject/Receiver actant—see p. 247, n. 8]
hear

[nourishment—figuratively, for product of 'making' as consumers' spiritual nourishment]

feed/food

[respected chaste female]

daughter
goddess/*dea*
grace(demi-goddess)
lass
maid/may
muse

[injuring/penetrating]

breaking
saving [as contrary]
shooting
wasting
wounding

[modalizations of having (possessing)]:

pouvoir: being-able-to-have, not-being-able-to-have, being-able-not-to-have

loss (*pouvoir,* not-being-able-to-have)

leaving (*pouvoir*, being-able-not-to-have)

([virtuality of losing]

dread)

vouloir: wanting-to-have, wanting-not-to-have

love (wanting-to-have)
lust (wanting-to-have + virtual sexual activity and dysphoria)

Appendix 2, Part IIa.

Summary of Inventory Stages that Led to the Isotopic Lexemes

(Classematic words are inclusively recorded in the inventories but not in the following lists of indicators for kernel semes; classemes were considered separately.)

For Stage 1 (frequency at 27–41 occurrences in whole text):

aeglogue
can/conne
emblem
eye
find
flower
head
hear
honor
lust
make [craft]
muse
pipe
poems/poetry
spring
winter
wit/weet
worth

Four of these not recurring (at the determined frequencies) after stage 1:

eye
find
wit/weet
worth

For Stage 2 (at 6 and + occurrences in stage 1):

blossoms
break
commend
complaint/plain
fame
flock
learn
mantle
music
oaten
poet
praise
reed
rhyme
sheep
shepherd
show
sing
skill
tree
tune
verse

Excluded for next stage (6 or + occurrences but seemingly represents no set of parasynonyms in stage 1):

argument
god (included later)
head
heart
judgment
love (included later)
mean [signify]

name
season
sleep (included later)
summer
word
year

Repeats from initial list here again
frequent (6 or + occurrences):

    aeglogue
    can/conne
    emblem
    flower
    honor
    make
    muse
    pipe
    poem/poetry
    spring

For Stage 3 (at 7 or + occurrences
in stage 2):

    boy
    dance
    daughter
    feed
    feign
    frame
    gift
    goddess
    play
    scorn
    sleep
    study
    swain
    war
    waste
    wolf

Excluded for next stage (7 or
+ occurrences but seemingly
represents no set of
parasynonyms in stage 2):

argument
god (included later)
head
keep
lead [vb.] (included later)
love (included later)
matter
mean
name
turn
winter

Repeats from earlier stages here
again frequent (7 or +
occurrences):

    aeglogue
    can/conne
    fame
    flower
    hear
    honor
    learn
    lust
    make
    muse
    music
    oaten
    pipe
    poet
    poem/poetry
    praise
    reed
    rhyme
    sheep
    shepherd
    show
    sing/song
    skill
    spring
    verse

For Stage 4 (at 4 or + occurrences
in stage 3):

    call
    dread

god
grace
home
lamb
lead[vb.]
love
maid/may
save
shade
shoot
woods
work
wound

Excluded for next stage (4 and + occurrences but seemingly represents no set of parasynomyms in stage 3):

mean
name
summer
nature

Repeats from earlier stages here again frequent (4 or + occurrences):

break
complain/plain
fame
flock
flower
learn
make
music
pipe
poet
rhyme
sheep
shepherd
sing/song
spring [vb.]
swain
verse

For stage 5 at 7 or + occurrences in stage 4:

lass
lost/lorn

Excluded (7 or + occurrences but seemingly represents no set of parasynonyms in stage 4):

mean
name
wander

Repeats from earlier stages here again frequent:

flock
god
learn
love
lust
play
poet
sheep
shepherd
sing/song
sleep
wolf
waste
woods

Last new qualification variable (at 3 or + occurrences in stage 5):

leave

Excluded (seemingly represents no set of parasynonyms in stage 5):

[none]

Repeats from earlier stages here again frequent (3 or + occurrences):

flock
love
wolf

**Part IIb, Coalesced isotopically
significant lexemes:**

aeglogue
blossoms
boy
break
call
can/conne
commended
complaint/plain
dance
daughter
dread
emblem
fame
feed
feign
flock
flower
frame
gift
god
goddess
grace
hear
home
honor
lamb
lass
lead[vb.]
learn
leave
lost/lorn
love
lust
maid/may
make [craft]
mantle
muse
music
oaten
pipe
play
poems/poetry
poet
praise

reed
rhyme
save
scorn
shade
sheep
shepherd
shoot
show
sing
skill
sleep
spring
study
swain
tree
tune
verse
war
waste
wolf
woods
work
wound

Appendix 2, Part III

**The Constructed Sememes with
their Constituent Parasynonyms
(complete inventory occurrences
only, with location and context-
defining lexeme—see pp. 71 and
205)**

[pastoral 'maker' of artistic/
prophetic expression]

author2174wit
author132poet
author1719sing
author2351show
authority1457poet
authority48verse
authors38fame, poet
boy372scorn
boy's763complain(t)
boy[2]682tree
boy1719sing

boy2159emblem
boy265aeglogue, complaint,
    shepherd
boy273shepherd, winter, waste
boy718poet, swain
boy743poet, shepherd
boy783shepherd
boy841make, sing
boy884shepherd
boys1576flock
boys2691shepherd
boys615shepherd, aeglogue
goatherds192shepherd
goatherds1515conne, muse
grooms652play, shepherd
herdsman's372boy, scorn
herdgroom1837eye
herdgrooms527verse
neatherd's1719boy
pastors2008flock
pastors210shepherd, poems
poet's2333honor, work
poet's2419love, praise
poet's727work
poet1004goddess
poet1457grace/pers.
poet14learn
poet17conne, fame
poet2236love
poet2295music
poet2304show, skill
poet2341fame
poet2345praise
poet2598tree
poet2751study
poet2754goddess
poet2769make
poet322worth, aeglogue
poet38fame
poet69worth
poet743boy, shepherd
poet873worth, goddess
*poeti*936honor
poets'618god, love
poets1254feign
poets1261feign
poets1477god

poets1635shepherd
poets1644feign, god, wood
poets1676eye
poets2216dread, play
poets2218worth
poets2279make
poets2327honor, show
poets2338show, worth, war
poets2349honor
poets2382play
poets2523muse
poets2535honor, muse
poets2537call
poets2568fame, wit, gift/ve
poets2572feign
poets2580feign
poets38fame
poets42sing
poets709feign
poets718boy, swain
poets858make, rhyme, verse
poets860make
poets887daughter, muse, feign
poets915feign
poets935fame
poets939feign, goddess
poets987feign
shepherd's[2]1953swain
shepherd's1406love
shepherd's1498swain
shepherd's1508learn, lust
shepherd's173waste
shepherd's2010call
shepherd's2054call
shepherd's2453conne
shepherd's2458call, home, scorn,
    swain
shepherd's2622hear, oaten, reed
shepherd's2638feed, swain
shepherd's265aeglogue,
    complain(t), boy
shepherd's2678frame, pipe
shepherd's273boy, winter
shepherd's276sheep
shepherd's3flock
shepherd's743boy
shepherd's783boy, love

shepherd's818goddess, swain
shepherd's883wit, daughter, boy
shepherd's8sing, swain
shepherd1064play
shepherd1378show
shepherd1433swain
shepherd1518flock, sheep
shepherd1538lead/vb/
shepherd1555flock
shepherd1635feign, poet
shepherd1689god
shepherd1745save, swain
shepherd1945sheep, waste
shepherd2040break, sheep, sleep,
    wolf
shepherd2064sleep
shepherd2133aeglogue
shepherd2296skill
shepherd2428daughter, maid
shepherd2465verse
shepherd2509verse
shepherd2527god
shepherd2555love
shepherd2615spring
shepherd2636muse, music, sing
shepherd2774feed, sheep
shepherd371lust
shepherd512home
shepherd593aeglogue
shepherd902poems
shepherds'1075god
shepherds'1080swain
shepherds'1381hear, scorn
shepherds'1583wit
shepherds'2180lead[v]/, rhyme
shepherds'2410swain
shepherds'2448daughter, make,
    sing
shepherds'2462lead[vb]
shepherds'2641god
shepherds'2691boy
shepherds'282god, love
shepherds'449daughter, flower
shepherds'615aeglogue, boy
shepherds'652play
shepherds'746love
shepherds'800grace/pers., god

shepherds'830daughter
shepherds'905worth, god
shepherds1006aeglogue
shepherds1025sing
shepherds1037play
shepherds1048god
shepherds1081learn
shepherds1083sheep
shepherds1099wit
shepherds1197god
shepherds1354flock
shepherds1389conne, make, head,
    god, love
shepherds1403feed, flock
shepherds1493aeglogue,
    commended, honor, make
shepherds1515skill
shepherds1523feed, flock
shepherds1557lust
shepherds1639feed, flock
shepherds1727dance, pipe
shepherds1846hear
shepherds1881home, pipe
shepherds1975lead[vb]
shepherds1aeglogue
shepherds2009sheep
shepherds2032flock, god
shepherds20aeglogue, worth, god
shepherds211poems
shepherds2441flock
shepherds2462dance
shepherds2618god
shepherds2622tune
shepherds2731skill
shepherds419make
shepherds45rhyme
shepherds792make, spring, tune
shepherds910god
swain1498shepherd
swain1508lust, learn, shepherd
swain1745shepherd, save
swain1758hear, sing
swain1953shepherd
swain2433shepherd
swain2458scorn, shepherd, call,
    home
swain2638feed, shepherd

swain3flock
swain659shoot, spring
swain718boy, poet
swain818goddess, shepherd
swain8shepherd, sing
swains1080shepherd
swains2410shepherd

[canine (incompetent or parody
'maker' of auditory art/prophecy)]

ball/bawl/2039learn, call
bark2039sleep, learn, call
barketh98feed
bark2035shepherd
barking99conne
beast's1745swain, shepherd, save
beast2453conne
beastliness1231rhyme
beastly1992shepherd
beasts2476learn
beasts2659learn
beasts2743fame
bite2034shepherd
creep1117god
creep2008flock
creeping1148complain(t)
cur's2039wolf, learn, call
cur2035shepherd
currish98feed
dog1609poems
dog1964conne, lose
dog2034shepherd
dogs2025shepherd
fox1011feign
foxes2016wolf
fox/he/1154conne
foxes1180shepherd
fur2025shepherd
hound2195music
jaws1744wolf, lamb
paws1745shepherd, swain, save
wolf's1744lamb
wolf2036lamb
wolf2040sleep, break, sheep,
    shepherd, call
wolf771break, lamb

wolfish2042sheep
wolves1347dread, flock, lose
wolves1519save
wolves2477sheep
wolves2627waste, wood, dread

[plant—vegetal maker of
excrescence—figuratively artistic/
prophetic 'maker']

arbor/tree/936honor, poet
avena2261oaten
avena2261reed
bush1345tune
bush2649lead/vb/
bush656hear
bushes1017blossom, flock, wood
bushy2615shepherd, spring
buskets1018home
fir968god, tree
forest1859work
forest2627dread, wood, waste, wolf
forests2476learn
grass626spring
grass1016wood
grove1383play, pipe, shade
grove1866sleep
grove1866eye
*herbis*2744poet
*herbis*2754goddess
herbs2744poet
herbs2754goddess
herbs963flower
ivy2244muse
moss456blossom
mossy1279blossom, lust
oak440tree
oak552learn
oak578poet
oak2631spring
oak484conne
oak490waste
oaten2420sleep
oaten1375muse, pipe
oaten2182pipe
oaten2211hear, reed
oaten2261reed

oaten2419praise, pipe
oaten2622hear, reed, shepherd,
    tune
oaten313break, muse, pipe
olives829war
olive2481muse
olive972spring, war
plants2425winter
reed2211oaten, flock
reed2622hear, oaten, shepherd,
    tune
reed2693pipe, tree, winter
reeds2182oaten, pipe
reeds2261oaten
reeds900pipe, make
salow2725wood
timber2656learn, frame, save
timber562tree, wood
toadstool2651frame, work
tree2424muse
tree2598poet
tree2693muse, pipe, reed, winter
tree682boy, shoot
tree968god
trees/2/562wood
trees1397wood
trees1467spring
trees269flock, winter
trees290shade, lose
vine1743war
witch/hazel/1353shepherd
wood1027dance, music, home
wood1111play
wood1644feign, poet, god
wood2043lamb, waste
woods1397tree, learn
woods1855complain(t), waste
woods2627waste, wolf, dread
woods2699lamb, love, sheep

[dysphoric 'plant']

bramble2469play, lead[vb]
bramble2650wood
brambles2671blossom
briar1018home
briar508scorn

briar1353shepherd
briar2615shepherd, spring
briar451sing
briar463complain(t)
briar469complain(t)
briar552learn
weed1404lass
weed2644wit
weed2664conne
weeds1542feed

[product of artistic/prophetic
expression]

aeglogue1006shepherd
aeglogue1335complain(t)
aeglogue1493commended, honor,
    make, shepherd
aeglogue1716make
aeglogue20shepherd, worth, god
aeglogue2133aeglogue, shepherd
aeglogue2252make
aeglogue2259sing
aeglogue2305skill
aeglogue2396emblem
aeglogue2401maid
aeglogue2403make
aeglogue2606complain(t)
aeglogue265complain(t), shepherd,
    boy
aeglogue323poet
aeglogue615boy, shepherd
aeglogue760honor, praise
aeglogues194head
aeglogues1shepherd
aeglogues2323feed, flock
aeglogues2761complain(t), sheep
aeglogues523shepherd
attune2426sing
bucolics2324war, sing, dread
*cana*1463verse
cantion2259aeglogue, sing
carol2208sing, lust, lead/vb/, love
carol415learn, love
charm2248pipe
charm713verse
charm2394verse

charms2394verse, make
complain2431gift/ve
complainest386winter
complaineth2169kstudy, poems
complaineth265aeglogue, boy,
     shepherd
complaining1335aeglogue
complaining763boy, love
complaint1147hear
complaint2606aeglogue
complaints2761aeglogue
complaints29love
ditties2185winter
ditties2622hear, oaten, reed,
     shepherd, tune
ditty282shepherd, god, love
emblem1481poems
emblem1487aeglogue
emblem1701poems
emblem1919poems
emblem2396aeglogue
emblem365poems
emblem677god, love
emblem848goddess
emblem995poems
fable1330verse
fiction1423poems, feign
hymns416praise, pipe, lass
hymns2411honor, love, lass
idyllion1894aeglogue
idyllion2252aeglogue, make
idyllion725love
lay[n]1854tune
lay[n]792tune
lay[n]791sing
lay792shepherd
lay879sing
lays2449praise
lyric2341fame
music's2636shepherd, sing
music[2]2275frame, verse
music1358make
music1460dance, muse
music1722frame
music1729dance, learn
music2270gift/ve, wit
music2288war

music2297poems
music2300eye
music2461sleep, lead[vb]
music2708poems
music309scorn, shepherd
musical1028home, wood
musical2282make
*musicam*2708music, poems, poet
nightspell715god, wood
odes2766wit, work
panegyrics2269learn
plain304love
plained279flock, feed, sheep
plained279lead[vb]
plaintive1366verse
plaints1388god
plaints1855waste, wood
plaints2494god, goddess
poesie1487aeglogue, emblem
poesie1701emblem
poesie1919emblem
poesie365emblem
poesie995emblem
poesie2277play
poetical1423feign
poetical2257wit
poetical2304show
poetical902shepherd, god
poetical925honor, muse
poetry211wit
poetry2137commended
poetry2169complain(t), study
poetry2297music
poetry2352show
poetry2708music
poetry2765learn, wit, work
poetry768sing, skill
poetry859skill
refrain99conne
rhyme584verse, make, scorn
rhyme858make, poet, verse
rhymers107scorn
rhymers2565wit
rhymes1370hear
rhymes1386flock, wit, feed
rhymes2180shepherd, lead[vb]
rhymes2222spring

rhymes2430gift/ve
rhymes2435conne
rhymes45shepherd
rhyming2356learn, skill, wit
rhyming766conne, pipe, sing, study
riddles2180rhyme, lead[vb],
   shepherd
rounde1788eye
roundel1834hear
roundelays1370hear, rhyme
roundelays879sing
roundels1846hear, shepherd
sing[2]2448shepherd, make,
   daughter
sing1365conne, pipe, tune, love
sing1371waste
sing1758hear
sing2201war
sing2205worth
sing2208lead/vb/, love, lust
sing2213dread, war
sing2271music, praise, verse
sing2409love
sing2426muse
sing2480dance
sing2616pipe
sing3flock
sing821play
sing823dance
sing8shepherd, swain
singing1025lust
singing2260make, commended,
   learn, aeglogue
singing2324dread, war
singing42poet
singing766conne, pipe, rhyme
song1373frame, spring, shade
song1384praise
song1719boy
song1758hear, sing, swain
song1852hear
song1900make, praise, love
song2404make
song2479verse
song2508verse, waste
song2622shepherd
song2636music, shepherd

song768poems, skill, make
song841boy, make
song998worth
songs1874sleep
songs2408muse
songs2419love, poet
songs2448make, shepherd, sing,
   daughter
songs2616pipe, sing, learn
songs310make, pipe
songs778break
sonnet2335worth
sonnet2622hear, oaten, reed,
   shepherd, tune
sonnets2364sing
sonnets936honor, poet
spell713verse
sung2622oaten, reed, tune
tale1011feign
tale509shepherd
tale512home, shepherd
tale552learn
tale586emblem
tale746love, shepherd
tales1477god
tales438love, make
tales548praise
teen[plaint]2430gift/ve, rhyme
verse1847make
verse1879boy
verse2214hear
verse2216play, poet, dread
verse2238head
verse2445break, pipe
verse2450flower
verse2465shepherd
verse2479sing
verse2484muse
verse2489dread
verse2494god
verse2508sing, waste
verse334gift/ve
verse583rhyme, conne, hear
verses2322work
verses351love
verses1366make
verses2271praise, sing

verses2275frame, music
verses2330fame
verses2394make
verses2509shepherd
versify1479make
versify858make, poet, rhyme
virelays2419sing
virelays2522sing
virelays879sing
virelays2418lust
woodspell715god

[organic excrescence—figuratively
artistic/prophetic expression]

apple1672gift/ve
bear1404flower
bear1556love, lass
bear1986god
beard1129break
bare2639pipe
begot800shepherd, god, grace/pers.
berries473blossom, flower
birth2635shepherd
blossom294waste
blossoming1017flock, wood
blossoms1115lust, spring
blossoms1279lust
blossoms292flower
blossoms473flower
blossoms566flower
born2341fame
boughs2671blossom
boughs2481muse
boughs293lust
boughs296eye
boughs445waste
boughs477spring
branch413lose
branch2478wound
branches2481muse
branches446honor
branches475break
branches479work
branches820muse
branches934honor
bred303god, love

breed303love, god
bud1155blossom, spring, lust
budded1129break
budded402spring
budding413lose
buds1017blossom, flock, wood
buds2220poems
buds292blossom, flower
buds294blossom, waste
chaplet1778head
corn403pipe
corn1573sheep
coronation[carnation]975flower
coronation976flower
damsons993gift/ve
ermines802maid
*faecundi*2374verse
fleece1040flock
fleece1076flock
fleece1573sheep
fleece297flock
flourish798sing, flower
flourish1124lust
flourished889honor, study
flower292blossom
flower629head, call
flower798sing
flower1404lass
flowered2625spring
flowered284spring
flowering473blossom
flowers1124lust
flowers2464muse
flowers2560mantle
flowers2750learn, study
flowers449daughter, shepherd
flowers478honor, wound
flowers689fame, goddess
flowers693goddess
flowret2450verse
flowreth2452mantle, spring
flowrets566blossom
fruit1671blossom
fruit2598tree
fruit2654gift/ve, spring
fruit306gift/ve
fruit984scorn

fruitful1354flock
grain2198praise
grew440tree
grew552learn
grew2674flower
grew446honor
grow1395fame
grow968tree, god
groweth2377verse
grown2651frame
hairs1279blossom
hairs1365sing, tune
hairs1279lust
hairs1365conne, pipe, love
hairs58honor
hay2413shade, winter
horns1115head, lust, spring
horns1125head
horns1155blossom
horns423lass
ivory1375oaten, muse, pipe
kingscups836love
leaf1959tree
leaf2035shepherd
leaf293lust
leaves1017blossom, flock, wood
leaves1373sing, spring, shade
leaves2558maid
leaves290shade, tree, lose
leaves455lust, maid
lily454flower
locks1368love, lose
locks2558maid
locks480flower
locks776scorn, shepherd
moss, mossy [cf. under 'plant]
nuts2633tree
pinions2229fame
pinions2359
primrose567worth
progeny903grace/pers.
queenapples1366make, verse, gift/
    give
queenapples1463verse
quill1381shepherd, hear, scorn
quill2426sing, muse
quill2426muse

sops-in-wine975flower
straw1538lead[vb]
unfruitful743poet, shepherd
vellet[velvet]1114head, shoot
vellet1114shoot
walnut2633tree
wither2222rhyme
withered1959tree
wreathe2725wood
wreathed1114shoot, head

[product of partial artistic/prophetic
expression]

dance1026play, pipe, maid
dance1359pipe
dance1459grace/pers., muse, music
dance1729learn, music
dance2462lead[vb], shepherd
dance2480sing
dance632lead[vb], love, sleep
dance824grace/pers., sing
dancing1727pipe, shepherd
heydeguys1459grace/pers., dance
hornpipe1026maid, dance, play
miller's/round2208lead[vb]
miller's/round2317dance
tripping883daughter

[activity of artistic/prophetic
'making']

device309music, scorn, shepherd
devise1109conne
devise2186feed, flock
devise905worth
devised125poet
devised1676eye, poet
devised1925shepherd
devised2585poet
devising28wit
disorder1250sheep
disorderly66show
feign1254poet
feign1635poet, shepherd
feign2221shoot
feign2562poet

feign2572poet
feign915poet
feigned1261poet
feigned1644god, poet, wood
feigned2509god
feigned2580poet
feigned709poet
feigned736shoot
feigned939poet, goddess
feigned969war
feigned987poet
frame1373sing, spring, shade
frame1722music
frame2651work
frame2656learn, save
frame2678pipe, shepherd
frame278conne, pipe, tune
framing2275music, verse
invention926verse
invention1468poems
invention194aeglogue, head
invention2267poems
labor16poet
labor2173learn
labored2212flock, reed, feed
labored75poet
laboring53work
laboring2323feed, flock
made255god
made(craft)403pipe
made1366verse
made1493aeglogue, commended, shepherd
made1847verse
made2216worth, poet
made2394verse
made2403aeglogue, sing
made2448shepherd, sing, praise, daughter
made284spring
made583rhyme, scorn
made769honor
made792shepherd, spring, tune
make1358music
make1389conne, shepherd
make1479verse
make2413play

make2617learn, love
make310pipe, sing
make418shepherd
make438love
make781skill
make858poet, rhyme, verse
make860poet
makedst286mantle, winter
makers2279poet
maketh1900praise, sing, love
maketh68music
making18skill, worth
making841sing, boy
making858make, poet, rhyme, verse
*poiein*860make, poet
prophesying2362sing
tune1365conne, pipe, sing, love
tune1854pipe
tune278conne, pipe, frame
tuned2622hear, oaten, reed, shepherd
tuned792make, shepherd, spring
unfeignedly1424poet
work2333honor, poet
work2441waste
work2663sleep
work2766wit
work727poet
working2280music
working2651frame
works154sleep
works2322verse
works2765learn, poems, wit

[covering—secrecy (being/non-seeming—veridictory modalization, figuratively, as activity of 'making')]

adorn831grace/pers.
adorned2173learn
adorned879sing
array1076flock
bedight2230love
bower2650wood
bower2194shepherd
bower2469play

burials2554honor
buried220winter
buried2451winter
buried2527shepherd
cave1522shepherd
close/vb/1866sleep
close1148complain(t)
close1866eye
close789flock, shade
closely2527god, shepherd
clothe456waste, lust, maid
clothed426flock
clothing2038sheep, sleep
coat1562shepherd
coffer2347work
color1081learn, shepherd
color1156sheep
color196learn
colored210shepherd
coloreth354love
colors2473mantle
cover2007feign
coverlet2560flower, mantle
coverture1507waste
decked990praise
decked877flower
dight/2/879sing
dight1933wit
dight2677flower
dight1367gift/ve, shade
dirks/darks/456waste, blossom
dressed1387frame
envelopeth359fame
folded2775flock, sheep
folds2046flock, eye
folds2696winter
folded2775flock
folded2775sheep
folds2046flock
gilded660tree
glove416praise, pipe, lass
girt2244muse
hid1105lamb
hidden2644wit
hood430head
mantle2451winter
mantle2452flower

mantle2452spring
mantle2560flower
mantle286winter
mantled2560flower
mask1013love
mask2417praise, muse
overcast2691boy
overlaid1558shepherd, lust
paint449shepherd, daughter
painted469complain(t)
private1424poet
privily1148complain(t)
privy1856sing
privy2751poet, study
privy635break
privy638sheep
secret2280music, work
secret2617learn, make, love, shade
secret369aeglogue
secret539maid, love
secret619love, scorn
secretly323aeglogue, poet
shade1367gift/ve
shade1383pipe, play
shade2413play
shade2617learn, make, love
shades1342wander
shady1373frame
shady290lose
shadow2615shepherd, spring
shadowed117show
shadoweth323aeglogue, poet
shadoweth355love
shady1373sing, spring
shady290tree
shield1500learn
shield165learn, conne, gift/ve
shield1500god
shield2060god
shroud1373sing, spring, frame,
    shade
shrouded789flock
shrouded655hear, god
shrouded790shade
trussed/up106frame
wear821play
weed[clothing]1564feed

weeds[clothing]1565god
wrapped1393sheep, feed
yclad1016wood
yclad2038sleep, sheep
yclad2214verse
yclad802head, maid
ygurt1568shepherd

[uncovering—being/seeming or
truth (another veridictory
modalization—figuratively, as
activity of 'making')]

abroad1111wood, play
abroad633sleep
appear2568fame, poet, wit
appear378eye
appeared1642god
appeareth2741work
appeareth2367worth
appeareth626spring
bald445waste
bare1072sheep
bare79verse
bared1588love
bared2478wound
bewray353feign
bewray1870hear
bred786daughter
breed2696winter
breed756flower
breed288waste
bring/forth3flock
bring/forth8shepherd, sing, swain
bringeth/forth2654spring, gift/ve
call(out)2010wander
call[cry]2040
call2459gift/ve, home, scorn
call273boy
called939feign
calleth864daughter
cried463complain(t)
cries1856sing
cries1869tune
cries1877hear
crowing403pipe

cry aloud1211hear
cry out86hear
cry817lamb
cry1150eye
cry1207gift/ve
display2304poet, show
display2452mantle
display2203muse
display2303poems
display2452flower, spring
display2645love
exposition143work
express1001worth
forth1115spring
forth659spring
leaped/forth2389head
leaped/forth2389lust
let/fly1589head
let/out2047wolf
looser2680lass
lowted1552conne
lowted1663honor
manifest927goddess
naked290tree, shade, lose
naked475break
naked659swain, shoot
open1171call
opened1166show
outcries1211hear
paint/out1388complain(t), frame,
    god
picture1894aeglogue
picture1895hear
picture378eye
pour/out1388complain(t), god
poured/out2279poet, scorn, love
poured/out2440verse
poured2173learn
put/forth154sleep, work
set/forth53work
set/forth763love
set forth1716aeglogue
set forth2335worth
set forth378eye
set forth763complain(t), boy
set/forth2564complain(t)

set/out156commended
set/out746shepherd, love
shoot forth1280lust
shoot out1114head
shouting1025sing
show forth2079head
show1377skill, shepherd
show1394skill
show2304poems, poet, skill
show646head
showeth118conne, muse, skill
showeth2327poet, honor
showeth2338poet, worth, war
showeth2352poems
shrieking1212dread
shrilled2445break, verse
spew/out107rhyme, scorn
sprang/out972war
sprang800grace/pers., god
spring forth1115lust
spring/water/792make
spring1373frame, shade
spring1396head
spring2451winter, flower
spring2625flower
spring2654gift/ve
spring284flower
spring892muse
spring954goddess
springeth478wound
springing1467spring
springing410scorn, skill
sprung/forth659shoot
sprung/forth659swain
sprung2222rhyme
sprout1115lust, spring
sprout1155blossom
sprout1279blossom, lust, shoot
tell forth509shepherd
thrust out808head
truest1406love
unbridled2648love, lead[vb]
unfolding738love, wound, lust
utter882shepherd
uttering29complain(t), love

utter629flower, head, call
yells1871complain(t)

[repose/inactivity (not-doing,
negation of 'making')]

abed2218poet
abed2218worth
abide2441flock, shepherd, waste
abide2507shepherd
abide2765learn, poems, wit
abode887muse, poet, daughter
abye313break, muse, oaten, pipe
asleep2698love
asleep2300music
asleep2409sing, love
asleep1857spring
asleep2300eye
awake632dance, sleep, lead/vb/,
    love
awake659swain, spring, shoot
awoke635break
cease2219learn
cease2508verse, waste, sing
*domi*710verse
ease2218poet, worth
ease512shepherd, ease
ease312muse
ease512home
home1411flock
home1881shepherd, pipe
home2458shepherd, gift/ve
home512shepherd
home594boy
home641flock
lazy386complain(t)
leisure486home
lulled2698love
rest1051sleep
rest2205sing, worth
rest2222spring
restless2663sheep, sleep, work
slack2315verse
sleep1861eye, love
sleep1866eye
sleep1870hear

sleep1874sing
sleep1877break, hear
sleep2040break, sheep, shepherd,
    wolf
sleep2064play, shepherd
sleep2420oaten, pipe
sleep254work
sleep2663sheep, work
sleepeth632dance, lust, lead[vb],
    love
sleeping703love
sleeps2461music
sleeps2462lead[vb]
slumber[2]707love
slumbereth2408muse, sing
still[unmoving]1975lead[vb]
tranquility1096call
unquietness2718love
unrest1388god
unrest1388complain(t), frame
wake1393sheep
waketh2035shepherd
wander1347wolf, flock, dread, lose
wander2010call, shepherd
wandered138love
wandering1342shade
wandering2477sheep, wolf
wandering2648love
wandering653shoot
wandering725love

[pouvoir modalization of artistic/
prophetic expression:
competence—being

able to 'make']
able2270learn, music, wit
able2270gift/ve
artp[2]2172gift/ve, commended,
    worth
art2637conne
*artem*2708music, poet
can1389shepherd, make
canne425lust, flock
con1515skill
cond2054shepherd
conne118muse, show

conne1380muse, skill, daughter
conne2435rhyme
conne327conne, skill
conning2436muse
conning766pipe, rhyme, sing, study
conningly584hear, verse
couth1365pipe, sing, tune, love
couth1391love
couth2456praise, shepherd
couth278pipe, tune, frame
couth327skill
crafty1180shepherd
fainting279lead[vb], feed, sheep,
    flock, complain(t)
feeble2475flock, verse
feeble297flock
kydst2665wound
kydst2644wit
learn1081shepherd
learn1396head, spring, wood
learn1508lust, shepherd, god
learn2475head
learn2616sing, make, love, shade
learn415love
learn631scorn
learned1396head, spring
learned14poet
learned1516god
learned1691head
learned1729dance, music
learned1830love
learned2039call
learned2219wit
learned224head
learned2361commended, sing
learned2656frame, save
learned2765poems, wit, work
learned340love
learning165conne, gift/ve
learning2356skill
learning2565rhyme
learning2750flower, poet, study
learning2766wit
learning895muse
learning973study
puo[be able to]1884emblem
skill118conne, muse, show

skill1378show
skill1380conne, muse, daughter
skill1394show
skill1515conne, muse
skill18make, worth
skill2296shepherd, music
skill2304show, aeglogue
skill2309praise
skill2356learn
skill2731shepherd
skill327conne
skill410scorn, spring
skill768poems, sing
skill781make, love
skill859poems
skills2355–56wit
studies171commendéd
studies2169complain(t), poems
studies2750flower, learn
studies766conne, pipe, rhyme, sing
studies889honor
studies973learn
study2751poet
unable1001worth
uncouth1964lose
uncouth17fame, poet
unlearned1322shepherd
weak1092work
weak297flock
weak425flock
wit2766work
wit2270gift/ve
wit2568gift/ve
witless1511eye
witless2664conne, wit
witless72head
wits211poems
wits2765poems
wits757lust
yconned1154learn

[figurativization of 'being able to
    'make']

bagpipes1722frame, music
bagpipe771break, wolf, lamb

mazer1891feign
pipe901lose
pipe/2/2693tree
pipe/2/313break, oaten
pipe1027dance
pipe1365conne, sing, tune, love
pipe1375muse, oaten
pipe2616sing
pipe2639flock
pipe2678frame, shepherd
pipe2693reed, winter, muse
pipe270break
pipe278conne, tune, frame
pipe310make, sing
pipe313muse
pipe416praise, lass
pipe778break
pipe900reed, make, love
piped2182oaten, reed
pipes1854tune
pipes1881home, shepherd
pipes2419praise, oaten, sleep
pipes2445break, verse
pipes403scorn
pipes740head
piping1383play, shade
piping1727dance, shepherd
piping766conne, rhyme, sing, study
reed1732love
reed2211oaten, flock, feed
reed2622hear, oaten, shepherd,
    tune
reed2693pipe, tree, winter
reed898god
reeds2182oaten, pipe
reeds2261oaten
reeds900pipe, make

[competition—activity of
actualizing competence]

advance2205sing, worth, love
advance2411honor, love, lass
advance2481muse
t'advance430head, wit
attained2567learn
battle2386goddess

conquered1214break
conquerors935fame
conquerors935poet
deserved179praise
deserved2309praise
deserves2419poet
deserves2419praise
deserves2419sing
deserveth1902praise
excell797praise
foes1100scorn
jousts2201war, sing
lead forth2469play
lead[vb]632dance
lead1934flock
lead2180rhyme, shepherd
lead2208love
lead2462sleep, dance, shepherd
lead632love, sleep
leads1538shepherd
led/forth274flock
led1975shepherd, sheep
led279complain(t), sheep
match1722frame, music
match1079love
peace2303wound
peace829war
peaceable973study
passing1394show
passing1394skill
play[music]1383pipe
play1037shepherd, flock
play1111wood
play1383shade
play2064shepherd, sleep
play2216poet, verse, dread
play2413shade, love
play2649lead/vb/
play321sing
play652shepherd
played1026dance, maid
played2285music
players2382poet
playing2277poems
playing2370love
playing352love

race800grace/pers., god, shepherd,
    spring
strife1891feign
strife1099shepherd, wit
strife2633tree
strife1718aeglogue
strife464god
strive1384praise
strive1385shepherd
strive1737rhyme
strove969feign
strove1564flock, feed
strove1381hear
*triomphale*936poet
triumphs935fame
triumphs935poet
victi/win/1883emblem
victorious907fame
victory2272gift/ve, praise
victory934honor
vincenti[winners]1883emblem
vinto[overcome]1883emblem
*vittoriosa*936honor, poet
war1674fame
war2303wound
war2288music
war969feign
war972spring
warlike2288music
wars2201sing
wars2213sing, dread
wars2324sing, dread
wars2338poet, worth, show
wars829shepherd
win784gift/ve
win1384praise, shepherd
win1922conne
won2361commended, learn, sing
won1753lose

[recognition, of successful
competing]

account1043shepherd
account2338poet
account2356learn, skill
account1041muse

account2171honor, worth
ashamed869verse
blame1483worth
blame72head, wit
blame1384praise, sing
blamest1093shepherd
commendable2171worth, gift
commendable171study
commendation207love
commendation1493aeglogue, honor,
    make, shepherd
commendation2137poems
commendation2361learn, sing
commendations156worth
commended2329fame, poems
commendeth2134flock
contempt211poems, wit
contempt2169poems, complaint(t),
    study
contempt2352poems,show
contempt2433shepherd, swain
credit1010gift/ve
credit1274gift/ve
credit1318gift/ve
deserved1483worth
deserved179praise
deserved2309praise, worth
deserves1400worth
deserves2419praise, sing, poet, love
deserveth1902gift/ve, praise, love
deserveth28wit
deserveth880worth
entitled2worth
fame1386feed, flock, wit
fame26worth
fame892–3spring
famous1674war
famous17conne
famous2329commended, verse,
    poems
famous2345praise
famous2568gift/ve, poet, wit
famous38poet
famous689flower, goddess
famous891spring
famous935poet
favor1114head, shoot

favor1552conne
favor2076god
granted677god
granted677love
hailed663shoot
hery415learn, love
hery2515honor
honor1493commended, shepherd,
    aeglogue, make
honor2171worth
honor2190lust
honor2220poems
honor2327poet, show
honor2350poet
honor2411love, lass
honor2506god
honor2535muse, poet
honor478flower, wound
honor760aeglogue, praise
honor769make
honor889study
honor925muse, poems
*honor*936poet
honor9feed
honorable2311worth
notable2544flower
note972spring
praise1384sing
praise1900make, sing, love
praise1902gift/ve, love
praise2271sing, verse
praise2345fame
praise2417muse
praise2419poet, sing, love
praise2448make
praise2456conne
praise416pipe, lass
praise760aeglogue, honor
praise797worth
praises2309worth
preferred346love
renown1384praise, shepherd
renown893fame, spring
renowned2333poet, work
renowned2311honor, worth
renowned2333honor
reprove309scorn

respected2333poet, work
reward993gift/ve
rewards2197feed
scorn107rhyme
scorn1381hear, shepherd
scorn2458swain, call, home,
    shepherd
scorn309music, shepherd
scorn403pipe
scorn410spring, skill
scorn776lass, love
scorned372boy
scorned619love
scornfully631learn
scorning2277play, love
scorning583make, rhyme
shame2178head
shame2657make, save
shameful2220honor
shameful2220poems
taunt1322shepherd
taunt1323learn
unknown539maid
unknown1484shepherd
unknown1970lose
unknown2527shepherd, god
unknown187aeglogue
unknown2105conne
unknown2403aeglogue, make
unknown24conne

[recognition, figuratively]

bay820muse
bay934honor
bays2481muse
garland2447flower
garland2480dance, sing
garland2677flower
garland566blossom, flower
garlands1367gift/ve, shade
garlands2244muse
garlands449shepherd, flower,
    daughter
gift2172commended
gifts165conne, learn
gifts2270music, wit

gifts2431complain(t)
gifts2568fame, poet, wit
gifts334verse
give1367shade
given590god
gives307love, lass
giveth1053god
giveth1902love
mazer1891feign
prize2189praise
kissed26fame
titles117show
titles3learn
titles2worth
unkissed17fame, poet, conne
unkissed24conne

[herd animal (figuratively, *materielle*
of pastoral 'making')]

bullock98feed
cosset2430gift/ve, rhyme
cosset2533lamb
dewlap423lass
ewed545lamb
ewe646show, head
ewes427lose
flock's427lose
flock1017blossom
flock1347lose, wolf
flock1386fame, rhyme, wit, feed
flock1518sheep, shepherd, feed
flock1556lass, love
flock1748lamb
flock1768feed
flock1934lead[vb]
flock2046eye
flock2134commended
flock269tree, winter
flock274lead[vb]
flock2775sheep
flock279complain(t), sheep, feed,
    lead[vb]
flock393winter
flock425conne, lust
flock641home
flock8shepherd, sing, swain, feed

flocking2186feed
flocking2639pipe
flocks1038feed, sheep
flocks1403feed, shepherd
flocks1411home
flocks1523feed, shepherd
flocks1555shepherd
flocks1563love, feed
flocks1576boy
flocks1639feed, shepherd
flocks2032god, shepherd
flocks2212feed
flocks2323aeglogue, feed
flocks2441shepherd, waste
flocks2474verse, head
flocks2619lamb, save
goats2248pipe
herd1599wander
kid1109conne
kid1114head, shoot
kid1129break
kid1164love
kid1171call
kid1551sheep
kid2043lamb, waste, wood
kids305gift/ve
kidden2664conne
kiddy1147hear
lamb1744wolf
lamb1748flock
lamb2036wolf
lamb2043waste, wood
lamb818goddess
lambkins2619flock
lambs2699love, sheep, wood
lambs428lust
lambs771break, wolf
prey2042wolf, sheep, lamb
ram544flock
sheep's2047wolf
sheep1038feed, flock
sheep1083shepherd
sheep1250feed
sheep1518flock, shepherd
sheep1736love
sheep1945shepherd, waste
sheep1975lead[vb]

sheep2009shepherd
sheep2038sheep, sleep
sheep2040break, sleep, wolf
sheep2393feed
sheep2477wolf
sheep2656save, make
sheep2663sleep, work
sheep2699lamb, love, wood
sheep2761aeglogue, complain(t)
sheep276shepherd
sheep2774feed, flock
sheep279complain(t), flock, feed,
    lead[vb]
sheep2942wolf
sheep316boy, head, home
weanell2043lamb, wood, waste
weanell2152waste

[consumer/sanctioner of artistic/
prophetic expression]

fauns1644feign, poet, god, wood
god's115feed
god[2]2641shepherd
god1074shepherd
god1197shepherd
god1388complain(t)
god1477poet
god1516learn
god1689shepherd
god2032shepherd
god20aeglogue, shepherd, worth
god2618shepherd
god282love, shepherd
god303love
god590gift/ve
god618love, poet
god655hear
god677love
god800grace/pers., shepherd
god906shepherd
god910shepherd
god968tree
gods1495complain(t)
gods1644feign, poet, wood
gods2494verse
gods2506honor

gods2589feign
gods279feed, love
gods876eye, lose
gods898reed
gods902poems, shepherd
iddio/god/515emblem
sylvans1644feign, poet, god, wood

[hearing/consumption of 'making']

ear1207gift/ve
ear2213sing, war, dread
ears42poet, sing
ears1445dread
hear1370rhyme hear1846shepherd
hear1852sing
hear1870sleep
hear1877break, sleep
hear2211oaten
hear2214verse
hear2622oaten, reed, shepherd
hear584conne, verse
heard1381shepherd
heardest1758sing, swain
hearken2623feed
heedless72head
heedless72wit
heedless2626lust
listened510worth
listeneth1854pipe
listening656hear

[nourishment—figuratively, for
product of 'making' as consumed)]

ambrosia[2]2509god
ambrosia2505god
ambrosia2589feign
banquets2550shepherd
cakes2457shepherd
cakes2550shepherd
cracknelles306gift/ve
cracknelles2457shepherd
crusts1572sheep
cups2374verse
damsons993gift/ve
drink2509god

drink2589feign
drinks2505god
drunk2523poet
fasting1578flock
fat1583shepherd
fed1393sheep
fed2638shepherd, swain
fed279complain(t), flock, sheep,
    lead[vb]
fed3flock
fed9honor
feed115god
feed1386wit
feed2323aeglogue
feeds2197eye
feed1251sheep
feed1386fame, flock, rhyme
feed1403flock, shepherd
feed1523flock, shepherd
feed1564flock, love
feed1639flock, shepherd
feed1768flock
feed2186flock
feed2212flock, reed
feed2323flock
feed2774shepherd, sheep
feeding1250sheep
feeding1517flock
food2509god
food2475head, flock
food2589feign
food1782sheep
food2475flock
fostered1669shepherd
fruit [cf. also under "vegetal
    excrescences" for fruit, apple,
    berries, corn, damsons, grain,
    nuts, queenapples, walnut]
glutted2036lamb
grain2198praise
graze789flock
harvest2667waste
harvest2673waste
honey[2]678love, emblem
honey1076flock
honey2650wood
hungry98feed

leany1578flock
nectar2505god
nectar2509god
nectar2589feign

[respected chaste female]

bellibone978maid
beloved1635feign, poet, shepherd
beloved906shepherd, god
bonibell978maid
bonilass978maid
damsel899reed
damsel2389head, lust
darling872goddess, poet
daughter2428shepherd, maid
daughters937grace/pers.
daughters1380conne, muse, skill,
    scorn
daughters2448make, shepherd, sing
daughters449flower, shepherd
daughters829shepherd
daughters887muse, poet
DEA1004poet
*dea*2744poet
dea[goddess]848emblem
goddess1495complain(t)
goddess689flower
goddess693flower
goddess696honor
goddess789fame
goddess818shepherd, swain, lamb
goddess872poet, worth
goddess954spring
goddesses939feign, poet
grace/2/824gift/ve, dance
grace/her/800spring, god
grace48verse
graces1356conne
graces1456eye
graces1458poet, eye, dance
graces822hear
graces937daughter
harlot689fame, flower, goddess
idol873worth, poet
ladies895learn, muse
lady1030flock

lady2562poet
lady824gift/ve, dance, grace/pers.
lass's416praise
lass1336love
lass1556love
lass2411love
lass266love
lass307gift/ve, love
lass352love, play
lass772love
lass776love, scorn
may[as'maid']2428shepherd,
    daughter
maid1026dance, play
maiden456waste
maiden-queen802head
maiden2401aeglogue
maiden455lust
mistress354love
muse's2426sing
muse2408sing
muse2417praise
muse2436conne
muse2464flower
muse2484verse
muse2535honor, poet
muse2635shepherd
muse2692pipe
muse313break, oaten, pipe
muse973learn
muses'1515conne
muses'2424tree
muses118conne, show, skill
muses1375oaten, pipe
muses1380conne, skill, daughter
muses1460dance, music
muses1515skill
muses2238head
muses2523poet
muses887daughter, poet
muses891spring
muses893spring
muses895learn
muses925honor, poems
nymphs1356grace/pers., conne
nymphs1459grace/pers., dance
nymphs2480sing, verse, dance

nymphs2639flock, muse
paragon359fame
paragon2299eye
paramour2299eye
princess829war, shepherd
princess922daughter
queen's885hear
queen1029home
queen2404sing, make
queen456waste, lust, maid
queen760praise
queen792shepherd
queen802maid
sorceress2743fame
virgins887daughter, poet, muse
virgins798sing
virgo/virgin/847emblem

[injuring/penetrating]

abuse689fame
abuses1926sheep
bane303god, love
beat477spring
beaten445waste
beating1959tree
bewitched1972wit
bewray1869tune
blast2694winter
blast624winter
blasts381winter
blasts600dread, god
blinded994poems
blindness577tree
brained1700poet
bruised1590break
burn2294poet
burned2685spring
burnt1156sheep
condemn72head, wit
confound1378shepherd
confounded1378show
cure2655wound
cureless1813love
cured2007feign
destroying2340poet
devoured1083sheep, wolf

gall1936love
gall678love
greete1904complain(t)
greete850complain(t)
hurt646show
hurtless2641god
lop413lose
marred1729dance, learn, music
marred286mantle, winter
mischief2012call
mischief2052god
mischief2619save
misusage1571lead/vb/
mord/biting/2513emblem
offended876god
poisoned736feign, shoot
pinching780love
plunged776love, lass
quell626spring
rankling2655wound, conne
ravenous2013wolf
requite2080god
rob1951shepherd
robbed270break, pipe
robbing476shade
safe1872home, waste
safely1393feed
safely2477wolf, wander
safety1704praise
save1745shepherd[contrary]
save2619flock
save2657sheep, frame
save1519wolf
save1745swain
slay986daughter
slew2300music
slew1824eye
slew2300eye
spared2183muse
spill1524shepherd
spill1769shepherd
spill2677flower
spill410spring
starved1966lust
starved428lamb, lust
stealing1411home, flock
stealing1411flock

stole1673lust
strike2470verse
stroke972spring, war
stroke1129break
stroke2289music
stroke2470verse
stroke2633tree
stroke490waste, wound
thieves715god, wood
tormenteth751love
treachery1401lass
unbruised2203muse
unwounded2303war, wound
vengeance600dread, god
vengeance876lose, eye, god
waste1872home
waste2043lamb, wood
waste2441flock, shepherd
waste2630winter
waste490wound
wasted1945sheep, shepherd
wasted2508sing, verse
wasted283winter
wasted294blossom
wasteful1855complain(t), wood
wasteful2627dread, wolf, wood
wasteful273boy, winter
wound2665conne
wounded744love, boy
wounded783boy, shepherd, love
wounding738love, lust
woundless2303war
wounds478flower, honor
wounds490waste
ytost1347wolf

[selected 'injuring' with sememe of 'rending']

break707love
break1877sleep, hear
break2040sheep, shepherd, sleep, wolf
break2445pipe, verse
breaketh270pipe
broke771lamb, wolf
broke313oaten, muse, pipe

broke778pipe
carve1953swain, shepherd
cut/off584verse, conne, hear
cut2575verse
gashes574wound
hew2389head
lop413lose
mord/biting/2513emblem
rent2182oaten, reed
rent297flock
scathe2746lose
tear[rip]1519wolf, save
tear[rip]776scorn, shepherd
yrent2013wolf
yshend1846shepherd
ytorn771wolf, break, lamb

[selected 'injuring,' with sememe of 'piercing']

arrow736feign, shoot
biteth2595emblem
bolt/arrow/655god
dart406shoot
dart784gift/ve
point1399love
pierce1399love
prick1483worth
shaft666play
shoot1998head
shoot2220poems, feign
shooting2486learn
shooting652play, wander
shot659spring, swain
shot682boy, tree
shot736feign
sting2626lust

[having(possessing)— modalizations]:

pouvoir modalization—
being-able-to-have, being-able-not-to-have, not-being-able-to-have:

cote/2/1953swain, shepherd, sheep [figuratively]

cotes2656save, frame, learn
cotes2724shepherd
　　[sheepcote2054shepherd, call
　　sheepcotes2724shepherd
　　sheepfold884shepherd, boy]
forlorn308lose
forlorn772love, lass
forsake1423feign
forsaken723love
forsaking1481love
hold1067god
keep1072sheep
keep1083sheep, shepherd
keep1108flock
keep1551sheep
keep1662flock
keep1966lust
keep2619flock
keeps775flock
keeping1661sheep
keeping2760love, sheep
keeps579shepherd
kept1673lust
kept99conne
lack1371sing
lack1581lose
leave/off2004lose
leave1081learn
leave1782sheep
leave2195music
leave224learn
leave2691boy
leave652play
leaves[vb]1970lose
left behind1052lose
left1234lose
left1556lass, love
left2104lose
left2211oaten, reed
left2642lose, love
lorne2642love
loss1368love
lost290shade, tree
lost420love
lost876god
lost901love
lost1347wolf, flock, dread

miss2486learn
miss[lack]2506god
miss2486shoot
need1967home
needeth489tree
paradise1347lose
paradise1638shepherd
paradise2585poet
shed1397wood, tree
sheddeth2198praise
takest/keep2619lamb
want111rhyme
want1861love, sleep
wanted2566learn
wants[lacks]1343work
wants823dance

[virtuality of losing]

afraid666play
beware682tree
beware1112wit
beware1318gift/ve
danger2501shepherd
danger2626lust
dangerous1009show
dread1347wolf, flock, lose
dread2213war, sing
dread2324war, sing
dread2627waste, wolf
dread2216poet, verse, play
dreaded2489verse
fear1704praise
fear598god
fear610god
fear989shepherd
feared1073shepherd
fear1837eye
fear2626lust
fear405winter
quake2214verse
security1078shepherd
spaventa[frightens]515emblem
warn1318gift/ve

vouloir modalization of 'having'—
wanting-to-have, wanting-not-to-
have:

chase1356grace/pers.
chase2477wolf
cherish1060god
coveting50study
coveting962love
covetise1976sheep
craveth1870sleep
curse1962lose
derision2355–56wit
despite316sheep, boy, home
despising594boy
disdain1158swain
disdain305gift/ve
disdain2460verse
disdained723love
disdaining584verse, hear, conne
enamored1336love, lass
enamored266love, lass
gained1839lamb
hateth151work
hateth309scorn, music, shepherd
loathe2235love, eye
loathsome756flower
longing1086love
love's2409sing
love's2649lead[vb]
love's707break
love(s ed)776lass
love[2]307gift/ve, lass
love[as lady]1902gift/ve
love1336lass
love1365conne, pipe, sing, tune
love1368lose
love1390head, shepherd
love1406shepherd
love1556lass
love1627shade
love1830learn
love1861eye, sleep
love1900make, praise, sing
love1902praise
love207commended
love2208lead[vb], lust, sing
love2235eye, poet
love2277play, scorn
love2370play
love2413play

love2419poet, praise
love2617learn, make
love265complain(t)
love2713lust
love279feed
love280god
love282god, shepherd
love29complain(t)
love304complain(t), god
love340learn
love346lust
love351verse, play, lass
love415learn
love420lose
love438make
love616spring
love618poet, scorn, god
love632dance, sleep, lust, lead[vb]
love677god
love703sleep
love707break
love738wound
love746shepherd
love748emblem
love776scorn
love782skill, shepherd, boy
love901make, pipe, lose
loved1564feed, flock
loved2216verse
loved2411honor
loved2699lamb, sheep
loved763complain(t), boy
loved772eye, lass
loved776scorn
lover's1736sheep
lover2555shepherd
lovers'[2]280god
loveth2205worth
lust1086love
lust1115spring, blossom
lust1279blossom
lust1508shepherd
lust1557shepherd
lust2190honor
lust2713love
lust346love
lustful1280shoot

lustful738love, wound
lustful757wit
lustihedde2208lead[vb], love, sing
lustless425conne, flock
lustless428lamb
lusty455maid
lusty633love, sleep
mislike1100scorn
passion2611love
passion366love
pursue1349god
pursued897love
scorn107rhyme
scorn1381hear, shepherd
scorn2458swain, call, home,
    shepherd
scorn309music, shepherd
scorn403pipe

scorn410spring, skill
scorn776lass, love
scorned372boy
scorned619love
scornfully631learn
scorning2277play, love
scorning583make, rhyme
seek115god
seek2650wood
seek304love
spite2489dread
spite273boy, waste, winter,
    shepherd
spite1400worth
spite2677flower
spite480flower, work
unlustiness372scorn

Appendix 2, Part IV:

Selected Lexeme Co-occurrence Patterns (from Part III, above)—the most frequent co-occurrences for certain lexemes

With the lexemes:

Word Co-occurrences:

the set "dance, heydeguys,
    hornpipe, millers round,
    tripping"

grace (demi-goddess)3
lead [vb] 3
pipe 3
maid 2
music 2
play 2
shepherd 2
sing 2

the set "daughter, goddess/*dea*,
    grace, lass, maid/may, muse"

poet 14
shepherd 11
love 11
dance 7
can/conne 7
sing 6
flower 5
skill 4
spring 4

"poet"
feign 10
god 7
fame 6
honor 5
worth 5
goddess 4
make 4

"feign"
poet 11
god 3
shoot 2

"can/conne" (conning, couth,
etc.)
skill 4
muse 3
pipe 3
shepherd 3

"skill"
show 4
muse 3

Notes

Chapter 1. Introduction

1. See chapter 2 for fuller explanation of the square, and for its definition A.-J. Greimas and Joseph Courtés, *Semiotics and Language: An Analytical Dictionary*, trans. Larry Crist, Daniel Patte, et al. (Bloomington: Indiana University Press, 1982); from *Sémiotique: Dictionnaire raisonné de la théorie du langage* (Paris: Hachette-Classiques, 1979). Roughly speaking, contradiction means the presence vs. the absence of some term, while contrariety means the term vs. itself in another form, namely its forceful obverse. To illustrate loosely, the contrary of love is hate, while its contradictory is indifference. Thus one can write the semantic category of love as

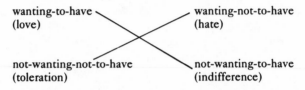

    wanting-to-have   wanting-not-to-have
    (love)   (hate)

    not-wanting-not-to-have   not-wanting-to-have
    (toleration)   (indifference)

2. In terms of neo-Marxism Jameson, after long wrestling and through a concept of different "horizons" of study, takes an Althusserian view of the relative autonomy of social-structural levels (the economic, the cultural, the political), though still insisting on the economic or modes of production as the "ultimate ground" and "untranscendable limit" of theorizing (100–102).

3. Erotic or quasi-erotic desire, in these concepts, is viewed not as the will to get something lacked but as an energy produced by, so to speak, interactive psychic and social moving parts, analogous to the capacity for desire produced in a child by the machinic coupling of baby's mouth and breast or bottle, which can continue or break the flow of milk.

4. See Jameson's enthusiastic "Foreword" to a well chosen set of Greimas's writings, *On Meaning: Selected Writings in Semiotic Theory*, ed. and trans. Paul J. Perron and Frank H. Collins (Minneapolis: University of Minnesota Press, 1987). Jameson's book is *The Political Unconscious. Narrative as a Socially Symbolic Act* (Ithaca: Cornell University Press, 1981).

5. See A.-J. Greimas and Joseph Courtés, *Dictionary*, I. Volume 2 has now appeared: Group de Recherches Semio-Linguistiques, A.-J. Greimas, ed. *Sémiotique: Dictionnaire raisonné de la théorie du langage, Tome 2: Compléments, débats, propositions* (Paris: Hachette-Classiques, 1986); for an American study of Greimas see Ronald Schleifer, *A.-J. Greimas and the Nature of Meaning: Linguistics, Semiotics and Discourse Theory* (London: Croom Helm, 1987).

6. Such values can be modal, like competence to do something, or pragmatic, such as a desired material object. My former student Swift Dickison once vividly described the Greimassian narrative program formula as a kind of "grabbology." In

the perspective of applying it here to the ideologeme, Deleuzean "partial objects"—such as baby's mouth and mother's breast, which each alternatingly facilitate and break the other's flow, producing desire—are considered correlatable with certain factors (namely the two subject positions) in the Greimassian "base narrative program," viewed as representing an aggressional discoursive motion that potentially generates aggressional reader response.

7. My own perspective is not Marxist, neither in the older sense of teleologically oriented commitment to a classless society nor in Jameson's sense of Marxism as an approach that claims "radically historicizing" study of class conflict to be the "ultimate critical operation, that which subsumes all others."

8. An earlier book by the feminist theorist cited below is Teresa de Lauretis, *Alice Doesn't: Feminism, Semiotics, Cinema* (Bloomington: Indiana University Press, 1982). Among other topics, she reviews narrativity theories of Jurij Lotman and Umberto Eco, with the overriding intent of asking "in what ways does narrative work to engender the subject in the movement of its discourse," and thus further, "how can we think of women outside of the man/non-man dichotomy, the 'sexual difference' on which all discourse is based?" (10). Whether all discourse is based on sexual difference is not an issue I can treat here, but part of my argument will be the suggestion that all ideologemes, at any rate, include it, not as man vs. non-man but as culturally constructed maleness vs. femaleness, a binary classematic opposition.

9. See Julia Kristeva, *Desire in Language: A Semiotic Approach to Literature and Art*, trans. Leon S. Roudiez, et al. (New York: Columbia University Press, 1980).

10. See, for example, Silvia Albertazzi, "'Shut In, Shut Off': Ruth Prawer Jhabvala's 'Mythology of Captivity'," *CE&S* 8 (1985): 45–55; and Jules Zanger, "Living on the Edge: Indian Captivity Narrative and Fairy Tale," *Cliol* 13 (1984): 123–32.

11. See, for example, Louis Waldman, "Spenser's Pseudonym 'E. K.' and Humanist Self-Naming," *Spenser Studies* 9 (1988—publ. 1991): 21–31, who offers the good suggestion that the initials are for Edmundus Kedemon, a hellenization of Spenser's name in its meaning of "steward." S. K. Heninger, Jr. ("Spenser and Sidney at Leicester House," *Spenser Studies* 8 [1987; publ. 1990]: 239–49) asserts that Gabriel Harvey was "E. K.," a point addressed in my own article's view that Harvey did parts of the apparatus, and the rest is Spenser addressing Harvey in various voices, including those of banter and of respectable scholarliness. L. Staley Johnson, in *"The Shepheardes Calender": An Introduction* (University Park: Pennsylvania State University Press, 1990), 7, likewise suggests that E. K. was Harvey. A discussion of these issues similar to parts of my 1990 article is Richard Rambuss, *Spenser's Secret Career* (Cambridge: Cambridge University Press, 1993), 50–56.

12. On other models and projects in discourse analysis, including socio-political discourse analysis, see Teun A. van Dijk, ed., *Handbook of Discourse Analysis* (London: Academic Press, 1985), 4 vols.

13. See Teresa de Lauretis, *Technologies of Gender. Essays on Theory, Film, and Fiction* (Bloomington: Indiana University Press, 1987), 112.

14. Ibid., 10.

15. Mary Jacobus, *Reading Woman: Essays in Feminist Criticism* (New York: Columbia University Press, 1986), 288.

16. Stephen Greenblatt, *Renaissance Self-Fashioning from More to Shakespeare* (Chicago: University of Chicago Press, 1980), 4.

17. Ibid., 8.

18. Ibid., 6.

19. Jameson sees Marxism, in the sense of radical historicizing and economic

contextualizing of all mental operations, as the most inclusive, the umbrella method-
ology (see the opening of chapter 4 below), while semiotics he says is an array of
locally useful concepts that one can "steal" or "bricolate" for particular purposes of
societally focused analysis. See his "Foreword" to the Greimas selections in *On
Meaning: Selected Writings in Semiotic Theory*, viii.

20. Richard Halpern, *The Poetics of Primitive Accumulation: English Renaissance Culture and the Genealogy of Capital* (London & Ithaca: Cornell University Press, 1991),
8–12.

21. They apparently have not yet been found to offer support for such a claim.
The passage from Fallopius alleged to indicate positive attitudes to male masturbation recommends a therapy for young boys (*aetatis infantilis*) who are not in very
robust health or with small penises, to help promote later reproductive potency: the
doctor, with nurse assistants and the child's parents attending, should stimulate the
organ and, using warm towels to help reduce the child's discomfort, keep it aroused
for a brief period. Such a recommendation, while interesting for study of the history
of sexuality and early modern family life, hardly constitutes a blanket sanctioning
of masturbation. See the chapter "Removing Seed" in Winfried Schleiner's study,
Medical Ethics in the Renaissance, forthcoming, Georgetown University Press.

22. Jonathan Culler has advocated this view in several books (see Bibliography).

23. More precisely, Kristeva spells out these last two items as follows: "[they]
revise back in the direction of] the logico-symbolic processes that function in the
predicative synthesis toward establishing the language system, . . . [and of] 'operations' establishing *functions* between the signifying code and the fragmented body
of the speaking subject as well as . . . his partners." See Julia Kristeva, "The System
and the Speaking Subject" (1973), reprinted in *The Kristeva Reader*, ed. Toril Moi
(New York: Columbia University Press, 1986), 28–29.

24. See, for example, Marc Eli Blanchard, *Description: Sign, Self, Desire. Critical
Theory in the Wake of Semiotics* (The Hague: Mouton, 1980); and also Claes Schaar,
The full voic'd quire below: Vertical Context Systems in Paradise Lost (Lund: CWK
Gleerup, 1982).

25. See *On Meaning: Selected Writings in Semiotic Theory*, 140–42, or *Du Sens, II*
(1983), 93ff.

26. See, for example, his essay "De la colère" from *Du Sens, II:* in English titled
"On Anger," in *On Meaning*, 148–64.

27. See Eco, *Semiotics and the Philosophy of Language* (London: Macmillan, 1984),
ch. 4.

28. Keir Elam described this project at a Folger Shakespeare Library Workshop,
"Words Made Flesh: Language, the Body, and the Passions in Shakespeare," Oct.
6–7, 1989. His earlier books are *The Semiotics of Theatre and Drama* (London: Methuen, 1980), and *Shakespeare's Universe of Discourse: Language-games in the Comedies*
(Cambridge: Cambridge University Press, 1984).

29. Umberto Eco, *Semiotics and the Philosophy of Language* (London: Macmillan,
1984), 4ff.

30. For my Kristevan studies of Shakespeare and Milton in this light see Louise
Schleiner, "Latinized Greek Drama in Shakespeare's writing of *Hamlet*," *SQ* 41
(1990): 29–48; and "Pastoral Male Friendship and Edenic Marriage: Textual Systems
Transposed," *Lit* 2 (1990): 41–58.

31. Concerning H. R. Jauss's reception aesthetics I would note a qualification
of principle: I do not see the possibility of an empirically grounded structuralist
hermeneutic in his terms—indeed, with Stanley Fish, I see reason to think such a

hermeneutic or poetics will not prove possible; thus, if we speak of a reader-group's "horizon of expectations" for a given kind of text, we must bear in mind that concept's problematic nature. For example, Fish would vigorously protest the structuralism of Jauss's view that a definedly fixed genre could be part of a reading community's 'horizon of expectations'; he points out that individual readers' value-installation will in part determine their concept of even, say, the genre applicable to a particular work, which genre could not, then, be objectified, as part of a group-competence model (see Fish "Resistance and Independence," 120).

32. Fredric Jameson in *The Political Unconscious* deals most effectively with this objection—see the epigraph quote at the beginning of my chapter 5.

33. Umberto Eco, Lecture Series for Clare College, Cambridge University, April 1990.

34. Thoroughly collaborative research is now the stage of things within Greimas's own project: the new volume of the semiotic dictionary, *Semiotique: Dictionnaire raisonné de la théorie du langage*, Tome II (1986), has been written almost entirely by his co-workers and former students of the Groupe de Recherches Semio-linguistiques, and various debates are shown in progress.

35. Jonathan Goldberg, *Endlesse Worke: Spenser and the Structures of Discourse* (Baltimore: Johns Hopkins University Press, 1981).

36. For the English translation of this chapter see "Knowing and Believing: a Single Cognitive Universe," *On Meaning*, 166ff.

37. By reader-response approaches I am referring to hermeneutics of various sorts, whether study of the literary text as a "writerly" one with multiple significances that readers inscribe in their readings (see Roland Barthes, *Writing Degree Zero*, trans. Annette Lavers and Colin Smith [New York: Hill & Wang, 1968], and *S/Z*, trans. Richard Miller [New York: Hill & Wang, 1974]); texts as "self-consuming artifacts" provoking readers' engagement, and the concept of "interpretive communities" determining meanings of texts (see Stanley Fish, *Self-Consuming Artifacts: The Experience of Seventeenth-Century Poetry* [Berkeley: University of California Press, 1972], and *Is There a Text in this Class? The Authority of Interpretive Communities* [Cambridge: Harvard University Press, 1980]); self-investment in reading to create literary experience (see Hans Georg Gadamer, *Truth and Method*, trans. Garrett Barden and John Cumming [New York: Seabury, 1975]); or reception aesthetics with its concept of readers' changing "horizons of expectations" (see Hans Robert Jauss, *Towards an Aesthetics of Reception*, trans. Timothy Bahti [Minneapolis: University of Minnesota Press, 1982]).

38. Fish, *Is There a Text in this Class*, 170.

39. Wolfgang Iser, *Spenser's Arcadia: The Interrelation of Fiction and History* (Berkeley: Center for Hermeneutical Studies, 1980).

40. For some accounts of these much discussed matters, see Elizabeth Jenkins, *Elizabeth the Great* (London: Victor Gollancz, 1958); Conyers Read, *Lord Burghley and Queen Elizabeth* (London: J. Cape, 1960), and his *Mr. Secretary Cecil and Queen Elizabeth* (New York: Knopf, 1955); Neville Williams, *Thomas Howard Fourth Duke of Norfolk* (London: Barrie and Rockliff, 1964); Marie Axton, *The Queen's Two Bodies: Drama and the Elizabethan Succession* (London: Royal Historical Society, 1977); and Mack P. Holt, *The Duke of Anjou and the Politique Struggle during the Wars of Religion* (Cambridge: Cambridge University Press, 1986).

41. Bruce R. Smith, "On Reading *The Shepheardes Calender*," *Spenser Studies: a Renaissance Poetry Annual* 1 (1980): 89.

42. See Patrick Cullen, *Spenser, Marvell, and Renaissance Pastoral* (Cambridge: Harvard University Press, 1970) on the bi-partite pastoral tradition Spenser knew (otiose and Mantuanesque); Louis Adrian Montrose's insights about Rosalind, Eliza,

and Dido as "Petrarchan lady" figures who unite the love eclogues around the theme of redirection of erotic into artistic power (see "'The perfecte paterne of a Poete': the Poetics of Courtship in The Shepheardes Calender," *TSLL* 21 [1979]: 34–67; "'Eliza, Queene of shepheardes,' and the Pastoral of Power," *ELR* 10 [1980]: 153–82; and "Interpreting Spenser's February Eclogue: Some Contexts and Implications," *Spenser Studies: A Renaissance Poetry Annual* 2 [1981]: 67–74); David Norbrook's balanced and informed account of the *Calender*'s political context (*Poetry and Politics in the English Renaissance* [London: Routledge, 1984]); and Anthea Hume's carefully oriented statement of the *Calender*'s place in the religio-political spectrum of its milieu, in *Edmund Spenser: Protestant Poet* (Cambridge: Cambridge University Press, 1984). Other recent works on the *Calender* are John D. Bernard, *Ceremonies of Innocence: Pastoralism in the Poetry of Edmund Spenser* (Cambridge: Cambridge University Press, 1989); and David R. Shore, *Spenser and the Poetics of Pastoral: A Study of the World of Colin Clout* (Montreal: McGill-Queen's University Press, 1985).

43. Paul E. McLane, *Spenser's Shepheardes Calender: A Study in Elizabethan Allegory* (Notre Dame, Ind.: Notre Dame University Press, 1961), 27–33.

44. Richard Mallette, *Spenser, Milton, and Renaissance Pastoral* (Lewisburg, Pa.: Bucknell University Press, 1981), 63.

45. "April" and "October" are the swing pieces here, prominent in both patterns, and as constant anthology choices they have been the highlights of the *Calender* for non-specialist modern readers.

46. I would qualify Roland Greene's view (*The Shepheardes Calender*, Dialogue, and Periphrasis," *Spenser Studies* 8 [1987; publ. 1990]: 31 n.8) that the tripartite E. K. scheme, because it is only "an element of the text supposedly under critical scrutiny," should therefore not be an important part of critics' analysis. The E. K. apparatus displays, among other things, Spenser and Harvey themselves playing editorial interpretive annotators on the eclogues, singly and as a group. The schemes thus presented are not at the diegetic level of something spoken by a petulant Cuddie or enraptured Piers: they are paratextual—designed as part of a vestibule (*seuil*, in Gerard Genette's term) between the centered text and its desired potential readerships, including us. There is no reason to discount their measure of explanatory power, though indeed one would not want (as Greene warns against) to let them "control the reading of the whole."

47. As Shore notes, the comment appears, for instance, in Peter Bayley, *Edmund Spenser: Prince of Poets* (London: Hutchinson, 1971), 33; and see Bruce R. Smith, "On Reading," 77.

48. For a brief use of the concept of actantial functions in relation to drama (referring to Propp, Souriau, and Greimas), see Keir Elam, *The Semiotics of Theatre and Drama* 126–31. It should be noted, though, that since the time of this reference by Elam, Greimas has made a quite basic change in his system of actants, now proposing only four actants (subject-object, sender-receiver) rather than six: what he formerly called the helper-opponent pair of actants he now regards as the actorialization of the pouvoir modality (being-able-to-do/ not-being-able-to-do).

49. See, for example, Sir Philip Sidney, *An Apology for Poetry*, ed. Forrest G. Robinson (Indianapolis: Bobbs-Merrill, 1970), especially 17–38.

50. In A. C. Hamilton, "The Argument of Spenser's Shepherdes Calender," *ELH* 23 (1956): 171–83; republished in Harry Berger, Jr., ed. *Spenser: A Collection of Critical Essays* (Englewood Cliffs, N.J.: Prentice-Hall, 1968), 30–39 (see especially 36).

51. Bruce Thornton, "Rural Dialectic: Pastoral, Georgic, and *The Shepheardes Calender*," *Spenser Studies* 9 (1988): 1–20, makes a good case that we should use a broader

term such as "bucolic," since so-called pastoral regularly involves a dialectic of georgic and properly pastoral modes, respectively emphasizing painful labor and *otium*. But I have stuck to conventional usage of "pastoral" as an umbrella term.

52. Hamilton, "Argument," 33.

53. Cullen, *Spenser, Marvell,* 80, 98, 108, 121–26.

54. Joseph A. Wittreich, Jr., *Visionary Poetics: Milton's Tradition and His Legacy* (San Marino, Calif.: Huntington Library, 1979), 106.

55. Roland Greene, 28–29.

56. Wittreich, *Visionary Poetics,* 108.

57. Donald Cheney in "The Circular Argument of *The Shepheardes Calender,*" in *Unfolded Tales: Essays on Renaissance Romance* (Ithaca: Cornell University Press, 1989), 139, 148–52) also sees Colin's "December" 'death' as one of dying into winter only until spring comes; he is studying Spenser's combination of pastoral and calendric genres. My own emphasis in treating this seasonal 'death' will be on its political and personal reference for Spenser.

58. The point generally accords with Jonathan Goldberg's insight ("Colin to Hobbinol: Spenser's Familiar Letters," in *Displacing Homophobia: Gay Male Perspectives in Literature and Culture,* ed. Ronald R. Butters, et al. [Durham, N.C.: Duke University Press, 1989], 119) that "as Colin moves beyond the pastoral world, Hobbinol stays behind, representing what must be refused in order to advance." But I argue that Spenser leaves Harvey behind not just after writing the *Calender,* but in and through the process of organizing and completing it in 1579.

59. D. M. Rosenberg, *Oaten Reeds and Trumpets: Pastoral and Epic in Virgil, Spenser, and Milton* (Lewisburg, Pa.: Bucknell University Press, 1981), treats all three, but in a classificatory manner.

60. Judith M. Kennedy, "The Final Emblem of The Shepheardes Calender," *Spenser Studies: A Renaissance Poetry Annual* 1 (1980): 95–106.

61. Louis Adrian Montrose, "'Eliza, Queene of shepheardes,' and the Pastoral of Power," *ELR* 10 (1980): 154; see also his "Of Gentlemen and Shepherds: The Politics of Elizabethan Pastoral Form," *ELH* 50 (1983): 415–59.

62. Roland Greene, "Calling Colin Clout," *Spenser Studies: A Renaissance Poetry Annual* 10 (1989): 229–44.

63. *Spenser: Poetical Works,* ed. J. C. Smith and E. De Selincourt (rpt. 1969; London: Oxford University Press, 1912), 416–18.

64. For valuable accounts of the ecclesiastical politics and agenda of the Leicester faction and of the bishops associated with them and praised (or dispraised) in the *Calender,* see David Norbrook, *op. cit.,* Anthea Hume, *Edmund Spenser, Protestant Poet,* and John N. King, *Spenser's Poetry and the Reformation Tradition* (Princeton: Princeton University Press, 1990), especially 17–46. I have not entered the debate on whether the Spenser of the *Calender* should be termed a "puritan"; for modern historians the term seems more commonly to refer to groups and positions arising some two decades later and persisting in the seventeenth century. I have preferred here to speak of the Leicestrian faction of the 1570s and early '80s as actively "reformist" since it was still pushing for Protestant changes in the state church, such as diminished prelatical wealth and power, and more homiletic independence and better education for clergy. The opponents to such reform I have termed conservative-prelatical. As King characterizes its affiliation, "The *Calender* reflects the academic taste that prevailed in a university setting [Cambridge, early 1570s] that produced the tightly knit group of committed Protestant reformers, including bishops, privy councilors, and members of Parliament, who attempted to implement

a religious settlement more radical than that desired by their cautious queen" (King, *Spenser's Poetry*, 31). On why the queen was "cautious," see above.

65. Jonathan Goldberg sees the queen, in "April" and "October," as presiding over an Orphic realm of death or Elisium, holding a defining "place" in these eclogues' "economy of death" (*Voice Terminal Echo: Postmodernism and English Renaissance Texts* [London: Methuen, 1986], 52–53). The point holds all the more for "November," but one must also look to its political dimensions of the threatened death of a cause.

66. See Bruce R. Smith, "On Reading," 79. In the 1611 edition, the apparatus even appears in larger print than the eclogues do.

67. Ruth Samson Luborsky, "The Allusive Presentation of *The Shepheardes Calender*" and "The Illustrations to the The Shepheardes Calender," *Spenser Studies: A Renaissance Poetry Annual* 1 & 2 (1980/1981), 29–67 and 3–53. See also Michael McCanles, "*The Shepheardes Calender* as Document and Monument" and Bruce R. Smith, "On Reading," especially 83–85, for generic analysis of the woodcuts.

68. See Richard Helgerson, *Self-Crowned Laureates: Spenser, Jonson, Milton and the Literary System* (Berkeley: University of California Press, 1983); and Rambuss, *Spenser's Secret Career*.

69. Greenblatt, *Renaissance Self-Fashioning*, 172–79.

70. Foster Provost, review of *Renaissance Self-Fashioning*, *Spenser Newsletter* 13 (1982): 13–14.

71. Queen Elizabeth's proposed French Catholic marital alliance (with d'Alençon), along with her rage at the Protestant party vigorously opposing it, has always been recognized as the central feature of the immediate political scene at the time of the *Calender's* publication. See the *Variorum*, and especially Paul E. McLane.

72. I suspect Spenser was influenced, in his generic innovations here, by Gascoigne's "Adventures of Master F. J." as an experiment in submerged narrative implied by poems, with prose apparatus—E. K. praises Gascoigne in a "November" gloss.

73. Cf. John Moore, "Colin Breaks his Pipe."

74. Cf. Helgerson, *Self-Crowned Laureates*, 69–70.

CHAPTER 2. THE GREIMAS MODEL AND THE *CALENDER'S* PERSPECTIVAL FRAMING

1. A.-J. Greimas and J. Courtés, *Semiotics and Language: An Analytical Dictionary*, trans. Larry Crist, Daniel Patte, et al. (Bloomington: Indiana University Press, 1982).

2. These include de Saussure, Propp, Lévi-Strauss, Jakobson, Hjelmslev, Tesnière, Benveniste, Chomsky, Genette, Dumézil, and Barthes.

3. The earlier *Dictionary* volume had said that "all categories, even the most abstract (including syntactic structures), are semantic in nature" (I:133); thus the category "logico-semantic" represents the unitary and deepest level of the generative trajectory. This makes semantics somehow more ultimate than syntax, since as Zilberberg notes, it makes syntax "a mere 'animation,' a putting in motion of the semantic." Zilberberg disagrees: he proposes that syntax should be seen as the prior term, and the category "logico-semantic" be replaced by the "thymico-semantic" (which interrelates syntax and semantics); calling the thymic "in a word, the price that thinking pays to living," ("d'un mot, le prix que le pensant acquitte au vivant"), he adds that his new category "signifies, in accord with the contemporary episteme, the

primacy of doing over being and, by corollary, of syntax over semantics" ("Signifie de plus, en accord avec l'épistéme contemporaine, le primat du *faire* sur l'*être* et corollairement de la syntaxe sur la sémantique")—*Sémiotique: dictionnaire raisonné de la théorie du langage,' II: Compléments, débats, propositions* (Paris: Hachettes-Classiques, 1986), 98. But the second half of Vol. II's entry *parcours génératif* (generative trajectory), by Daniel Patte, reasserts Greimas's original view (which had always accorded the thymic a certain semantic role, in sharpening, valorizing, or putting into play whatever oppositions exist at the deep level). Like Zilberberg, Patte expands and elaborates the importance of the thymic category at various levels and sub-layers of the trajectory, though in a pattern different from his, but Patte maintains the primacy of the semantic over (or we should say 'behind') the syntactic by arguing that syntax necessarily presupposes semantics, which is thus the primary instance (*"La syntaxe fondamentale,* en tant que structure syntaxique élémentaire virtuelle, appartient à l'instance *ab quo* du parcours génératif tout comme la sémantique fondamentale, bien qu'elle présuppose cette derniere" [Considered as a virtual elementary syntactic structure, fundamental syntax is part of the instance *ab quo* of the generative trajectory entirely in the same way as fundamental semantics is, even though the former presupposes the latter] *Dictionnaire,* II:101). This disagreement within Greimas's research group appears to be a new version of an old philosophical argument.

4. Patte is one of the translators of the English version of vol. I of the *Dictionary.*

5. The actant is not, as Jameson asserts (*Political Unconscious,* 122–23), merely another anthropomorphic substitute for the concept of a character: it can be actorialized by abstractions and metaphoric figures (as well as characters); it is a position or function within the syntax of the meta-sentence, the narrative program, that formularizes the structure of a given discourse. Greimas admits that because of the way language works, "as soon as we open our mouths to talk about functions, we substantify" (*Du Sens II: Essais Sémiotiques* [Paris: Seuil, 1983]), but to substantify is not necessarily to anthropomorphize.

6. For a version of level 2 divided into three subsidiary layers, see Daniel Patte, "Parcours génératif," B, *Dictionnaire* II: 103.

7. On the exception see nn. 8 and 9.

8. The Sender/Receiver pair (indicated in this instance by upper case letters) can also in one kind of circumstance constitute a pair of narrative actants, namely in "ethno-literary, philosophical, or juridical discourses" where a "transcendent Sender" offers "modal values" but without losing them itself (as would happen in an exchange). See the *Dictionary* entries "Sender-Receiver" and "participative communication."

9. There can be "cognitive subjects" or subjects of knowing, represented in a text as observer or informant, which one might consider actants of communication, though they do not seem to be so classified—rather as a separate third category. For the exception the other way, in which a Sender (with capital "S") becomes an actant of narration, see nn. 8 and 12 and the *Dictionary* entries under "actant," "subject-object," and "sender-receiver."

10. See A.-J. Greimas, *On Meaning: Selected Writings in Semiotic Theory,* ed. Paul J. Perron (Minneapolis: University of Minnesota Press, 1987), 102–4: "The universe of values, which is, in the strictest sense of the term, semantic, has thus [through the preceding theory of their discoursivization] been placed within the framework of those elementary syntactic structures that assure their being grasped and account for their narrativization." The essay there translated dates from 1973.

11. Zilberberg defines its fundamental category, tensivity, as the interface between time and space ("interface du temps et de l'espace," *Dictionnaire,* II:98).

12. Greimas himself has been offering some related explorations, e.g., in his chapter "De la colère" ["On Anger"] in *Du sens, II*. Let me try a redrawing of the chart "Generative Trajectory," as it would appear to have been supplemented and partly revised by Zilberberg's article. He does not redraw it himself, so I am hypothesizing. (See *Dictionnaire*, II:97–100.)

"Generative Trajectory": Zilberberg's Apparent Adaptation

		syntactic component	thymic component	semantic component
Semiotic and narrative structures	deep levels:	FUNDAMENTAL SYNTAX	TENSIVITY ASPECTUALITY	FUNDAMENTAL SEMANTICS
	surface levels:	SURFACE NARRATIVE SYNTAX	MODALITY	NARRATIVE SEMANTICS
Discoursive structures		DISCOURSIVE SYNTAX		DISCOURSIVE SEMANTICS
		Discoursivization actorialization temporalization spatialization	Pleasure-Satisfaction	Thematization Figurativization

13. As I noted in chapter 1 and will discuss again in chapter 5, it does so in a way that makes the Greimassian formula, when operative at the ideologeme level, commensurate with Deleuze and Guattari's idea of "partial objects" together functioning as "desiring machines"—i.e., the partial objects are equivalent to the formula's interacting Subjects.)

14. Greimas notes that this is a "horizontal" transformation rather than a "vertical" one (*Dictionary*, I:350), the latter being the name for the movement of a given term from deep to surface structure.

15. While "NP" in linguistics usually means "noun phrase," note that here it instead means "narrative program."

Chapter 3. *The Shepheardes Calender* Analyzed through the Greimas Model

1. Segmentation divides the text into surface units, each defined and held together by both syntactic and semantic demarcators, working in conjunction. (See appendix 1 for more detail.)

2. A fifth category of words is also excluded from the chosen list to be used for each successive new inventory selection, though these are included in the listings of words co-occurrent with each of the chosen ones, so that they may be observed and used as elements of co-occurrence patterns: namely, terms of the binary categories known as classemes, such as human/animal or living/nonliving. This is because one is out eventually to identify what are called kernel semes, upon which classemes are attendant (they will be shown thus in diagrams of the constructed sememes later).

3. The definition of "frequently occurring" cannot be numerically fixed, of course, discourses being of no fixed length. More is said on this point above and in appendix 1.

4. As I began the first extraction from the above list, I wondered if genre might be overdetermining diction, such that some of the high frequency words might not be isotopically significant (mere inevitable props on the generic stage, so to speak). So I began by inventorying the lower half of the high-frequency range, to see whether the highest-frequency words would appear (frequently) among the words co-occurring with subsequent groups. In fact, they all eventually did and were thus in turn inventoried, though a few from the lower half (of the intitial high-frequency range) proved not to be isotopic, i.e., did not recur in later inventory stages.

5. One will of course want computer help for these operations, which would otherwise be enormously painstaking.

6. This step is my own suggestion, not so far as I know proposed by Greimas.

7. A measure of disruptive subjectivity may be part of the process here, an issue to be worked on by future researchers, to see whether there may be ways to minimize it. Up to this point, it is highly unlikely that someone else following the procedures, with the same text, and understanding the concepts of the semiotic model, would come up with a list much different from mine. But might the seventy-odd words be sorted into categories much different from mine? It appears unlikely but not impossible.

8. The word 'god' also belongs here, as will be explained below.

9. The term means words that are not strictly synonymous but that share one or more kernel semes.

10. It must be borne in mind that the following semic/sememic inventories (unlike a complete semic analysis of a lexeme *per se*, such as of 'head' [*tête*] in Greimas' *Structural Semantics* [35ff.], as ultimately comprised of "extremity" + "superativity") are only partial analyses, semic and in part sememic descriptions of the components of the word's acceptation in the particular discourse.

11. The kind of classeme identified here is described under part "a" of the entry for "classeme" (Greimas and Courtés, *Semiotics and Language. An Analytical Dictionary*), and under the "categorization" entry, namely those classemes that "serve as a framework for the categorization of the world . . . in its overall perception by our senses" (26, 28).

12. The other two terms are fiction (non-being/non-seeming) and lie (seeming/ non-being); see appendix 1, section IV on "structuration."

13. A "narrative Sender" actant such as this is not part of the NP formula *per se*, but part of its installation in the discourse.

14. "Values" are of course not always modal, they may be "descriptive" (pots of gold, husbands, etc.); but 'competence for making' is the only one of any sort found in our list of isotopic sememes.

15. From the composite list of inventoried words, each with its line number and extraction base-word, I compiled sub-lists of parasynonym groupings (for example, all words carrying the sememe for {respected chaste female}); I then counted word co-occurrences to see what patterns of highly frequent co-occurrence emerged (see appendix 2, part IV).

16. See the entry "modality," *Dictionary*, 195, on the "tensional trajectory" of modalities, "virtualizing, actualizing, realizing."

17. *Dictionary*, 293–94. Sender and receiver are usually communication actants, which can however also have this special function as narrative actants. See chapter 2, nn. 8 and 12.

18.   I thee beseche (so be thou deigne to hear,
        Rude ditties tund to shepheards Oaten reede,
        Or if I euer sonet song so cleare,
        As it with pleasaunce mought thy fancie feede)
        Hearken awhile from thy greene cabinet,
        The rurall song of carefull Colinet.
                                        ("December," ll. 13–18)

19. In Stockinger's terms, this instrumental NP would be F (p-> ⁻p), or written out without the new abbreviations he has introduced, F [(S₂ ^ Oᵥ)-> (S₂ U Oᵥ)], "création de l'etat actualisé" (*Dictionnaire*, II, 179).

20. In Stockinger's terms, it would be F (-p-> p).

21. Greimas might call this allegorical fable an "annex NP" of the case just noted as the interactions of Cuddie, Thenot, Phyllis, and lack of approval (*Dictionary*, 246).

22. In Stockinger's terms, this one would be written as F (-p->⁻p), "maintien de l'etat actualisé."

Chapter 4. Isaiah: Excrescence as Expression and the Figurative Isotopy

1. This figurative dimension of the results is, in Greimas's theory, partly accounted for by his concept of "figurativization of a thematic role"; for an introduction to this concept see *On Meaning*, 116–19.

2. That is, each of the terms in the base narrative program instance that we derived at the end of the previous chapter (pastoral-prophetic maker, respected chaste female) is represented in the occurrent frequent-word groupings not only by several parasynonyms of the term itself, but also by several frequent-words metaphorically representing the formula-term. (See appendix 2.) These correlations represent the pattern described here.

3. Palinode in all probability evoked Gabriel Harvey's enemy Andrew Perne, vice-chancellor at Cambridge, who apparently changed his religious-politics for convenience, thus being dubbed Palinode by the undergraduates (see chapter 7, n. 13 for sources of these and further references). Morrell of "July" called to mind the high-church Bishop John Elmore or Aylmer, and the unfortunate Diggon Davie of "September" most probably Bishop Richard Davies of St. David's in Wales, who had allowed rich noblemen to plunder diocesan holdings before realizing what had been lost.

4. Cf. Edward Dering's sermon before the queen of February 1570, complaining about unworthy churchmen: "Some [are] blind guides and cannot see, some dumb dogs and will not bark," cited in M. M. Knappen, *Tudor Puritanism: A Chapter in the History of Idealism* (Chicago: University of Chicago Press, 1939), 223.

5. See Sir Philip Sidney, *The Old Arcadia*, ed. Katherine Duncan-Jones (Oxford: Oxford University Press, 1985), 94; and *The Poems of George Herbert*, ed. Helen Gardner (London: Oxford University Press, 1961), 72.

6. The suggestion of castration here is noted by Patrick Cullen, *Spenser, Marvell, and Renaissance Pastoral* (Cambridge: Harvard University Press, 1970), 33–39.

7. Ovid, *Metamorphoses*, bk. I, cited in E. K.'s "April" gloss. Elizabethans commonly read the translation by Arthur Golding of 1560.

8. For a more detailed analysis of this metaphoric construct and its source in Gabriel Harvey's work, see my article "Spenser's E. K. as Edmund Kent (Kenned/ of Kent)," *ELR* 20 (1990): 374–407.

9. Louis A. Montrose makes the same point in "The Elizabethan Subject and

the Spenserian Text," in *Literary Theory, Renaissance Texts*, ed. Patricia Parker and David Quint (Baltimore: Johns Hopkins University Press, 1986), 319–20.

10. On Marot and this pastoral imaging of God as dwelling in a "green cabinet" see Annabel Patterson, "Re-opening the Green Cabinet: Clement Marot and Edmund Spenser," *ELR* 16 (1986): 44–70.

11. In the Graeco-Roman metamorphosis concept, trees that were formerly human beings may bleed and suffer pain. Ovidian tales (as well as their Virgilian and Dantesque analogues) like that of Myrrha, the incestuous daughter who became a tree, or of Baucis and Philemon, the couple who became intertwined leafy shade trees at death, thus expressing their life-long love, are also relevant to Spenser's metaphoric thinking here.

12. See Cullen, *Spenser, Marvell*, especially 98–108.

13. John D. Bernard in *Ceremonies of Innocence: Pastoralism in the Poetry of Edmund Spenser* (Cambridge: Cambridge University Press, 1989), 64–76, reads the several pastor figures of the eclogues in just this way, though without reference to discourse analysis. Of the ecclesiastical ones he notes: "in each case the eclogue turns on a public issue of the day and features a Colin-like shepherd, normally young and callow . . . , who is vulnerable to a threatening world" (64). Likewise he sees Cuddie in "October" and Willye in both "March" and "August" as "parodies of Colin" (67). The overall progression of states for these Colin-like figures Bernard sums up in saying, "Spenser is making full use of the linear aspect of the calendar-form to exhibit his hero's 'progression' from an ideal of pastoral community . . . to a narrowed focus on the individual's spiritual destiny that renders the idea of an earthly community . . . all but irrelevant" (73). On this last point—to what end the coalesced pastoral figure moves—my reading differs from Bernard's, seeing Colin not as retreating into individualism or other-worldliness but as silenced unless and until a restored prophetic season may come.

CHAPTER 5. THE CALENDER AS PROPHECY AND THE CAPTIVE WOMAN IDEOLOGEME

1. Jameson, *Political Unconscious*, 48.

2. "Have control of/govern," and "disjoin from" are also relations within the formula and would not necessarily be found represented at the textual surface as a most-frequent-word category. That they are so represented in the *Calender* indicates that Spenser's narrative program there is both an auto-reflexive one—i.e., thematically concerns a writer's taking possession of his own competence—and so to speak a meta-"narrative program." It is as if the structure of narrativity itself is conceived to be politically at stake in his prophetic text.

3. Also as was noted, in applying Jameson's concepts of the literary work as a socially symbolic act and of the ideologeme as the basic unit of antagonistic inter-class discourse, I am neither endorsing nor refuting his broader claim that "Marxism [methodologically defined as "the radical historicizing of mental operations"] . . . is the 'untranscendable horizon' that subsumes . . . apparently antagonistic or incommensurable critical operations, assigning them an undoubted sectoral validity within itself, and thus at once canceling and preserving them" (ibid., 10).

4. I do not find a citation of its origin in *The Political Unconscious*—Kristeva is footnoted more generally. Kristeva drew the term (see *The Kristeva Reader*, ed. Toril Moi [New York: Columbia University Press, 1986], 87,n. 12) from *The Formal Method in Literary Scholarship*, trans. A. J. Wehrle (1928; Baltimore: Johns Hopkins University Press, 1978), attributed to P. N. Medvedev though perhaps written by Mikhail

Bakhtin (on the vexed authorship issue see Gary Saul Morson and Caryl Emerson, *Mikhail Bakhtin: Creation of a Prosaics* [Stanford, Calif.: Stanford University Press, 1990]).

5. See *Kristeva Reader*, 62–63. In analyzing the emergence of the novel as a genre, Kristeva identifies an "ideologeme of the sign" underlying the novel (vs. an ancient and medieval "ideologeme of the symbol" underlying the epic), the former representing "a move to another way of thinking" (a metaphysically more guarded and pluralistic way of thinking) than that of the epic, which had depended on a view of the world as innately symbolic, seen from within a unitary culture. For further comments on Kristeva see chapters 1 and 7.

6. On masculinity-femininity as an opposition existent within and only within the system of language, see Julia Kristeva, "Il n'y a pas de maître à langage," *Nouvelle revue de psychoanalyse* 20 (1979): 119–40.

7. See the beginning of the section in chapter 1 above on "Colin Clout, Prophetic Pastor or Sickly Dying Lover" for a little fuller evocation of the political moment; and see J. J. Higginson, *Spenser's "Shepheardes Calender" in Relation to Contemporary Affairs* (New York: Columbia University Press, 1912), 45.

8. Paul E. McLane, *Spenser's Shepheardes Calender: A Study in Elizabethan Allegory* (Notre Dame, Ind.: Notre Dame University Press, 1961).

9. David Norbrook, *Poetry and Politics in the English Renaissance* (London: Routledge, 1984), 66.

10. See Mack P. Holt, *The Duke of Anjou and the Politique Struggle during the Wars of Religion* (Cambridge: Cambridge University Press, 1986), 116–28, and the second section of chapter 1 above.

11. Richard Helgerson, *Self-Crowned Laureates: Spenser, Jonson, Milton and the Literary System* (Berkeley: University of California Press, 1983), has explored this matter of Spenser's place as a professional poet in a society that, until then, had no place for such a career. See also Richard Rambuss's partial challenging of Helgerson's view, in *Spenser's Secret Career* (Cambridge: Cambridge University Press, 1993).

12. It could still be used literally as 'to draw' an image. For an instance of this usage see the Euphuist tale *Narbonus* by Austen Saker (London: 1580), 67.

13. Greimas & Courtés analyze the category of 'veridiction' as a two-generation semiotic square on the term of "being" (*Dictionary*, 367 and p. 74 above). A second-generation semiotic square consists of the relations between the relations comprising a first generation one.

14. Jonathan Goldberg, *James I and the Politics of Literature* (Baltimore: Johns Hopkins University Press, 1983), 69.

15. Joseph A. Wittreich, Jr., *Visionary Poetics: Milton's Tradition and His Legacy* (San Marino, Calif.: Huntington Library, 1979), 105–10.

16. Anthea Hume's chapter on the *Calender* (*Edmund Spenser Protestant Poet* [Cambridge: Cambridge University Press, 1984], 13–58) details evidence of its reception in the 1580s, by writers such as Webbe. Abraham Fraunce's recasting of the *Calender*, in effect, as a casebook of rhetorical figures (in *The Lawyer's Rhetorike*, for his patroness the Countess of Pembroke, Sidney's sister), would also be noteworthy in possible study of its reception in Protestant activist circles.

17. It has been noted again by Stephen Greenblatt in terms of Spenser's devotion to power, in the Spenser chapter of *Renaissance Self-Fashioning from More to Shakespeare* (Chicago: University of Chicago Press, 1980.) Of older studies, see those in my bibliography by Wilson, Strong, Yates, and Wells.

18. See the Kirby volume in E. H. Fellowes, ed., *The English School of Lutenist Song Writers*. Series 1 & 2 (1920; 2d ed. London: Stainer & Bell, 1959).

19. Donald Cheney interestingly recalls that tradition also offered an alternative Dido figure to Virgil's love-lorn suicide, one who was faithful to her husband Sychaeus. This Dido could be echoing through "November" too, as the 'good' model for Elizabeth, to stick to her commitment to her "first" husband (kingdom) alone.

20. John N. King, throughout *Spenser's Poetry and the Reformation Tradition* (Princeton: Princeton University Press, 1990), contests the applicability of the word "puritan" to Spenser and the Leicestrian party. I believe the important point is to be aware of their reformist activism and particular ecclesiastical/political agenda, whether one terms them activist Protestant or puritan (a term not yet in common usage in the 1570s). See the characterization summarized from Norbrook above.

21. Hume, *Edmund Spenser*, 55.

22. Dido is one of the few female greats of antiquity not discussed in Robin Headlam Wells's comprehensive treatment of "the cult of Elizabeth" and its many figurations of her (*Spenser's Faerie Queene and the Cult of Elizabeth* [London: Croom Helm, 1983]). Harry Berger, Jr., *The Allegorical Temper: Vision and Reality in Book II of Spenser's "Faerie Queene"* (New Haven: Yale University Press, 1957), 125, pointed out the allusion to her in Spenser's description of Belphoebe *(Faerie Queene,* II, iii, 31), which draws upon *Aeneid* I, 493: "Such as Diana by the sandie shore / Of swift Eurotas," etc.

23. Cheney too emphasizes that this is only a seasonal death, or as it were hibernation, leaving Colin ready for springtime resurrection.

24. Louis A. Montrose, "Of Gentlemen and Shepherds: The Politics of Elizabethan Pastoral Form," *ELH* 50 (1983): 415–59.

25. An essay well documenting this point is Derek Attridge, "Puttenham's Perplexity: Nature, Art and the Supplement in Renaissance Poetic Theory," in *Literary Theory/ Renaissance Texts*, ed. Patricia Parker and David Quint (Baltimore: Johns Hopkins University Press, 1986), 257–79.

26. See Thomas Girtin, *The Golden Ram: A Narrative History of the Clothworkers Company—1528–1928* (London: Hunt, 1958), 52.

27. See M. B. Donald, *Elizabethan Monopolies: The History of the Company of Mineral and Battery Works from 1565–1604* (London: Oliver and Boyd, 1961), esp. 1–15 and 31ff. As soon as he became Lord Treasurer, Burghley also called in and reminted the whole, largely devalued Elizabethan coinage, to eliminate the practice of melting it down for resale of its metal content abroad at a better price than its face value.

28. John M. Keynes, "Economic Possibilities for Our Grandchildren," in *Collected Writings of John M. Keynes* (London: Macmillan, 1930), ix.

29. *Tudor Puritanism: A Chapter in the History of Idealism* (Chicago: University of Chicago Press, 1939), 232, 249.

30. See M. E. Bratchel, "Alien Merchant Colonies in Sixteenth-Century England: Community Organisation and Social Mores," *JMRS* 14 (1984): 39–62, which treats colonies in various continental cities as well as in England.

31. See Winfried Schleiner, "Divina virago: Queen Elizabeth as an Amazon," *SP* 75 (1978): 163–80, for a reproduction and discussion of such maps.

32. Greimas considers the concept of "factitivity" as a single modal category to be an over-simplification, preferring to discuss 'causing-to-do' as a contractual matter of a manipulator/Sender sending a narrative program to a subject/Receiver. That need not concern us here; since we are not doing a complete analysis of the square's component sememes into semes, we simply note 'causing-to-do' without determining whether it is a seme or a sememe.

33. A third but here less salient square (less closely parallel to the first) can also

be articulated, on the term of the factitive modality itself, with the same combinant semes and sememes:

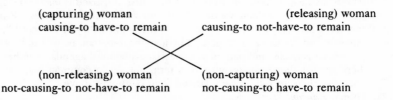

(capturing) woman   (releasing) woman
causing-to have-to remain   causing-to not-have-to remain

(non-releasing) woman   (non-capturing) woman
not-causing-to not-have-to remain   not-causing-to have-to remain

This illustrates the point that syntagmatic, as opposed to paradigmatic, articulation of a semantic category reverses the positions of the contrary and contradictory terms.

34. On iconographic as well as verbal images of Elizabeth as Amazon and capturer, for example, see Winfried Schleiner, "Divina virago."

35. Witches (mostly peasant or working/class women) as portrayed in, for example, ballads and court reports cause men impotence or madness but not physical captivity or detention.

36. These categories of course do not exclude imported motifs and figures. The point is that an ideologeme's terms draw suitable materials, whether domestic or imported, to themselves as if magnetically. In the case of the imported, this would be part of the process of 'Englishing' them.

37. See under the Countess of Pembroke in chapter 6 for bibliographical work on new studies of women writers of the period.

38. Jameson uses this metaphor to say that an ideologeme often continues functioning for a while after the political situation appropriate to it no longer exists.

39. For a brief definition of the three oppositions see Ronald Schleifer, introduction to *Structural Semantics An Attempt at a Method,* trans. D. McDowell, R. Schleifer, and A. Velie (1966; Lincoln: University of Nebraska Press, 1983), xxxiii.

40. Robin Headlam Wells (in *Spenser's "Faerie Queene",*) stresses especially the image of the virgin queen Eliza as a Protestant substitute for the lost figure of the Virgin Mary.

41. Smith asserts that Parliament holds absolute power in England, a statement that has made some historians proclaim him a herald of the new parliamentary power under James, though this view has been more recently disputed; see the introduction to Mary Dewar, ed., Sir Thomas Smyth, *De Republica Anglorum. The maner of Gouvernement or policie of the Realme of England* (1583; facs. Charlottesville: University Press of Virginia, 1968).

42. Ibid., 58.

43. For example, the husband should "bring in the necessaries" and the wife "well kepe them," says Edmund Tilney, *The Flower of Friendship: A Renaissance Dialogue Contesting Marriage,* ed. Valerie Wayne (Ithaca: Cornell University Press, 1992), 120.

44. See Louis Montrose, "'Shaping Fantasies': Figurations of Gender and Power," *Representations* 2 (1983): 61–94.

45. In discussing Conrad's Lord Jim, for example, Jameson concedes that the opposition he sets up is not logically accurate (that is, does not "compare comparable entities") but claims that this does not matter (*Political Unconscious,* 254). It appears that some of Jameson's squares are non-compelling attempts to map arbitrary oppositions (perhaps of the third sort—see n. 22 and above). Since he does not spell out his squares in fuller sememic definition, I am not sure. The distinction does matter,

since if one does not stick to genuine semantic categories, analysts will not be able to agree on what if anything the squares show.

46. See, for example, Linda Woodbridge, *Women and the English Renaissance: Literature and the Nature of Womankind* (Urbana: University of Illinois Press, 1984), 1540–1620; Coppèlia Kahn, *Man's Estate: Masculine Identity in Shakespeare* (Berkeley: University of California Press, 1981); Katherine Henderson and Barbara F. McManus, *Half Humankind: Contexts and Texts of the Controversy about Women in England, 1540–1640* (Urbana: University of Illinois Press, 1985); Elaine V. Beilin, *Redeeming Eve: Women Writers of the English Renaissance* (Princeton: Princeton University Press, 1987); and for further reading the bibliographical essays by Hageman, Robertson, and Beilin in my bibliography.

Chapter 6. The "Captive Woman" at Work

1. Dominant medical thinking of the time—including that of Fallopius, who discovered the tubes named for him but not their functioning—held that women, like men, have "seed" in their genital fluids (Winfried Schleiner, "The Moral Dilemma of Removing Seed," a chapter in *Medical Ethics in the Renaissance*, forthcoming, Georgetown University Press.

2. The lack of ultimate closure in *The Faerie Queene* was a much pursued topic in deconstructionist analysis of Spenser; see especially Jonathan Goldberg, *Endlesse Worke: Spenser and the Structures of Discourse* (Baltimore: Johns Hopkins University Press, 1981); and Maureen Quilligan, *Milton's Spenser: the Politics of Reading* (Ithaca: Cornell University Press, 1983).

3. See Winfried Schleiner, "*Divina Virago:* Queen Elizabeth as an Amazon," *SP*, 75 (1978), 163–80.

4. Thomas H. Cain, *Praise in the "Faerie Queene"* (Lincoln: University of Nebraska Press, 1978), 152.

5. Donald V. Stump, "The Two Deaths of Mary Stuart," *Spenser Studies* 9 (1988): 99.

6. Kate M. Warren, ed., "Introduction" to *The Faerie Queene*, vol. 3 (Westminster: Constable, 1904), xx, suggested that Radigund might represent the queen herself in certain moods and moments. Thus her better self is being made to defeat her worse self.

7. In a discussion that treats "maleness-femaleness" as if it could be mapped onto a semiotic square (of contrariety/contradiction) rather than as a classematic opposition, i.e., an arbitrary, culture-specific one (see p. 125 above), Lauren Silberman vividly describes Britomart as female aggressor, illustrating part of the entrepreneurial definition of femaleness:

"While Britomart's enchanted spear lends symbolic (and practical) potency to her quest, the Martial Maid's courage is not simply the product of one phallic symbol. Rather, her chastity itself is the female equivalent of the Hermaphrodite's manhood. In fashioning a female hero, one who dons armor in pursuit of love, Spenser moralizes and transforms Ovid's paradox that the triumph of Hermaphroditus' manhood is also its loss into the paradoxical giving and withholding of the self that defines chastity in Book III. ("The Hermaphrodite and the Metamorphosis of Spenserian Allegory," *ELR* 17 [1987]: 216)

8. Sir Walter Raleigh, "A Report of the Truth of the Fight . . . betwixt the *Revenge* . . . and an Armada," in *The Renaissance in England*, ed. Hyder E. Rollins & Herschel Baker (Lexington, Mass.: Heath, 1954), 894.

9. Thomas Cain, *Praise*, 112, similarly describes Philotime as a negative image of Gloriana (Elizabeth), being "what she is not"; he terms this an instance of the rhetorical figure of *vituperatio*, "one of the poem's subtle encomiastic strategies." I see such imaging as a kind of warning to the queen (under the cover of praise), to think which pole of the opposition she and her court more nearly resemble.

10. It would probably turn out to be recognizable as an instrumental narrative program, if the text were analyzed.

11. See her soliloquy, "O me, unfortunate wretch . . . what poisonous heats be these that thus possess me? How hath the sight of this strange guest invaded my soul? What entrance found this desire . . . . O ye stars, judge rightly of me; and if I have willingly made myself a prey to fancy, or if by any idle lusts I framed my heart fit for such an impression, then let this plague daily increase in me till my name be made odious to womankind" (Sir Philip Sidney, *The Old Arcadia*, ed. Katherine Duncan-Jones [Oxford: Oxford University Press, 1985], 97–98).

12. See Sir Philip Sidney, *The Countess of Pembroke's Arcadia*, edited by Maurice Evans (New York: Penguin, 1977); subsequent in-text citations are to this edition. Whether the change represents Sidney's own intent or was an editorial revision by the Countess of Pembroke does not matter for my purposes: in the revision, the reprehensible sexual forcing of a woman takes a new form, and leads well into the new plot material of captivity by Cecropia.

13. On the nature of the position see Frederic S. Boas, "Queen Elizabeth, the Revels Office, and Edmund Tillney," in *Queen Elizabeth in Drama and Related Studies* (London: Allen & Unwin, 1950); and on Lyly's efforts to get it, R. Warwick Bond, ed., *The Complete Works of John Lyly* (Oxford: Clarendon, 1902), vol. I, 60–72.

14. See, e.g., Boas, "Queen Elizabeth in Elizabethan and Later Drama," 9–35.

15. The name Bagoa comes from the servant/ go-between of Ovid's *Amores;* a *miles gloriosus* of the comic sub-plot marries her, who incidentally may be a parody of Gabriel Harvey, as Bond notes.

16. See Bond, ed., *Complete Works of John Lyly*, vol. III, 236 and 555; vol. II, 256n.; and vol. I, 63–64, 383, and 389–90.

17. See Louise Schleiner, "Ladies and Gentlemen in Elizabethan Fiction," *SEL* 29 (1989): 1–20.

18. Cited from Edmund H. Fellowes, *English Madrigal Verse 1588–1632* (Oxford: Clarendon Press, 1967), 481–82.

19. *The Riverside Shakespeare*, ed. G. Blakemore Evans et al. (Boston: Houghton, Mifflin, 1974), 107.

20. Louis B. Wright, *Middle-Class Culture in Elizabethan England* (1935; 2nd ed. Ithaca: Cornell University Press, 1958), 473, describes the library of Captain Cox, a Coventry mason.

21. Cited from *An Anthology of Elizabethan Prose Fiction*, Paul Salzman, ed. (Oxford: Oxford University Press, 1987), 155.

22. See *The Winter's Tale*, J. H. P. Pafford, ed. (London: 1981), xxx, who thus interprets the ending. Paul Salzman, ibid., xix, disagrees. My treatment here owes a debt to a stimulating conversation with Jackie Christman.

23. G. B. Harrison, ed., *Willobie His Avisa, 1594. with an Essay on Willobie His Avisa* (1924; rpt. New York: Barnes & Noble, 1966), 181–270.

24. Wright (*Middle-Class Culture*, 476) makes this observation.

25. The seeming clue is repeated in one of the dedicatory poems, which locates Avisa in the "West of Albion's Isle."

26. For a convenient list of 'Avisa's' numerous scriptural and classical allusions see B. N. De Luna, *The Queen Declined: An Interpretation of "Willobie his Avisa"* (Oxford:

Clarendon Press, 1970), 14–15. I do not find De Luna's argument that Avisa is allegorically Queen Elizabeth convincing. Elements of the text that contradict this interpretation are not adequately explained (as when De Luna claims that the 'west' of England, twice given as Avisa's home, somehow really means the 'east'), and the supposed links to Elizabeth's heraldic symbols of roses and lillies involve metaphors too generally appropriate to any praise of admired chaste ladies for them necessarily to evoke Elizabeth. Perhaps my own analysis of the Chaste Britannia Militant articulation of the ideologeme, though, can suggest why De Luna and others might well feel that the figure of Avisa has something to do with the queen. I believe that it does, on the socio-linguistic level, since the captive woman ideologeme functioned in constant interplay with her government's activities.

27. De Luna notes (ibid., 106–7) that one of the mottoes had appeared in George Whetstone's *Rocke of Regard* and one in George Turberville's *Tragical Tales*, besides the five from the *Calender*. The fact that a whole set of them comes from the Calender suggests an intended allusion to it.

28. From Eusebius he cites the cases of a mother and daughters who drowned themselves rather than be raped, and of one Blandina, who learning that the tyrant Maxentius had ordered her brought to be "ravished," in her chamber "tooke a sword and perced her selfe to the hart" (*Willobie His Avisa*, ed. Harrison, 14).

29. Sir Philip Sidney, *An Apology for Poetry*, ed. Forrest G. Robinson (New York: Bobbs-Merrill, 1979), 20.

30. Southampton was affiliated with Essex, who had inherited the leadership of the Leicester party in the 1590s. Thus if he was indeed the target one might question how he and his group, including Shakespeare, could be perceived as squirearchist, given this affiliation (certainly my analysis of Shakespeare here indicates a squirearchist bent on his part, into which he may have tried to draw or influence the youthful Southampton). In the absence of more conviction about who were the *Avisa*'s intended targets, all such speculation has limited merit. But in any case it is long recognized that under Essex the faction did not have the degree of ideological unity for which it had been noted under Leicester. It seems to have been a loose coalition of people who had in common a disaffection with the long unshakeable dynasty of Burghley and his now succeeding son Robert Cecil.

31. Louis A. Montrose, "'Shaping Fantasies': Figurations of Gender and Power," *Representations* 2 (1983), 61–94; reprinted in *Representing the English Renaissance*, ed. Stephen Greenblatt (Berkeley: University of California Press, 1988), 35.

32. See the bibliography articles by Elaine V. Beilin, "Current Bibliography of English Women Writers, 1500–1640," in *The Renaissance Englishwoman in Print. Counterbalancing the Canon*, ed. Anne M. Haselkorn and Betty S. Travitsky (Amherst: University of Massachusetts Press, 1990), 347–60; Elizabeth H. Hageman, "Recent Studies in Women Writers of the English Seventeenth Century (1604–1674)," *ELR* 18 (1988): 138–67; and "Recent Studies in Women Writers of Tudor England. I: Women Writers, 1485–1603," *ELR* 14 (1984): 409–25; and by Josephine A. Roberts, "Recent Studies in Women Writers of Tudor England. II: Mary Sidney, Countess of Pembroke," *ELR* 14 (1984): 426–39. Several more articles on women writers have since appeared in *ELR*.

33. Mary Sidney Herbert, Countess of Pembroke, *The Triumph of Death and Other Unpublished and Uncollected Poems*, ed. Gary F. Waller (Salzburg: Universität Salzburg, 1977), 88–91 and 181–83.

34. Margaret P. Hannay, *Philip's Phoenix: Mary Sidney, Countess of Pembroke* (Oxford: Oxford University Press, 1990), traces this factor in the Countess's activities through the late 1590s.

35. Herbert, ed. Waller, 209.

36. See the very thorough essay on Elizabeth as Astraea in Frances A. Yates, *Astraea: The Imperial Theme in the Sixteenth Century* (London: Routledge, 1975). Henri IV's pragmatic conversion to Catholicism in mid-1593 dampened English Protestant enthusiasm for him, but he remained their ally of choice, as he tried to institute toleration for Huguenots.

37. Spenser indirectly but clearly evokes both in the succeeding stanzas (9 and 10) concluding the Proem to *Faerie Queene* V, his climactic epic plea for the internationalist Protestant faction's political agenda, including continued support of Henri IV despite his apostasy. That is, stanza 9 is a retelling of the Astraea myth, calling her "justice" who "sate high ador'd" during the golden-age reign of Saturn, while stanza 10 evokes David and Solomon as enforcers of her justice (see n. 50 below).

38. For an insightful essay on this issue see Constance Jordan, "Representing Political Androgyny: More on the Sienna Portrait of Queen Elizabeth I," in Haselkorn and Travitsky, *Renaissance Englishwoman*, 157–76. In the same collection, Josephine A. Roberts, "Radigund Revisited: Perspectives on Women Rulers in Lady Mary Wroth's Urania," 193–94, also comments on the masculinity of the queen's body politic and the necessity not to treat it too literally.

39. Hannay, *Philip's Phoenix*, 91–97, discusses the tradition of citing Old Testament figures in flattering metaphors concerning Queen Elizabeth, and particularly David, mentioning the *Coronation of David* by Edmund Bunny (1588), where popish practices are compared to the attempts on David's life.

40. Again, for thorough demonstration of the French Protestant uses of the David figure for Henri IV, see Yates, *Astraea*.

41. For the general point that some features of her Psalm translations themselves show political motivation, see Margaret P. Hannay, "'Princes you as men must dy': Genevan Advice to Monarchs in the *Psalmes* of Mary Sidney," *ELR* 19 (1989): 22–41.

42. See Roy Strong, *The Cult of Elizabeth: Elizabethan Portraiture and Pageantry* (London: Thames & Hudson, 1977), 43ff.

43. A good source for the military situation recalled in these paragraphs, even though biased in Burghley's favor, is still Conyers Read, *Lord Burghley and Queen Elizabeth* (London: Jonathan Cape, 1960), because it quotes so extensively from primary documents.

44. Ibid., 481.

45. Ibid., 483.

46. See Michael Brennan, "The Date of the Countess of Pembroke's Translation of the Psalms," *RES* 33 (1982): 434–36.

47. See *The Poems of Queen Elizabeth I*, ed. Leicester Bradner (Providence: Brown University Press, 1964).

48. Read, *Lord Burghley*, 483.

49. Elkin Calhoun Wilson, *England's Eliza* (New York: Octagon, 1966), chaps. 1 and 2.

50. For several examples of such extensional or indirect comparisons see Wilson, *England's Eliza*, 418–19, 439, 444, 446, 453; Robin Headlam Wells, *Spenser's "Faerie Queene" and the Cult of Elizabeth* (London: Croom Helm, 1983), 19; and Hannay, *Philip's Phoenix*, 90–97. Spenser used the David trope for Elizabeth likewise indirectly in the Proem, st. 10, to *Faerie Queene*, bk. V, where Elizabeth is said to 'sit in God's own seat' for dealing justice (cf. 1st Chron. 29:23, where exactly this is said of David and his son Solomon).

51. Cf. Hannay, *Philip's Phoenix*, 92.

52. David was referred to as the "man after God's own heart": see 1st Sam. 13:14 and Acts 13:22.

53. See Bradner ed., *Poems of Queen Elizabeth*.

54. See Strong, *Cult of Elizabeth*, plate 82, following 169.

55. See James E. Phillips, "Elizabeth I as a Latin Poet: An Epigram on Paul Melissus," *Renaissance News* 16 (1963): 289–99,

56. Bradner and Phillips consider the issue of whether Melissus himself or perhaps a secretary of the queen's could have written the poem. Both note that she was perfectly capable of it, and Philips adds that she had at this time political motivation to take time to do something to show her good will to the emperor, having switched her supposed marital interests from the Archduke of Austria to the French d'Alençon. About the first suggestion, I would add that while writers did sometimes 'put words into the mouth' of a patroness as a kind of acceptable fiction (as when Nicholas Breton wrote a supposed "Countess of Pembroke's Passion," imagining her persona speaking it though it was a work of his own—see Grosart ed. of Breton), it seems very unlikely that, at the level of sensitive diplomatic interactions between the emperor and the queen, a poet would dare to publish something claimed to have been penned by her if he did not believe it to be so.

CHAPTER 7. COMPOSITIONAL ORDER AND COLIN'S FRAMING OF MALE AND FEMALE LOVES IN *THE SHEPHEARDES CALENDER*

1. The "you" is asked to look with indulgence on Colin Clout as a mere "shepherd's boy—no better do him call" (minor employee of a bishop).

2. Gerard Genette, *Seuils* (Paris: Seuil, 1987), 8. The translations are my own; subsequent citations are in-text.

3. William W. E. Slights ("The Edifying Margins of Rennaissance English Books" *RenQ* 42 [1989]: 682–716) has briefly discussed *The Shepheardes Calender* in connection with Genette's analysis of paratexts. And Louis Montrose has mentioned the importance of the apparatus for the *Calender* as Spenser planned its impact; he does not, however, cite Genette (*Seuils* was not yet published) but refers to paratexts as "discursive forms characterized by distinctive modes of address to readers" ("The Elizabethan Subject and the Spenserian Text," in *Literary Theory, Renaissance Texts*, ed. Patricia Parker and David Quint [Baltimore: Johns Hopkins University Press, 1986], 320).

4. A similar view of the *Calender* apparatus, though without reference to Genette, is adopted by Evelyn Tribble, "Glozing the Gap: Glossing Traditions and *The Shepheardes Calender*," *Criticism* 34 (1992): 155–72. She sees glossing as an interested undertaking, E. K. as constructing an unreliable and evasive system of significance.

5. Richard Halpern, *The Poetics of Primitive Accumulation: English Renaissance Culture and the Genealogy of Capital* (Ithaca: Cornell University Press, 1991), 193 and 187. Halpern thus sees the *Calender* as marking—through its strategic juxtaposing of discursive positions—a transition from one to the next sub-phase of increasing accumulation of capital in England, dismantling of local feudal culture, and deterritorialization of workers and means of production. If his scheme is right, I would apply it to the "February" eclogue in a way different from his; he sees the Briar of "February" as allegorizing the scientific, rhetorical pragmatics of international humanism, while the erstwhile protector and victim the Oak represents native English "narrative pragmatics." However, I, like most students of the *Calender*'s topicality, believe the Briar refers to the crypto-Catholic Earl of Oxford, one of the prominent advocates

of the remnant of feudal ideology, as was also his cousin the Duke of Norfolk (the Oak), who had tried to marry Mary Stuart and had been executed by Elizabeth; Spenser and many other people thought, probably erroneously, that Oxford had betrayed his cousin Norfolk in some manner. In other words the fable shows two earlier allied affiliates of "narrative pragmatics" (by Halpern's terms) in conflict, the corrupt younger one destroying the older.

6. As mentioned, I have elsewhere argued ("Spenser's E. K. as Edmund Kent: Kenned, Kissed, and Kunning/Conning," *ELR* 20 [1990]: 374–407) from extensive evidence that E. K. is a persona of mixed voices created by Spenser with the partly savy and partly unwitting help of Harvey. But even if one considers him an actual person—who must then have collaborated extremely closely with Spenser on the glosses while yet presenting himself in some passages as distant from "the author"— my points here about the interactive functioning of text, paratext, and readership remain the same. A description of the apparatus akin to mine (L. Staley Johnson, *"The Shepheardes Calender": An Introduction* [University Park: Pennsylvania State University Press, 1990]: 26–28) presenting E. K. as "the creation of Spenser" appeared in the same year as my "E. K." essay; Johnson refers to the glosses' comic dimensions and some similar satires of scholarly pomposity by Sidney and Langham (25–30). Halpern (*Poetics of Primitive Accumulation*, 177–82) also discusses the apparatus in a way quite similar to mine, noting that it "is poised unstably between the serious and the ludic." See Chapter 1, n. 11 for more of such recent views.

7. J. Michael Richardson (*Astrological Symbolism in Spenser's "The Shepheardes Calender"* [Lewiston, N.Y.: Edwin Mellen, 1989]) in an appendix offers various readings whereby the erroneous naming of the fish as sign for "November" might be an astrological riddle. Johnson (*"Shepheardes Calender,"* 199–201) makes another such suggestion, that Spenser meant "to evoke" the word haspe instead of haske, which would then refer to the haspe or "knot" of Pisces, i.e., the star Alpha Piscium (it remains unexplained how this star's conjunction with the sun at the vernal equinox should relate to November; and in any case, in each woodcut the zodiac sign is cradled in a hassock or basket-shaped cloud, so there is no need to emend "haske" to "haspe"—see Johnson, 200). Donald Cheney ("The Circular Argument of *The Shepheardes Calender,"* in *Unfolded Tales: Essays on Renaissance Romance* [Ithaca: Cornell University Press, 1989], 157–59) offers further riddle possibilities but admits that none of them "makes sense of the claim that the sun is in Pisces in November." He mentions as an alternative "that this would have been a February eclogue in a *Calender* that started the year with March"—I believe the sensible explanation.

Seeing the Pisces mention as an error Spenser or the printer failed to correct would not mean, as Richardson thinks (503), that the calendric framework was a mere "hastily contrived and imposed" format. Clearly Spenser was working with his seasonal thematics in all the eclogues, but the present "November" death lament could have served well for "February" too, as the "death" or end month of the equinoctal year—that is exactly what the lines about Phoebus weary of his year-long course suggest. One can always forget to make a needed adjusting correction in a manuscript, or editorial confusion can arise. Possibly Spenser added the fitting November zodiacal gloss, which now appears just before the "Pisces" one, meaning for it to replace that now unsuitable one about the fish; but both notes were inadvertently kept, and the page-setter, seeing the obviously incorrect word "February" in the second one, put in "November" instead. This assumes that Spenser also intended some change in the referenced eclogue lines which likewise was neglected, so that they still refer to February.

8. See Richard Rambuss, *Spenser's Secret Career* (Cambridge: Cambridge University Press, 1993).

9. See n. 15 below on Morrell, and the highly probable evocations of other particular bishops.

10. Donald Cheney, "The Circular Argument of *The Shepheardes Calender*," in *Unfolded Tales: Essays on Renaissance Romance* (Ithaca: Cornell University Press, 1989), 156.

11. See J. J. Higginson, *Spenser's "Shepheardes Calender" in Relation to Contemporary Affairs* (New York: Columbia University Press, 1912), 45.

12. As further examples, about John Skelton's character Colin Clout, who like this Colin had daringly offered criticism of the church establishment, the "January" gloss mentions only the harmless-seeming point that there is a work of Skelton's with that title. And further, since the pastorals of Clement Marot and his self-imaging persona 'Colin' were essential models for the *Calender*, Spenser could not do without a citation to him when the name Colin was introduced. But he is given only feeble mention, perhaps because anti-French hostility was intense in England after the Parisian St. Bartholomew's Day massacre of Protestants in 1572; the gloss makes the essential Marot background as acceptable as possible by harumphing a bit over Marot (whose religious loyalty was considered ambivalent) and claiming merely that the name Colin had been chosen because Latin names are unrealistic for an English shepherd.

13. Of course not every character in the *Calender* necessarily referred to a contemporary person; Spenser's poet-courtier acquaintances such as Edward Dyer were possibly evoked for contemporaries—Paul MacLane made a good case for Cuddie as Dyer. Some other characters like Thenot or Willy are, so far as we know, purely literary personae, sometimes signaling derivations of material from particular poets: "Thenot," like "Colin," is a name from Marot.

14. See Leicester Bradner, *Edmund Spenser and the "Faerie Queene"* (Chicago: University of Chicago Press, 1948), 54; and Sam Meyer, *An Interpretation of Edmund Spenser's Colin Clout* (Notre Dame, Ind.: Notre Dame University Press, 1969), 166.

15. The conservative Morrell, i.e. Elmore, is politically allied with Palinode of "May," who with very high probability evoked Andrew Perne, vice-chancellor of Cambridge University and enemy of Gabriel Harvey, through many years dubbed "Palinode" (recantation) by the undergraduates for his practice of easily switching religious loyalty according to who was in power (on Perne see Virginia F. Stern, *Gabriel Harvey: his Life, Marginalia, and Library* [Oxford: Clarendon Press, 1979], 38–39 and 53–54; Higginson, 181–84; and Edmund Spenser, *Works: A Variorum Edition*, eds. Charles G. Osgood and Henry G. Lotspeich [Baltimore: Johns Hopkins University Press, 1943], vol. 7, *Minor Poems*, on "May."). Piers, Palinode's opponent of "May," probably alludes to John Pierce (*Variorum* 7:296), Young's predecessor at Rochester and a reform-minded bishop of whom Spenser would have approved; as John N. King notes (*Spenser's Poetry and the Reformation Tradition* [Princeton: Princeton University Press, 1990], 35), Thomalin of "July" suggests Thomas Cooper, Bishop of Lincoln; and Diggon Davie of "September" probably evokes Bishop Richard Davies of St. David's in Wales, portrayed to be disillusioned about his own policies after they have enabled noblemen to rob his diocese of certain holdings (*Variorum* 7: 354).

16. Ellen Moody ("Six Elegiac Poems, Possibly by Anne Cecil de Vere, Countess of Oxford," *ELR* 19 [1989]: 152–70), and others have argued that Oxford had expected, through this marriage, to influence Burghley to arrange a reprieve for Norfolk, and that Burghley's pressing ahead with the execution was a primary reason

why Oxford then repudiated his wife and claimed she had been unfaithful to him. If this is right, then the Oak and Briar satire of Oxford would have been outrageously galling to him, since he considered himself to be the one who had been double-crossed. The emphasis of Robert Lane (*Shepheardes Devises: Edmund Spenser's 'Shepheardes Calender' and the Institutions of Elizabethan Society* [Athens: University of Georgia Press, 1993], 89–110 & 142–145) on ecclesiastical satire, for example of noblemen's stealing of church lands in the "February" and "September" fables, might accord with those two eclogues' evocations, respectively, of Norfolk/Oxford and of Bishop John Young, as discussed here. Norfolk, shown as a victim in "February," was considered a supporter of educated Protestant preaching, church charity to the poor, and firm prelatical governance (his secret flirtation with Mary, Queen of Scots, was by many people not believed). And the unidentified "wolf" trying to raid Young's Rochester flock (Lane thinks by suing for a "concealed" property used as a charity hospital) might have been a Catholic-associated nobleman like Oxford. Lane's book was only available after the present one was in press, but I believe complements it in some ways.

17. For a recent lively retelling (which interestingly applies some of Pierre Bourdieu's concepts of class interaction) of the politically significant "tennis court" quarrel between Sidney and Oxford, as a live political performance played out before the French emissaries, see Maureen Quilligan, "Sidney and his Queen," in *The Historical Renaissance. New Essays on Tudor and Stuart Literature and Culture*, eds. Heather Dubrow and Richard Strier (Chicago: University of Chicago Press, 1988), 171–96.

18. Stern, op. cit., 65–66.

19. Higginson, op. cit., 46–71.

20. Louis A. Montrose, "Interpreting Spenser's February Eclogue: Some Contexts and Implications," *Spenser Studies: A Renaissance Poetry Annual* 2 (1981): 70.

21. Commenting on the contentious emblems, the glossator spins out opposite arguments, that old men are more pious and favored by God than young men, and vice versa. With debate-team suavity, he sounds quite convinced as he presents each case. Thus the gloss accords with the opening claim of the "Argument," that this eclogue is "moral and general."

22. See Charles Mounts, "Spenser and the Countess of Leicester," *ELH* 19 (1952): 191–202; Helena Shire, *A Preface to Spenser* (London: Longman, 1985), 45–47; and *The Yale Edition of the Shorter Poems of Edmund Spenser*, eds. William A. Oram, et al. (New Haven: Yale University Press, 1989), 58. Richard Rambuss, *Spenser's Secret Career* (Cambridge: Cambridge University Press, 1993), 21–24, goes beyond other scholars to suggest that this over-obvious allusion to Leicester's secret marriage may have been a deliberate though "misconceived" effort to warn Leicester, and even that it may have been, as the *Calender*'s separate eclogues were circulating in manuscript, the means by which the queen learned about the marriage, causing Leicester to release Spenser from his service.

23. Since Thomalin of "July," as an earnest Protestant "pastor" denouncing high-living clergy, is much more serious and mature than the Thomalin of "March," commentators have wondered whether Spenser meant the two Thomalins to be at all related to each other. Of course a naive boy lover could later become an earnest clergyman. In any event, Thomalin's identity or identities serve I think to becloud and thus tone down the Leicester allusion.

24. See Stern, *Gabriel Harvey*, 65–70; and Quilligan, "Sidney and his Queen."

25. John D. Bernard's reading of the *Calender* (in *Ceremonies of Innocence: Pastoralism in the Poetry of Edmund Spenser* [Cambridge: Cambridge University Press, 1989], 54–62) also emphasizes this framing function of what E. K. lists as the plaintive

eclogues. He calls "June" "the structural hinge or fulcrum of the work that appears to be its thematic centerpiece as well. Occurring virtually halfway through Spenser's calendar year, it is also the middle eclogue of three in which Colin appears in his principal role of thwarted lover" (54).

26. See ibid., 307–12.

27. See Parmenter, "Spenser's Twelve Aeglogues"; Miller, "Authorship," 226; and Cressy, "Bonfires and Bells..

28. They leave the country dialects and archaic words of the middle eclogues behind and primarily speak a lyric language of Spenser's own time, within the bounds of pastoral convention.

29. "October" too is seasonally non-specific—it might at first have occupied a different slot.

30. Johnson, *"Shepheardes Calender,"* 181.

31. The gloss asserts that Socrates' love for Alcibiades, as viewed by Plato and certain neo-Platonists, was not "fleshly" homosexuality such as that sanctioned by Pietro Aretino but spiritual male love, and thus a good kind of "pederastice," like the friendship of Hobbinol and Colin. The ensuing fierce denunciation of Aretino may refer to a book of pornographic dialogues ascribed to him, *La Putana Errante,* or perhaps to some work that has not survived but was included among the dialogues known in England as his "capricios." (Harvey's brother Richard in his treatise on "the Lamb of God" referred to the work meant here as Aretino's "infamous Capricio or apologie of Pederastice.") Harvey later denounced Aretino as pornographer in his pamphlet *Pierces Supererogation,* referring as this gloss does to a group of anti-Aretine humanist authorities beginning with Perionius, and including Cornelius Agrippa, Cardan, and Manutius (Harvey, *Works* 2: 271).

32. Bruce R. Smith, *Homosexual Desire in Shakespeare's England: A Cultural Poetics* (Chicago: University of Chicago Press, 1991), 94–96, has also noted Spenser's shift here from Virgil's pattern, with the pursuing lover as speaker, to that of the pursued beloved as speaker; Smith adds that the *Calender,* unlike Virgil's poem, sees the heterosexual attraction as fleshly, the male one as spiritual. For other treatments of Spenser on the pederasty issue see Stephen Orgel, "Nobody's Perfect: Or Why Did the English Stage Take Boys for Women?" *SAQ* 88 (1989): 22–23; and Jonathan Goldberg, "Colin to Hobbinol: Spenser's Familiar Letters," *South Atlantic Quarterly* 88 (1989): 107–26.

33. She is, incidentally, another figure about whom the interactive textual and glossarial hints represent the technique of obfuscating and titilating already noted in other instances. Most scholars have not agreed with Paul McLane's claim (*"Spenser's Shepheardes Calender": A Study in Elizabethan Allegory* [Notre Dame, Ind.: Notre Dame University Press, 1961]) that there was no private lady behind Rosalind, only the political referent, the queen. "Rosalind" could have referred both to a lady Spenser had courted or admired (perhaps less intensely than he makes out here) and to the queen. Some have followed the gloss's hint and sought the lady's name in the letters of "Rosalinde." The best guess so far is Elisa North [elisa nord], daughter of the translator Sir Thomas North, whose marriage in June 1579, corresponds to Rosalind's betrayal cited in "June." One can also see Elisa R[egina En-gl]ond in the name's letters. The verbs in this "January" gloss on Rosalind—feign, color, shadow, envelope, counterfeit—suggest the metaphor of the apparatus as wrapping, i.e., as both opalescent partial concealment and safe packaging for the eclogues' allusions.

34. The poem is given, and its uses in Catholic and Lutheran polemics discussed,

in Anne Lake Prescott, "English Writers and Beza's Latin Epigrams: The Uses and Abuses of Poetry," *StudRen* 21 (1974): 83–117.

35. The note for the passage in *Spenser's Minor Poems*, eds. William Oram, et al. (New Haven: Yale University Press, 1989) says that he has here Petrarchized Virgil, that is, shifted the scorned, intense love of Virgil's Eclogue II from a male to a female beloved, and treated it through imitating Petrarch. This is true as far as it goes but does not account for how Spenser managed to shift the character and gender constellation while retaining its libidinal force.

36. For reasons to think Harvey himself drafted this particular gloss see my "Spenser's E. K."

37. See Mack P. Holt, *The Duke of Anjou and the Politique Struggle during the Wars of Religion* (Cambridge: Cambridge University Press, 1986), 116–28, for a concise yet detailed account of the year's diplomatic events in England.

APPENDIX 1

1. Jonathan Culler, *Structuralism, Linguistics, and the Study of Literature* (Ithaca: Cornell University Press, 1975), 75–95; and Fredric Jameson, *The Political Unconscious: Narrative as a Socially Symbolic Act* (Ithaca: Cornell University Press, 1981).

2. The point here is not, as Culler seems to think, to obtain "no irritating collocations"; that is, to ensure that there will be no occurrent combinations of chosen lexemes that are unrelated to the patterns eventually emerging, but rather to leave infrequent or unique collocations aside and to discover instead the numerically prevalent ones, which serve as an "isotopy" or semantic reading-grid of frequently linked sememes, partly on the basis of which readers will, for example, disambiguate potentially ambiguous passages.

3. Whether the classematic element(s) interacting with the kernel semes in a given occurent lexeme be considered part of the lexeme itself (classemes per se) or rather, as Culler on good grounds suggests, functions of a classematic system of each given discourse, acting upon the lexeme—the distinction is not consequential for the present procedures and analysis; since a single discourse is being analyzed, results will be the same either way.

Bibliography

Albertazzi, Silvia. "'Shut In, Shut Off': Ruth Prawer Jhabvala's 'Mythology of Captivity'." *CE&S* 8 (1985): 45–55.

Alpers, Paul, ed. *The Singer of the Eclogues* [Virgil's eclogues and an English translation]. Berkeley: University of California Press, 1979.

Arroyabe, Estanislao. *Semiotik und Literatur.* Bonn: Bouvier, 1984.

Auberlen, Eckhard. *The Commonwealth of Wit: The Writer's Image and His Strategies of Self-Representation in Elizabethan Literature.* Tübingen: Narr, 1984.

Bakhtin, Mikhail [see Medvedev].

Ball, B. W. "George Peele's Huanebango: A Caricature of Gabriel Harvey." *RenP* (1968): 29–39.

Barthes, Roland. *Writing Degree Zero.* Translated Annette Lavers and Colin Smith. New York: Hill & Wang, 1968.

———. *S/Z.* Translated by Richard Miller. New York: Hill & Wang, 1974.

———. *L'Aventure semiologique.* Paris: Seuil, 1985.

Beilin, Elaine V. *Redeeming Eve: Women Writers of the English Renaissance.* Princeton: Princeton University Press, 1987.

———. "Current Bibliography of English Women Writers, 1500–1640." In *The Renaissance Englishwoman in Print. Counterbalancing the Canon,* edited by Anne M. Haselkorn and Betty S. Travitsky, 347–60. Amherst: University of Massachusetts Press, 1990.

Belenky, Mary Field, et al. *Women's Ways of Knowing: the Development of Mind, Voice, and Self.* New York: Basic Books, 1986.

Bentley, Thomas. *Monument of matrones: conteining seuen seuerall Lamps of Virginitie.* London, 1582.

Berger, Harry, Jr. *The Allegorical Temper: Vision and Reality in Book II of Spenser's "Faerie Queene."* New Haven: Yale University Press, 1957.

———, ed. *Spenser: A Collection of Critical Essays.* Englewood Cliffs, N.J.: Prentice-Hall, 1968.

Bernard, John D. "'June' and the Structure of Spenser's *Shepheardes Calender.*" *PQ* 60 (1981): 305–22.

———. *Ceremonies of Innocence: Pastoralism in the Poetry of Edmund Spenser.* Cambridge: Cambridge University Press, 1989.

Blanchard, Marc Eli. *Description: Sign, Self, Desire. Critical Theory in the Wake of Semiotics.* The Hague: Mouton, 1980.

Boas, Frederick S. "Queen Elizabeth, the Revels Office, and Edmund Tilney." In *Queen Elizabeth in Drama and Related Studies.* London: Allen & Unwin, 1950.

Bond, R. Warwick, ed. *The Complete Works of John Lyly.* 3 vols. Oxford: Clarendon Press, 1902.

265

Bond, Ronald B. "Supplantation in the Elizabethan Court: The Theme of Spenser's February Eclogue." *Spenser Studies: A Renaissance Poetry Annual* 2 (1981): 55–65.

Boudon, Pierre. "Le logos greimassien: Narrativité et discursivité (Première Partie)." *Recherches Sémiotiques/ Semiotic Inquiry* 3 (1983): 376–408.

Bradner, Leicester. *Edmund Spenser and the Faerie Queene.* Chicago: University of Chicago Press, 1948.

―――, ed. *The Poems of Queen Elizabeth I.* Providence, R.I.: Brown University Press, 1964.

Bratchel, M. E. "Alien Merchant Colonies in Sixteenth-Century England: Community Organisation and Social Mores." *JMRS* 14 (1984): 39–62.

Brennan, Michael. "The Date of the Countess of Pembroke's Translation of the Psalms." *RES* 33 (1982): 434–36.

Cain, Thomas H. *Praise in the "Faerie Queene."* Lincoln: University of Nebraska Press, 1978.

Caldwell, Ellen M. "John Lyly's *Gallathea:* A New Rhetoric of Love for the Virgin Queen." *ELR* 17 (1987): 22–40.

Chandler, Robert M., ed. *Gabriel Harvey's 'Rhetor': A Translation and Critical Edition.* Ann Arbor, Mich.: University Microfilms, 1984.

Cheney, Donald. "The Circular Argument of *The Shepheardes Calender.*" In *Unfolded Tales: Essays on Renaissance Romance,* 137–161. Ithaca: Cornell University Press, 1989.

Chomsky, Noam. *Aspects of the Theory of Syntax.* Cambridge: Massachussets Institute of Technology Press, 1965.

―――. *Language and Mind.* New York: Harcourt, 1972.

Copeland, James E., ed. *New Directions in Linguistics and Semiotics.* Houston: Rice University Press, 1984.

Cornelius, Patsy Scherer. *E. K.'s Commentary on The Shepheardes Calender.* Salzburg: Institut für Englische Sprache, 1974.

Cressy, David. *Bonfires and Bells: National Memory and the Protestant Calendar in Elizabethan and Stuart England.* Berkeley: University of California Press, 1989.

Cullen, Patrick. *Spenser, Marvell, and Renaissance Pastoral.* Cambridge: Harvard University Press, 1970.

Culler, Jonathan. *Structuralist Poetics. Structuralism, Linguistics, and the Study of Literature.* Ithaca: Cornell University Press, 1975.

―――. *The Pursuit of Signs. Semiotics, Literature, Deconstruction.* Ithaca: Cornell University Press, 1981.

de Lauretis, Teresa. *Alice Doesn't: Feminism, Semiotics, Cinema.* Bloomington: Indiana University Press, 1982.

―――. *Technologies of Gender. Essays on Theory, Film, and Fiction.* Bloomington: Indiana University Press, 1987.

Deleuze, Gilles, and Felix Guattari. *Anti-Oedipus: Capitalism and Psychoanalysis.* Translated by Helen R. Lane, et al. New York: Penguin, 1977.

De Luna, B. N. *The Queen Declined: An Interpretation of "Willobie his Avisa."* Oxford: Clarendon Press, 1970.

Deneef, A. Leigh. *Spenser and the Motives of Metaphor.* Durham, N.C.: Duke University Press, 1982.

Derrida, Jacques. *Of Grammatology.* Translated by Gayatri Chakravorti Spivak. Baltimore: Johns Hopkins University Press, 1976.

Dixon, Michael F. "Rhetorical Patterns and Methods of Advocacy in Spenser's *Shepheardes Calender.*" *ELR* 7 (1977): 131–54.

Dolezelova-Velingerova, Milena. Review of Jonathan Culler, *The Pursuit of Signs: Semiotics, Literature, Deconstruction. RSSI* 5 (1985): 76–82.

Donald, M. B. *Elizabethan Monopolies: The History of the Company of Mineral and Battery Works from 1565–1604.* London: Oliver & Boyd, 1961.

Ducrot, Oswald, and Tzvetan Todorov. *Encyclopedic Dictionary of the Sciences of Language.* Translated by Catherine Porter. Baltimore: Johns Hopkins University Press, 1979.

Eco, Umberto. *Semiotics and the Philosophy of Language.* London: Macmillan, 1984.

Elam, Keir. *The Semiotics of Theatre and Drama.* London: Methuen, 1980.

———. *Shakespeare's Universe of Discourse: Language-games in the Comedies.* Cambridge: Cambridge University Press, 1984.

Erickson, Wayne. "Spenser's Letter to Ralegh and the Literary Politics of *The Faerie Queene's* 1590 Publication." *Spenser Studies* 10 (1989): 139–74.

Fellowes, Edmund H., ed. *The English School of Lutenist Song Writers,* ser. 1 & 2. 1920; 2d ed. London: Stainer & Bell, 1959.

Fish, Stanley. *Is There a Text in this Class? The Authority of Interpretive Communities.* Cambridge: Harvard University Press, 1980.

———. "Consequences." In *Against Theory: Literary Studies and the New Pragmatism,* edited by W. J. T. Mitchell, 11–30 and 106–31. Chicago: University of Chicago Press, 1982.

———. "Resistance and Independence: A Reply to Gerald Graff." *NLH* 17 (1985): 119–127.

Fowler, Alastair. *Edmund Spenser.* Harlow, Essex: Longman, 1977.

Gabriel Harvey's Marginalia. Edited by G. C. Moore Smith. Stratford: Shakespeare Head, 1913.

Gadamer, Hans Georg. *Truth and Method.* Translated by Garrett Barden and John Cumming. New York: Seabury, 1975.

Gans, Nathan A. "Archaism and Neologism in Spenser's Diction." *MP* 76 (1979): 377–79.

Genette, Gerard. *Seuils.* Paris: Seuil, 1987.

Giora, Rachel. "Segmentation and Segment Cohesion: On the Thematic Organization of the Text." *Text* 3 (1983): 155–81.

Girton, Thomas. *The Golden Ram: A Narrative History of the Clothworkers Company—1528–1958.* London: Hunt, 1958.

Goldberg, Jonathan. *Endlesse Worke: Spenser and the Structures of Discourse.* Baltimore: Johns Hopkins University Press, 1981.

———*James I and the Politics of Literature.* Baltimore: Johns Hopkins University Press, 1983.

. ———. "Colin to Hobbinol: Spenser's Familiar Letters." *South Atlantic Quarterly* 88 (1989): 107–126.

Greenblatt, Stephen. *Renaissance Self-Fashioning from More to Shakespeare.* Chicago: University of Chicago Press, 1980.

————. *Shakespearean Negotiations: The Circulation of Social Energy in Renaissance England*. Berkeley: University of California Press, 1988.

Greene, Roland. *"The Shepheardes Calender,* Dialogue, and Periphrasis." *Spenser Studies* 8 (1987): 1–33.

————. "Calling Colin Clout." *Spenser Studies* 10 (1989): 229–44.

Greimas, A.-J., *Sémantique structurale*. Paris: Larousse, 1966. (Translated by Ronald Schleifer as *Structural Semantics*.)

————. *Du Sens*. Paris: Seuil, 1970.

————. "Narrative Grammar: Units and Levels." Translated by P. Bodrock. *MLN* 86 (1971): 793–807.

————. "The Cognitive Dimension of Narrative Discourse." *NLH* 7 (1976): 433–47.

————. *Du Sens (II). Essais Sémiotiques*. Paris: Seuil, 1983.

————. *Dictionnaire raisonné de la théorie du langage*, Tome 2: *Compléments, débats, propositions*, Groupe de la recherche semiotique, ed. A.-J. Greimas. Paris, 1986.

————. *On Meaning: Selected Writings in Semiotic Theory*. Edited by Paul J. Perron. Minneapolis: University of Minnesota Press, 1987.

Greimas, A. J. and Joseph Cortés. *Semiotics and Language: An Analytical Dictionary*. Translated by Larry Crist, Daniel Patte, et al. Bloomington: Indiana University Press, 1982. [From *Sémiotique: Dictionnaire raisonné de la théorie du langage*. Paris: Hachette-Classiques, 1979].

Gülich, Elisabeth, and Wolfgang Raible. *Linguistische Textanalyse: Überlegungen zur Gliederung von Texten*, 1974; reprint, Hamburg: Buske, 1979.

Habermas, Jürgen. *Communication and the Evolution of Society*. Translated by Thomas McCarthy. London: Heinemann, 1979.

Hageman, Elizabeth H. Recent Studies in Women Writers of Tudor England. I: Women Writers, 1485–1603." *ELR* 14 (1984): 409–25.

————. "Recent Studies in Women Writers of the English Seventeenth Century (1604–1674)." *ELR* 18 (1988): 138–67.

Halpern, Richard. *The Poetics of Primitive Accumulation: English Renaissance Culture and the Genealogy of Capital*. London and Ithaca: Cornell Univerity Press, 1991.

Hamilton, A. C. "The Argument of Spenser's *Shepherdes Calender*." *ELH* 23 (1956): 171–83; also in *Spenser: A Collection of Critical Essays*, edited by Harry Berger, Jr., 30–39. Englewood Cliffs, N.J.: Prentice-Hall, 1968.

Hannay, Margaret P. "'Doo What Men May Sing': Mary Sidney and the Tradition of Admonitory Dedication." In *Silent but for the Word*, edited by Margaret P. Hannay, 149–65. Kent, Ohio: Kent State University Press, 1985.

————. *Philip's Phoenix: Mary Sidney, Countess of Pembroke*. Oxford: Oxford University Press, 1990.

————. "'Princes you as men must dy': Genevan Advice to Monarchs in the *Psalmes* of Mary Sidney." *ELR* 19 (1989): 22–41.

Hardin, Richard. "The Resolved Debate of Spenser's 'October'." *MP* 73 (1976): 257–63.

Harrison, G. B., ed. *Willobie his Avisa, 1594, with an Essay on Willobie his Avisa*. 1924; rpt. New York: Barnes & Noble, 1966.

Harvey, Gabriel. *Gabriel Harvey's "Rhetor": A Translation and Critical Edition*. Translated by Robert M. Chandler. Ann Arbor, Mich.: University Microfilms, 1984 (*Rhetor, Vel duorum dierum Oratio, De Natura, Arte, & Exercitatione Rhetorica*, 1578).

————. *The Letter-book of Gabriel Harvey. A. D. 1573–1580*. Edited by Edward J. L. Scott. London: Camden Society, 1884.

————. *Works*. Edited by Alexander Grosart. 1884; reprint, New York: AMS Press, 1966.

Haselkorn, Anne M., and Betty S. Travitsky. *The Renaissance Englishwoman in Print: Counterbalancing the Canon*. Amherst: University of Massachusetts Press, 1990.

Helgerson, Richard. *Self-Crowned Laureates: Spenser, Jonson, Milton and the Literary System*. Berkeley: University of California Press, 1983.

Henderson, Katherine, and Barbara F. McManus. *Half Humankind: Contexts and Texts of the Controversy about Women in England, 1540–1640*. Urbana: University of Illinois Press, 1985.

Hendricks, William O. *Essays on Semiolinguistics and Verbal Art*. The Hague: Mouton, 1973.

Heninger, S. K., Jr. "Spenser and Sidney at Leicester House." *Spenser Studies* 8 (1987; publ. 1990): 239–49.

Herbert, Mary Sidney, Countess of Pembroke. *The Triumph of Death and Other Unpublished and Uncollected Poems*. Edited by Gary F. Waller. Salzburg: Universität Salzburg, 1977.

Hesse, Mary. *Revolutions and Reconstructions in the Philosophy of Science*. Bloomington: Indiana University Press, 1980.

Higginson, James Jackson. *Spenser's Shepherd's Calender in Relation to Contemporary Affairs*. New York: Columbia University Press, 1912.

Hoffman, Nancy Jo. *Spenser's Pastorals: The Shepheardes Calender and "Colin Clout."* Baltimore: Johns Hopkins University Press, 1977.

Hollway, Wendy, Julian Henriques, et al. *Changing the Subject: Psychology, Social Regulation, and Subjectivity*. London: Methuen, 1984.

Holt, Mack P. *The Duke of Anjou and the Politique Struggle during the Wars of Religion*. Cambridge: Cambridge University Press, 1986.

Hume, Anthea. *Edmund Spenser: Protestant Poet*. Cambridge: Cambridge University Press, 1984.

Iser, Wolfgang. *Spenser's Arcadia: The Interrelation of Fiction and History*. Berkeley: Center for Hermeneutical Studies, 1980.

Jacobus, Mary. *Reading Woman: Essays in Feminist Criticism*. New York: Columbia University Press, 1986.

Jameson, Fredric. *The Prison-House of Language: A Critical Account of Structuralism and Russian Formalism*. Princeton: Princeton University Press, 1972.

————. *The Political Unconscious: Narrative as a Socially Symbolic Act*. Ithaca, N. Y.: Cornell University Press, 1981.

Jenkins, Raymond. "Who is E. K.?" *Shakespeare Association Bulletin* 19/20 (1944–45): 147–55 and 22–38.

————. "A Note on E. K." *SP* 45 (1948): 76–79.

Johnson, L. Staley. "Elizabeth, Bride and Queen: A Study of Spenser's April Eclogue and the Metaphors of English Protestantism." *Spenser Studies: A Renaissance Poetry Annual* 2 (1981): 75–91.

————. *'The Shepheardes Calender': An Introduction*. University Park: Pennsylvania State University Press, 1990.

Jordan, Constance. "Representing Political Androgyny: More on the Sienna Portrait of Queen Elizabeth I." In *The Renaissance Englishwoman in Print. Counterbalancing the Canon*, edited by Anne M. Haselkorn and Betty S. Travitsky, 157–76. Amherst: University of Massachussets Press, 1990.

Kahn, Coppèlia. *Man's Estate: Masculine Identity in Shakespeare*. Berkeley: University of California Press, 1981.

Kennedy, Judith M. "The Final Emblem of The Shepheardes Calender." *Spenser Studies: A Renaissance Poetry Annual* 1 (1980): 95–106.

King, John N. *Spenser's Poetry and the Reformation Tradition*. Princeton: Princeton University Press, 1990.

Knapp, Steven, and Walter Benn Michaels. "Against Theory." In *Against Theory: Literary Studies and the New Pragmatism*, edited by W. J. T. Mitchell. Chicago: University of Chicago Press, 1982.

Knappen, M. M. *Tudor Puritanism: A Chapter in the History of Idealism*. Chicago: University of Chicago Press, 1939.

Kristeva, Julia. *Desire in Language: A Semiotic Approach to Literature and Art*. Translated by Thomas Gora, et al. New York: Columbia University Press, 1980.

———. *Revolution in Poetic Language*. Translated by Margaret Waller. 1974; New York: Columbia University Press, 1984.

———. *The Kristeva Reader*. Edited by Toril Moi. New York: Columbia University Press, 1986.

———. "Il n'y a pas de maître à langage." *Nouvelle revue de psychanalyse* 20 (Autumn 1979): 119–40.

Lacan, Jacques. *The Language of the Self: The Function of Language in Psychoanalysis*. Translated by Anthony Wilden. Baltimore: Johns Hopkins University Press, 1968.

Lane, Robert. *Shepheardes Devises: Edmund Spenser's 'Shepheardes Calender' and the Institutions of Elizabethan Society*. Athens: University of Georgia Press, 1993.

Lavers, Annette. *Roland Barthes: Structuralism and After*. London: Methuen, 1982.

Lévi-Strauss, Claude. *Myth and Meaning*. New York: Schocken, 1979.

———. *Anthropology and Myth: Lectures, 1951–82*. Translated by Roy Willis. Oxford: Blackwell, 1987.

Luborsky, Ruth Samson. "The Allusive Presentation of The Shepheardes Calender." *Spenser Studies: A Renaissance Poetry Annual* 1 (1980): 29–67.

———. "The Illustrations to The Shepheardes Calender." *Spenser Studies: A Renaissance Poetry Annual* 2 (1981): 3–53.

Lyly, John. *Gallathea and Midas*. Edited by Anne Begor Lancashire. Lincoln: University of Nebraska Press, 1969.

———. *Complete Works*. See R. Warwick Bond.

Lyotard, Jean-François. *Libidinal Economy*. Translated by Iain Hamilton Grant. 1974; Bloomington: Indiana University Press, 1993.

MacCaffrey, Isabel G. "Allegory and Pastoral in *The Shepheardes Calender*." In *Essential Articles: Edmund Spenser*, edited by A. C. Hamilton. Hamden, Conn.: Archon, 1972.

MacLean, Ian. *The Renaissance Notion of Woman*. Cambridge: Cambridge University Press, 1980.

Mallette, Richard. *Spenser, Milton, and Renaissance Pastoral*. Lewisburg, Pa.: Bucknell University Press, 1981.

Margolies, David. *Novel and Society in Elizabethan England.* London: Croom Helm, 1985.

Marot, Clement. *Oeuvres Lyriques.* Edited by C. A. Mayer. London: Athlone, 1964.

McCanles, Michael. *"The Shepheardes Calender* as Document and Monument." *SEL* 22 (1982): 5–19.

McLane, Paul E. *Spenser's "Shepheardes Calender": A Study in Elizabethan Allegory.* Notre Dame, Ind.: Notre Dame University Press, 1961.

McPherson, David C. "Aretino and the Harvey-Nashe Quarrel." *PMLA* 84 (1969): 1551–58.

Medvedev, P. N. [Mikhail Bakhtin ?]. *The Formal Method in Literary Scholarship.* Translated by A. J. Wehrle. 1928; Baltimore: Johns Hopkins University Press, 1978.

Meyer, Sam. *An Interpretation of Edmund Spenser's Colin Clout.* Notre Dame, Ind.: Notre Dame University Press, 1969.

Miller, David L. "Authorship, Anonymity, and The Shepheardes Calender." *MLQ* 40 (1979): 219–36.

———. *The Poem's Two Bodies: The Poetics of the 1590 Faerie Queene.* Princeton: Princeton University Press, 1988.

Mitchner, Robert. "Spenser and E. K.: An Answer." *SP* 42 (1945): 183–90.

Montrose, Louis Adrian. "'The Perfecte Patterne of a Poete': The Poetics of Courtship in *The Shepheardes Calender.*" *TSLL* 21 (1979): 34–67.

———. "'Eliza, Queene of shepheardes,' and the Pastoral of Power." *ELR* 10 (1980): 153–82.

———. "Interpreting Spenser's February Eclogue: Some Contexts and Implications." *Spenser Studies: A Renaissance Poetry Annual* 2 (1981): 67–74.

———. "Of Gentlemen and Shepherds: The Politics of Elizabethan Pastoral Form." *ELH* 50 (1983): 415–59.

———. "'Shaping Fantasies': Figurations of Gender and Power." *Representations* 2 (1983): 61–94.

———. "The Elizabethan Subject and the Spenserian Text." In *Literary Theory, Renaissance Texts,* edited by Patricia Parker and David Quint, 303–40. Baltimore: Johns Hopkins University Press, 1986.

Moody, Ellen. "Six Elegiac Poems, Possibly by Anne Cecil de Vere, Countess of Oxford." *ELR* 19 (1989): 152–70.

Moore, John W., Jr. "Colin Breaks His Pipe: A Reading of the 'January' Eclogue." *ELR* 5 (1975): 3–24.

Morris, Charles. *Foundations of the Theory of Signs.* 9th ed. Chicago: University of Chicago Press, 1959.

Morson, Gary Saul, and Caryl Emerson. *Mikhail Bakhtin: Creation of a Prosaics.* Stanford, Calif.: Stanford University Press, 1990.

Norbrook, David. *Poetry and Politics in the English Renaissance.* London: Routledge, 1984.

O'Connell, Michael. *Mirror and Veil: The Historical Dimension of Spenser's Faerie Queene.* Chapel Hill: University of North Carolina Press, 1977.

Osgood, Charles G., and Henry G. Lotspeich, eds. *The Works of Edmund Spenser. A Variorum Edition.* Baltimore: Johns Hopkins University Press, 1943.

Parmenter, Mary. "Spenser's *Twelve Aeglogves Proportionable to the Twelve Monethes.*" *ELH* 3 (1936): 190–217.

Patterson, Annabel. "Re-opening the Green Cabinet: Clement Marot and Edmund Spenser." *ELR* 16 (1986): 44–70.

———. *Pastoral and Ideology: Virgil to Valery.* Berkeley: University of California Press, 1988.

Phillips, James E. "Elizabeth I as a Latin Poet: An Epigram on Paul Melissus." *Renaissance News* 16 (1963): 289–99.

Prescott, Anne Lake. "English Writers and Beza's Latin Epigrams: The Uses and Abuses of Poetry." *StudRen* 21 (1974): 83–117.

Provost, Foster. Review of Stephen Greenblatt, *Renaissance Self-Fashioning. Spenser Newsletter* 13 (1982): 1–14.

Putnam, Hilary. *Reason, Truth, and History.* Cambridge: Cambridge University Press, 1981.

Quilligan, Maureen. *Milton's Spenser: the Politics of Reading.* Ithaca: Cornell University Press, 1983.

———. "The Comedy of Female Authority in *The Faerie Queene.*" *ELR* 17 (1987): 156–71.

———. "Sidney and his Queen." In *The Historical Renaissance. New Essays on Tudor and Stuart Literature and Culture,* edited by Heather Dubrow and Richard Strier, 171–96. Chicago: University of Chicago Press, 1988.

Rambuss, Richard. *Spenser's Secret Career.* Cambridge: Cambridge University Press, 1993.

Read, Conyers. *Mr. Secretary Cecil and Queen Elizabeth.* New York: Knopf, 1955.

———. *Lord Burghley and Queen Elizabeth.* London: Jonathan Cape, 1960.

Renwick, W. L., ed. *The Shepherd's Calendar.* By Edmund Spenser. London: Scholartis, 1930.

Richardson, J. Michael. *Astrological Symbolism in Spenser's "The Shepheardes Calender".* Lewiston, N.Y.: Edwin Mellen, 1989.

Riffaterre, Michael. *Semiotics of Poetry.* Indiana University Press, 1978.

———. *La Production du Texte.* Paris: Seuil, 1979. [Translated as *Text Production* by Terese Lyons (1983).]

Roberts, Josephine A. "Recent Studies in Women Writers of Tudor England. II: Mary Sidney, Countess of Pembroke." *ELR* 14 (1984): 426–39.

———. "Radigund Revisited: Perspectives on Women Rulers in Lady Mary Wroth's *Urania.*" In *The Renaissance Englishwoman in Print. Counterbalancing the Canon,* edited by Anne M. Haselkorn and Betty S. Travitsky, 193–94. Amherst: University of Massachussets Press, 1990.

Rosenberg, D. M. *Oaten Reeds and Trumpets: Pastoral and Epic in Virgil, Spenser, and Milton.* Lewisburg, Pa.: Bucknell University Press, 1981.

Rosenberg, Eleanor. *Leicester Patron of Letters.* New York: Columbia University Press, 1955.

Ruprecht, Hans-Georg. "La modalisation de la connaissance chez E. Husserl et A. J. Greimas." *RSSI* 3 (1983): 351–62.

Saccio, Peter. *The Court Comedies of John Lyly: A Study in Allegorical Dramaturgy.* Princeton: Princeton University Press, 1969.

Schleifer, Ronald. *A.-J. Greimas and the Nature of Meaning: Linguistics, Semiotics, and Discourse Theory.* London: Croom Helm, 1987.

———, trans. *Structural Semantics* (see Greimas).

Schleiner, Louise. "Spenser and Sidney on the Vaticinium." *Spenser Studies: A Renaissance Poetry Annual* 6 (1985): 129–45.

———. "Ladies and Gentlemen in Elizabethan Prose Fiction." *SEL* (1989): 1–20.

———. "Latinized Greek Drama in Shakespeare's Writing of *Hamlet.*" *SQ* 41 (1990): 29–48.

———. "Pastoral Male Friendship and Miltonic Marriage: Textual Systems Transposed." *LIT* 2 (1990): 41–58.

———. "Spenser's 'E. K.' as Edmund Kent: Kenned, Kissed, and Kunning/Conning." *ELR* 20 (1990): 374–407.

Schleiner, Winfried. "Divina virago: Queen Elizabeth as an Amazon." *SP* 75 (1978): 163–80.

———. *Medical Ethics in the Renaissance.* Forthcoming: Georgetown University Press.

Scholes, Robert. *Semiotics and Interpretation.* New Haven: Yale University Press, 1982.

Shire, Helena. *A Preface to Spenser.* London: Longman, 1985.

Shore, David R. "Colin and Rosalind: Love and Poetry in The Shepheardes Calender." *SP* 73 (1976): 176–88.

Sidney, Sir Philip. *The Countess of Pembroke's Arcadia,* edited by Maurice Evans. New York: Penguin, 1977.

———. *Spenser and the Poetics of Pastoral.* Montreal: McGill-Queen's University Press, 1985.

Silberman, Lauren. "The Hermaphrodite and the Metamorphosis of Spenserian Allegory." *ELR* 17 (1987): 207–23.

Slights, William W. E. "The Edifying Margins of Rennaissance English Books." *Renaissance Quarterly* 42 (1989): 682–716.

Smith, Bruce R. "On Reading The Shepheardes Calender." *Spenser Studies: A Renaissance Poetry Annual* 1 (1980): 69–93.

———. *Homosexual Desire in Shakespeare's England: A Cultural Poetics.* Chicago: University of Chicago Press, 1991.

Smith, Hallett. *Elizabethan Poetry.* 1952; 2d ed. Ann Arbor: University of Michigan Press, 1968.

Smith, Sir Thomas. *De recta et emendata linguae Anglicae scriptione, dialogus.* 1568; facs. Menston: Scolar Press, 1968.

———. *De republica Anglorum. The maner of Gouernement or policie of the Realme of England.* 1583; Mary Dewar, ed., facs. Charlottesville: University Press of Virginia, 1968.

Spenser, Edmund. *Poetical Works.* Edited by J. C. Smith and E. de Selincourt. 1912; rpt. London: Oxford University Press, 1969.

———. *Works: A Variorum Edition.* Edited by Charles G. Osgood and Henry G. Lotspeich. 11 vols. Baltimore: Johns Hopkins University Press, 1943.

———. *The Yale Edition of the Shorter Poems of Edmund Spenser.* Edited by William A. Oram, Einar Bjorvand, Ronald Bond, Thomas H. Cain, Alexander Dunlop, and Richard Schell. New Haven: Yale University Press, 1989.

Starnes, D. T. "Spenser and E. K." *SP* 41 (1944): 181–200.

Stephenson, Edward A. "Some Stylistic Links Between Spenser and E. K." *RenP* (1956): 66–71.

Stern, Virginia F. *Gabriel Harvey: His Life, Marginalia, and Library.* Oxford: Clarendon Press, 1979.

Stevenson, Laura. *Praise and Paradox: Merchants and Craftsmen in Elizabethan Popular Literature.* Cambridge: Cambridge University Press, 1984.

Strong, Roy. *The Cult of Elizabeth: Elizabethan Portraiture and Pageantry.* London: Thames & Hudson, 1977.

Stump, Donald V. "The Two Deaths of Mary Stuart: Historical Allegory in Spenser's Book of Justice." *Spenser Studies* 9 (1988): 81–105.

Thornton, Bruce. "Rural Dialectic: Pastoral, Georgic, and *The Shepheardes Calender.*" *Spenser Studies* 9 (1988): 1–20.

Tilney, Edmund. *The Flower of Friendship: A Renaissance Dialogue Contesting Marriage.* Edited by Valerie Wayne. Ithaca: Cornell University Press, 1992.

Tribble, Evelyn. "Glozing the Gap: Authority, Glossing Traditons and *The Shepheardes Calender.*" *Criticism* 34 (1992): 155–72.

Van Dijk, Teun A., ed. *Discourse and Literature.* Amsterdam: Benjamins, 1985.

———, ed. *Handbook of Discourse Analysis.* 4 vols. London: Academic Press, 1985.

Virgil. *The Aeneid,* trans. Robert Fitzgerald. New York: Random House, 1983.

Waldman, Louis. "Spenser's Pseudonym 'E. K.' and Humanist Self-Naming." *Spenser Studies* 9 (1988; publ. 1991): 21–31.

Warren, Kate M., ed. *The Faerie Queene.* Vol. 3. Westminster: Archibald Constable, 1904.

Wells, Robin Headlam. *Spenser's "Faerie Queene" and the Cult of Elizabeth.* London: Croom Helm, 1983.

Welply, W. H. "Some Spenser Problems." *N&Q* 180 (1941): 74–76 and 92–95.

Willobie his Avisa. See Harrison.

Wilson, Elkin Calhoun. *England's Eliza.* New York: Octagon, 1966.

Wittreich, Joseph A. *Visionary Poetics: Milton's Tradition and his Legacy.* San Marino, Calif.: Huntington, 1979.

Woodbridge, Linda. *Women and the English Renaissance: Literature and the Nature of Womankind, 1540–1620.* Urbana: University of Illinois Press, 1984.

Wright, Celeste T. "Anthony Mundy, 'Edward' Spenser, and E. K." *PMLA* 76 (1961): 34–39.

Wright, Louis B. *Middle-Class Culture in Elizabethan England.* 1935; Ithaca: Cornell University Press, 1958.

Yates, Frances A. *Astraea: The Imperial Theme in the Sixteenth Century.* London: Routledge, 1975.

Zanger, Jules. "Living on the Edge: Indian Captivity Narrative and Fairy Tale." *ClioI* 13 (1984): 123–32.

Index